# Dancing in the Sky

# Dancing in the Sky

*The Royal Flying Corps in Canada*

## C.W. Hunt

DUNDURN PRESS
TORONTO

Copy-editors: Shannon Whibbs and Andrea Waters
Design: Courtney Horner
Printer: Webcom

**Library and Archives Canada Cataloguing in Publication**

Hunt, C. W. (Claude William)
    Dancing in the sky : the Royal Flying Corps in
Canada / by C.W. Hunt.

Includes bibliographical references and index.
ISBN 978-1-55002-864-5

    1. Great Britain. Royal Flying Corps. 2. World War, 1914-1918--
Aerial operations, British. 3. World War, 1914-1918--Aerial operations,
Canadian. I. Title.

UG639.C3H85 2008          940.4'4941          C2008-903963-7


1  2  3  4  5      13  12  11  10  09

 Conseil des Arts du Canada    Canada Council for the Arts     Canada    ONTARIO ARTS COUNCIL CONSEIL DES ARTS DE L'ONTARIO

We acknowledge the support of the **Canada Council for the Arts** and the **Ontario Arts Council** for our publishing program. We also acknowledge the financial support of the **Government of Canada** through the **Book Publishing Industry Development Program** and **The Association for the Export of Canadian Books**, and the **Government of Ontario** through the **Ontario Book Publishers Tax Credit program**, and the **Ontario Media Development Corporation**.

Care has been taken to trace the ownership of copyright material used in this book. The author and the publisher welcome any information enabling them to rectify any references or credits in subsequent editions.

*J. Kirk Howard, President*

Published by Natural Heritage Books
A Member of The Dundurn Group
Printed and bound in Canada.

www.dundurn.com


Dundurn Press
3 Church Street, Suite 500
Toronto, Ontario, Canada
M5E 1M2

Gazelle Book Services Limited
White Cross Mills
High Town, Lancaster, England
LA1 4XS

Dundurn Press
2250 Military Road
Tonawanda, NY
U.S.A. 14150

This book is dedicated to William Taylor Hunt
journalist and photographer (1966–2005)

# TABLE OF CONTENTS

# Acknowledgements

This book began when RCAF Captain (Ret.) J. Alan Smith gave me material he had collected over twenty years of research. We agreed that I would write a book about it. Smith had interviewed former members of the Imperial Royal Flying Corps (IRFC), thereby preserving their experiences for posterity. As a result of our meeting, I set out on a journey that lasted a decade.

My brother, Pete Hunt, a detailed and thorough researcher, uncovered a great deal of information while combing through hundreds of newspapers. Many of the vignettes that flesh out the book are the result of his research.

I was always graciously assisted by Elizabeth Mitchell and Marie Wright of the Belleville Library. Marci Weese of Queen's University Library was particularly helpful. Euan Callender assisted in the early research.

Deseronto archivist Ken Brown guards his photos and documents more ferociously than any junkyard dog, but generously made several photos and documents available for use in the book. Master Warrant Officer Normand Marion at CFB Borden provided capable assistance on the material available there. He took me on a knowledgeable tour of a few of the original hangars that were built for temporary use in 1917 but still stand today.

Glen Martin of Fort Worth, Texas, researched the Texas camps over several years and provided information not available in Canada. The taped interviews of Texans long dead provided a useful insight into the social life of the British and Canadian airmen stationed in Texas during the winter of 1917–1918.

The National Archives, Canadian War Museum, and the Canadian Forces Directorate of History are treasure troves of information. The documents held by these institutions were essential in providing a detailed understanding of the Royal Flying Corps/Royal Air Force (RFC/RAF) training scheme in Canada. My thanks also to The Hastings County Historical Society, which has a small but excellent collection of photos from the Rathbun and Mohawk camps.

My late son, William Taylor Hunt, read parts of the manuscript. An excellent stylist, he helped clarify the work. Professor (emeritus) Arthur Bowler read the entire manuscript and made many useful suggestions, all of which I acted upon. Ren Duinker provided invaluable assistance with the photographs.

If I have missed anyone who assisted with the project, I apologize. My only excuse being that a project taking a decade to complete challenges an imperfect memory. My wife, Milli, was unwavering in her support and never complained of her status as a writer's widow. My thanks for her generous forbearance.

Any errors or omissions are entirely those of the author.

# INTRODUCTION

The Royal Flying Corps' plan to train pilots in Canada marked a dramatic turning point in the military relationships between Canada, Britain, and the United States. Today, that close alliance is taken for granted, yet, for over a century, both Britain and Canada regarded the emerging American giant with a mixture of envy and foreboding. In the last decade of the nineteenth century, relations had deteriorated to the point where the United States was threatening to go to war against Britain over an obscure boundary dispute in Venezuela.

The antipathy between the three nations had deep roots. During the American Civil War, Britain barely disguised its hope the American Union would break into two weaker nations; a divided America posed less of a threat to the hegemony of the British Empire. Canadians, on the other hand, were deeply suspicious of American expansionism. In the election of 1911, Sir Wilfrid Laurier proposed a reciprocity trading agreement with the United States. The proposed agreement was highly favourable to Canada, but the expression of annexationist sentiments by some American politicians so alarmed Canadians they defeated the popular Laurier, thereby killing a trade agreement that would have meant greater prosperity for the majority of the population. Canadians were so fearful of the United States that they threw out of office one of the most popular prime ministers in the nation's history because he had advocated a trading treaty that might have led to closer relations with the United States.

The memory of America's invasions into Canada during the War of 1812, the Fenian raids, plus the American desire to absorb Canada was etched deeply into the national consciousness. Despite Canada's fears and American resentment of British imperialism, Canadians and Americans joined in an Air Force Training Plan run by the British on both Canadian and American territory. The Plan was the beginning of the close alliance between the three nations that is now taken as a fundamental principle of their respective foreign policies.

At the outbreak of the conflict in Europe, both Canada and the United States had fallen far behind the British and the Europeans in aircraft technology. The Plan was the primary agent in dragging both Canada and the United States into the age of modern aviation.

While the Canadian government was a reluctant participant in the training scheme, its passive participation resulted in so many Canadians mastering the art of flying that it was Canadians and not Americans who mapped and pioneered the North American Arctic, thereby ensuring that this vast territory would fly the Maple Leaf rather than the Stars and Stripes.

There were benefits for America, as well. In 1917, the United States, while an industrial powerhouse, was militarily weak, lacking both the weapons and the trained manpower necessary for the creation of a modern military establishment. Although capable of raising a powerful citizens' army, the U.S. air force existed largely on paper. The RFC/RAF Training Plan jump-started the American Air Force, enabling it, in just a few months, to compete with the world's major air powers. Now the world's most powerful military nation, the United States trained many of its early military pilots at the aerodromes of Canada under British command. Its first aviation schools were modelled directly from the Aeronautical School set up by the RFC at the University of Toronto.

Curiously, the single most important individual to the success of the Training Plan was a British colonel who had spent most of his career in India. A graduate of Harrow and a professional soldier, Cuthbert Gurney Hoare was born into the rural gentry of Norfolk County. Fortunately, he had an appreciation for the practical mindset of Canadians and Americans, as well as a high regard for the talents of North American youth. He was able to wheel and deal with the Americans, to pick their pockets and leave them smiling. He was also a brilliant administrator and one of the first officers in the British Army to master the art of flying.

The First World War brought flying into the realm of the practical while endowing it with a unique glamour and romance. Pilots of the

Royal Flying Corps held a status similar to the early astronauts. Climbing into the open cockpit of those flimsy crates — wood and fabric held together with piano wire — held a powerful appeal to the adventurous and strong of heart. Not surprisingly, flying attracted the most talented young men from both countries. Although their country was not yet in the war, large numbers of young Americans flocked north to join the ranks of the niggardly paid Royal Flying Corps. Among those who rose to distinction were several American generals and naval officers. U.S. Naval Cadet James Forrestal, who learned to fly in Canada, rose to secretary of the Navy and was America's secretary of defence at the close of the Second World War.

The RAF in Canada also had its share of cadets who later excelled in the arts. The Nobel prize–winning author, William E. Faulkner, learned to fly with the RAF in Canada. While working as a nurse in Toronto, the most famous aviatrix in history, Amelia Earhart, was inspired by the RAF to take up the challenge of flying. But the most famous member of the Imperial Royal Flying Corps (IRFC) at the time of his enlistment was Vernon Castle, an instructor posted to Canada after a tour of France. British by birth, Castle immigrated to America, where he gained fame as a Broadway actor. He and his New England bride, Irene Castle, went on to popularize ballroom dancing and became international stars of the dance floor.

In subsequent years, the most prominent Canadian associated with the RAF in Canada was Lester B. "Mike" Pearson. Pearson began his post-war career as a University of Toronto lecturer and went on to become a prominent diplomat and minister of foreign affairs. In that capacity he brokered a United Nations agreement at the height of the Cold War that prevented a crisis in the Middle East from triggering a nuclear war. For his efforts, Pearson was awarded the Nobel Peace Prize. He subsequently became prime minister of Canada and was responsible for the Canada Pension Plan and the nation's universal health-care system.

Another prominent Canadian who trained with the IRFC in Canada was Roland Michener. He became speaker of the House of Commons and, eventually, governor general of Canada. Another cadet, Mitchell Hepburn, later became the eleventh premier of Ontario.

This is the story of the men and women of the RFC/RAF in Canada and Texas; how they trained, the risks they took, their often tragic love affairs, and the sudden death that came so unpredictably.

It is also the story of the incredible challenges facing those who had to organize and build the Royal Flying Corps in Canada, and who did so almost overnight. The impact on the three nations involved in that long-ago training plan was significant and enduring. Its effects are still being felt and are manifest in all three nations, even to the present war on terror as well as in various military alliances and trade arrangements.

# CHAPTER ONE
## CANADA'S FIRST AIR FORCE

> To us who have only armies and navies, it must seem strange that the sky, too, is about to become another battlefield no less important than the battlefields on land and sea. But from now on we had better get accustomed to this idea and prepare ourselves for the new conflicts to come. If there are any nations which can exist untouched by the sea, there are none which can exist without the breath of air. In the future, then, we shall have three instead of two separate and well-defined fields of battle.
>   — *Guilio Douhet, Italian theorist, addressing his countrymen, 1909*

Only a few Canadians believed that air power would be crucial to the outcome of the Great War; most thought the war would be fought almost entirely by the infantry, artillery, and cavalry. Navies would play their usual role of bottling up ports, disrupting supplies, and slowing or preventing the movement of troops. Navies would be important but the real battle would be fought on land, using the same weapons that had triumphed in South Africa against the Boers. Only a few "eccentric" inventors and airplane enthusiasts had any inkling that air power would play a critical role in the conflict; almost no one gave serious thought to air power as a necessary or even an important element in winning the war. The prophecy of Italian theorist Guilio Douhet had no impact on Canada.

In the first decade of the twentieth century, Canada was one of only three nations that had made significant progress in airplane building, design, and flight. In 1903, the Wright Brothers at Kitty Hawk, North

Carolina, flew the first heavier-than-air machine in a powered flight barely the length of a hockey rink. That flight was too brief to be spectacular. Moreover, the brothers avoided public exhibitions of their flights in order to prevent other inventors taking advantage of their pioneer experiments. They guarded their patents and designs zealously.

In France, a prize was offered to the first aviator-inventor to fly a powered, controlled, heavier-than-air vehicle the distance of a measured kilometre. In the fall of 1908, this feat was accomplished by Henri Farman. But Canadian inventors were close on the heels of the French and the Americans. In March 1908, a full six months before the Farman flight, a Canadian, Casey Baldwin, successfully flew the Red Wing from Lake Keuka, at Hammondsport, New York.

He was a member of the Aerial Experimental Association (AEA) founded by Alexander Graham Bell. The other members were Glen Curtiss, Lieutenant Thomas Selfridge, and another Canadian, J.A.D. McCurdy. Like Baldwin, McCurdy was a recent engineering graduate from the University of Toronto. It was this group that, in February of 1909, successfully flew the Silver Dart off Baddeck Bay in Nova Scotia; the first controlled and powered flight of a heavier-than-air machine in the British Empire. The group frequently met at Bell's summer home on the shores of Bras D'Or Lake where they discussed and experimented with problems of flight and aircraft design.

Having accomplished many successful flights with both the Silver Dart and the Red Wing, airplanes designed by their members, the Aerial Experimental Association was clearly challenging the Wright Brothers' leadership in aircraft design. Unfortunately, the AEA disbanded shortly after Glen Curtiss and Casey Baldwin left the group to set up a plant in Hammondsport, New York, for the purpose of manufacturing airplanes.

In Canada, the minister of militia, Lieutenant-Colonel Sam Hughes, ruled the army without regard for existing channels of communication, opinions of his fellow cabinet ministers, or even those of the prime minister. At the outbreak of the war, Hughes met with the pioneer airman, engineer, and inventor J.A.D. McCurdy. The aviator laid out a proposal to create a Canadian air force. Never one to understate his views, the minister decisively dismissed the supplicant: "My boy, the aeroplane is the invention of the Devil and will never play any part in such a serious business as the defence of the nation."[1]

Sam Hughes did not walk onto the world stage so much as stormed it; all elemental force and vanity; an immense ego draped in the resplendent red-tabbed uniform of a full colonel, a rank he didn't hold. Had he been offered a crown, Hughes would undoubtedly have donned it and, brandishing a sceptre, mounted his steed and ridden magisterially (and ramrod straight) amongst his troops, bullying his officers, countermanding their orders, and generally creating havoc and frenetic activity.

At the beginning of the war, Hughes disregarded the professional British generals who had carefully drawn up mobilization plans for Canada and ordered a massive mobilization of the Dominion's scattered local militia units to a camp not yet constructed, rather than to the already-functioning Camp Petawawa. Within six weeks of the declaration of war, Hughes had created an encampment in the bush north of Valcartier, Quebec, capable of accommodating over 32,000 troops. It was a remarkable achievement and took place with Hughes on site, directing the multitude on a day-to-day basis. His practice of riding amongst the men issuing orders — which he frequently reversed — added considerably to the chaos and confusion. Nevertheless, his infectious energy and determination, combined with his constant interference, was a powerful motivation for the contractors and workers

*Sir Sam Hughes, minister of militia. Courtesy of Allan R. Capon.*

to build the camp in record time; escaping the minister's constant interference was a powerful incentive.

While the Canadian troops were milling in the mud of Valcartier, Hughes inexplicably cabled Lord Kitchener, the British minister of war, inquiring if the services of aviators were required. The minister of war replied that six experienced aviators could be taken on at once and perhaps more later. Nothing was done. Only eight Canadians had earned a certificate from the Aero Club of America, the sole organization able to test aspiring pilots and issue flying certificates. The quixotic Hughes did not choose any of these men to serve in England's Royal Flying Corps but, despite his earlier declamation to McCurdy, suddenly decided to form a Canadian air force. Rather typically, he also failed to consult the prime minister or any of his fellow cabinet ministers. Moreover, the new corps was to be formed immediately as Hughes wanted his ad hoc air force to accompany the first contingent of troops leaving for England.

At this point, Ernest Lloyd Janney stepped onto the Alice-in-Wonderland stage, equipped with the improbable credentials of a motor mechanic from Galt, Ontario. Janney had absolutely no experience in flying, nor in building airplanes, but he was a gifted huckster who, in all probability, could have sold baby seal meat to Brigitte Bardot and Paul McCartney.

But something of Janney was known to the Canadian Militia. When Lieutenant-Colonel A.J. Oliver, commanding officer of the 29th Regiment based in Galt, heard of Canada's new Air Corps, he sent a letter to the assistant adjutant-general, 1st Division in London, stating what he knew about Janney. The letter eventually found its way to Ottawa, but far too late to influence events. In his letter, Oliver warned:

> It is the impression of a great many people here in Galt, to which city this party belongs, that absolutely no reliance should be placed in him in any way, shape, or form, and his statements in connection with flying have always been taken as a joke. He is a high flyer all right, but the meaning of the term is entirely different from that normally applied to an aviator.[2]

*Sam Hughes at Valcartier, Quebec, circa 1914. Hughes is on the horse on the left. Courtesy of Allan R. Capon.*

How the virtually unknown Janney gained access to Hughes is not known, but on 16 September 1914, the minister of militia made Janney the provisional head of the new Canadian Air Corps (CAC). Hughes also appointed Janney a captain in the Canadian Militia, and had him outfitted with a new uniform, Sam Browne belt, and shiny new service revolver.* All this was done without consulting any governmental authority or advising Major-General Alderson, commander of the Canadian Expeditionary Force (CEF). Moreover, Janney was never properly gazetted as a captain, although he drew pay from the militia as of the date of his probationary appointment.

Shortly after his initial meeting with Janney, Hughes appointed two more members of the CAC: Harry A. Farr was made a staff sergeant and

---

* Much to the distress of Canadian Militia officers, Hughes was in the habit of handing out promotions on the spot, often to the surprise of the recipient.

William Sharpe was made a lieutenant. Although neither of these men was ever properly gazetted in the CEF, they continued to draw pay from the date of their appointment, a fact that created some confusion for the paymasters of the CEF.

Prior to his meeting with the minister of militia, Janney had scouted for an aircraft in the United States where he met with executives of the Burgess-Dunne airplane factory at Marblehead, Massachusetts. Janney fixated on a used Burgess-Dunne float plane. The airplane needed a considerable amount of maintenance work on the engine, but the price was right.

After his appointment as captain in the Canadian Aviation Corps, Janney recommended to the minister of militia that he empower his provisional commander — himself — to purchase an airplane for the new Corps. Hughes hastily scribbled a note authorizing Janney to spend up to $5,000 for that purpose. With Hughes's written authorization in his pocket, Captain Janney returned to Marblehead and ordered the used float plane. The airplane was a two-seat, delta-wing, tailless machine manufactured at Marblehead, which had been extensively used as a demonstrator. This creaky, unreliable, and much-used float plane has the distinction of being Canada's first warplane.

As the flotilla in Quebec City was preparing to depart for England, Janney wanted the airplane delivered immediately, overruling company officials who advised Canada's strutting aviation commander that the aircraft had many hours of use and needed extensive overhauling, particularly the engine. The self-important Janney couldn't wait. The company employees were able to make some minor repairs, then hurriedly crated the machine and shipped it by rail to East Arlburg, Vermont, where it was reassembled on Lake Champlain and turned over to company pilot Cliff Webster. On 21 September, Webster, with Janney as passenger and student-pilot, took off for Valcartier on a short but memorable journey.

The Burgess-Dunne was so stable it could almost fly itself. Consequently, Webster was able to turn the controls over to Janney for about 40 percent of the trip. Janney might have had more time at the controls but — as if on cue in a Gilbert and Sullivan Opera — problems arose. Strong headwinds hampered the delta-winged aircraft's progress, resulting in the flying boat taking some two hours to cover the eighty miles to Sorel, Quebec, where the craft ran out of fuel. A large crowd awaited the aviators at the wharf where, once the Burgess-Dunne was safely moored, the local sheriff promptly stepped forward and arrested the aviators as spies. This mix-up resulted from an order-in-council passed under Canada's War Measures Act, which banned all airplane flights in Canada except with the militia's permission. Janney's situation was further complicated by the minister of militia's failure to advise his headquarters; no one in Ottawa had any idea that Sir Sam's air force was raggedly winging its way northward towards the plains of Val Cartier. Indeed, they had no idea Canada had suddenly acquired an air force.

The muddle was finally sorted after the sheriff was persuaded to phone the minister of militia himself. After a short consultation, the intrepid aviators were released and resumed what proved a most abbreviated journey. About forty-five minutes into the final leg, the engine began to vibrate ominously. Suspecting the bearings, Webster decided to land. Had Janney been less insistent on rushing the inspection at Marblehead, the problem would likely not have arisen and the flight would have been successful. At Janney's insistence, Webster reluctantly took off again, but the engine packed it in after about fifteen minutes and Webster had no choice but to land on Lake Champlain.

Sometime later, a boat found the stranded aviators and towed them and their warplane to Deschaillons where the Burgess-Dunne was dragged onto shore with more enthusiasm than caution, resulting in two holes being punctured in the main float. Mechanics brought spare parts from Marblehead and began a makeshift repair job. After a delay of several hours, the float was patched sufficiently for the wounded craft to be transported to Quebec City where troops were being loaded onto the thirty transport ships assembling for miles up the St. Lawrence River.

Prior to joining the troop ships leaving for England, Janney telegraphed some auto mechanics in Galt, ordering them to report to him for service with the Canadian Air Corps. They wisely checked to see if Janney had such authority and were advised that he did not. Provisional Commander Janney and his two officers had to board the SS *Franconia* without the extra mechanics. In the meantime, the CAC's only aircraft was lashed onto the deck of the *Athenia* where it would cross the Atlantic without supervision from Janney or either of the CAC's two crew members.

The Atlantic crossing drove the final spike into Janney's misadventure. The Burgess-Dunne was severely damaged during transit and never repaired. In February 1915, the Canadian Division moved from England's Salisbury Plain, but without the CAC's only warplane, which was inadvertently — or perhaps deliberately — left behind. Three months later, Canadian soldiers were ordered to locate the airplane, but no one was told what type of machine they were actually looking for. In June, the search was called off. A few rusty parts and two inner tubes were all that was found. Somehow, the inner tubes had wound up in a friendly pub. As for the Canadian Air Corps, the CEF reported that Janney had been absent without leave since 1 December 1914. The peculiar nature of his appointment created a problem, for how could the CEF discipline a man when there was no record of his enlistment? Captain Janney was therefore allowed to resign his commission although there were no documents confirming he had ever received one. As for Hughes, the rush of events in England and France so consumed his attention that he appeared to have forgotten all about the CAC.

Canada's first air force disappeared as ignominiously as an orphan on the doorstep of a Victorian workhouse. A more apt title for it would be, "Canada's first air farce."

Janney left further tracks, appearing from time to time in Canada and the United States, always claiming his captaincy and attempting to land some job in aeronautics; rather like an aspiring starlet who keeps showing up for rehearsals but never lands the part. Janney was truly a fey hero, frequently appearing on the Canadian aviation scene, well-intentioned and generally ineffectual.

The true story of aviation in Canada involves great achievement, mostly by young men and a few women, all of whom were venturing into largely unknown territory with courage and resourcefulness. Each did so in his or her own way, some with panache, some with reckless abandon, some cautiously, others shrewdly, most conscious that they were pioneers venturing into the frontiers of space and human endeavour.

# Chapter Two
## The Novelty of Flight

> They are the knighthood of this war, without fear and
> without reproach: they recall the legendary days of
> chivalry not merely by the daring of their exploits
> but by the nobility of their spirit.
> — *David Lloyd George, prime minister of England*

On a bitterly cold autumn day, Cadet Briggs Adams wrote to his parents
in New Jersey, telling of his adventure, attempting to describe the
experience of flying a heavier-than-air machine. In 1917, describing the
phenomena of flight was a daunting task. Until then, few people had
even seen a photograph of an airplane, and, like space travel today, only
a select few had actually experienced the sensation of flight.

*Camp Borden, 16 October 1917*
This afternoon the sky was full of those great masses
of thick, puffy white clouds, with the sky appearing
so clear and deep blue between them. I climbed up
between some until I was on top a thousand feet; then
I flew along for an hour or more, with the wheel just
touching the upper surface ... It seemed like riding in
a mythical chariot of the gods, racing along this vast,
infinitely white field, stretching off endlessly in every
direction. The clear open sky above ... is heaven as we
imagined it in childhood ... the world was completely
shut out. The celestial illusion was perfect, and it was
hard to come away from it — really quite a tug.

Then came the glide down — a wonderful sensation to pass through the air with the engine shut off so that you really seemed to be floating … making great swooping spiral curves … sometimes I would drop and tear through the air like a meteor … the wires shrieking with the wind, then nose up again and slow down.… It was so beautiful and to get away above the world that way — outside of it — in a heaven of absolutely unmarred beauty … you seem to expand with it — where there is no measure there are no bonds.[1]

The voice of Briggs Adams resonates across the ages, his voice awed by the epiphany of his experience. Since the beginnings of recorded history, humankind has yearned to conquer the skies and soar with the birds. In the middle ages, the great artist and theorist, Leonardo da Vinci, attempted to create a flying machine using only his observations of birds and his unlimited imagination. But mankind's dream of flying like the birds reaches back even into prehistory, before writing, when civilizations relied on oral tradition.

Two thousand years before Leonardo, the ancient Greeks recited the tale of Daedalus, an architect, inventor, and sculptor. Imprisoned by King Minos on the Island of Crete, Daedalus fashioned wings made from feathers and wax. Using these wings, Daedalus and his son, Icarus, flew out of prison to freedom. And so, even Daedalus, the ancient mythological Greek, dreamed of "slipping the surly bonds of earth."

In the summer of 1917, hundreds of young Americans, fuelled by the dreams of the ancients, travelled to Canada to enlist in the Royal Flying Corps so that they might penetrate the mysteries of flight. Holding that same dream, even more Canadians scraped together the money for the long train journey across the country. So strong was the urge to fly, that young men from the remote corners of the globe, from South Africa, from Venezuela, from Argentina, made their way to Canada so that they too might soar with the eagles.

This was the era before commercial air travel. Travel across oceans was possible only by ship. On land, the principal mode of transport was by steam-driven passenger trains. The automobile was just coming into common use, primarily for short hauls. Consequently, virtually all the recruits who travelled to Toronto did so by train. When they arrived they were billeted at the University of Toronto where they studied at Canada's first school of aeronautics. Created specifically for the training of RFC flight cadets, the school's instructors had only one type of aircraft with which to illustrate their lessons: the JN-4.

Having an actual airplane in the classroom made a lasting impact on the bright young men selected by the Imperial Royal Flying Corps. Most had only a vague idea as to what a flying machine looked like. When a JN-4 landed at the racetrack in Orillia, a reporter struggled to describe the strange craft, comparing it to a "motor car with small front wheels only" and having "wings cross-wise with the car" and driven by "motormen."[7]

*Lecture on rigging at the School of Military Aeronautics, Royal Flying Corps, University of Toronto, 1917. Courtesy of Library and Archives Canada/Department of National Defence C-020396.*

The first manned flight in Canada had taken place just eight years earlier. In February 1909, J.A.D. McCurdy had flown the Silver Dart a half mile over the frozen waters of Baddeck Bay, Nova Scotia. Neither McCurdy's achievement nor those of the famous Wright brothers appeared to herald a new air age. Indeed, airplanes were considered highly experimental and of little practical value by both governments and businessmen.

The rapidly changing nature of modern warfare would gradually demonstrate that a strategic new weapon had emerged. Initially, the airplane's function had been to observe and report on the enemy's troop movements. This role quickly expanded to include photographing the enemy's troops, bombing his installations, strafing his troops and, finally, attacking and destroying both his airplanes and the men who flew them. The famous aerial dogfights did not develop until the spring of 1915. This phase of the air war led to growing losses of pilots and a critical need to train replacements.

England had entered the war with just 113 first-line airplanes. These were distributed between the Royal Flying Corps and the Royal Naval Air Service (RNAS). Between them the two branches numbered about 2,000 crewmen. By war's end, British air power included 291,000 crew members and 22,000 aircraft, of which over 3,000 were first-line machines.[3] Modern air power was born during the First World War.

In order to supply the demands of this new weapon, England created a vast training establishment in the British Isles. With space running out and demands for pilots increasing daily, the RFC began expanding training facilities outside the motherland. The first of these was established in Egypt, at that time a part of the vast, globe-encircling British Empire.

The First World War became a contest of attrition; the Allied generals' strategy for victory came to be based on the calculation that they had greater populations than Germany and therefore could afford to lose more soldiers. But, even with the imposition of mandatory military service — conscription — the supply of young cannon fodder began drying up.

Only the best and brightest young men were eligible as pilots. Flying an airplane required perfect eyesight, quick, athletic reflexes, and a keen mind. Britons of this quality had been among the first to volunteer and were the first casualties; men of this calibre were soon absorbed by the rapid expansion of the RFC and the RNAS. The problem was exacerbated by the heavy losses experienced by the RFC at the front. At the Battle of the Somme, manpower losses in the air war averaged 300 percent a year. By September of 1916, the casualty rate had risen to 400 percent.[4] During March and April of 1917 the situation reached crisis proportions; Allied pilots were being killed, captured, or wounded faster than they could be replaced.

While the land war was frozen in both movement and strategy, the War in the Air changed rapidly. As it assumed greater strategic importance, both sides moved to expand their air forces. Sir Sefton Brancker at the British War Office developed an ambitious plan to increase the strength of the RFC from six to fifty squadrons. When he presented the plan to Lord Kitchener, the secretary of state for war, he said bluntly, "double it."[5]

Faced with a manpower crisis in England, General Brancker conceived a strategy to involve the overseas Dominions. Despite many roadblocks, his initiatives eventually led to the formation of RFC (Canada), also known as the Imperial Royal Flying Corps.

On New Year's Day 1916, Canada's prime minister, Sir Robert Borden, convinced that the future of civilization hung on the Allies winning the war, committed Canada to providing an army of half a million men. This from a nation whose total population numbered less than 8 million. Initially, the militia had sucked up men like a blotter, but with the majority of recent British immigrants already enlisted and the horror of trench warfare increasingly evident, enlistments in Canada began drying up. The government of Canada faced increasing resistance from the population as it struggled to maintain the half-million soldiers promised by the prime minister.

Faced with a manpower crisis in the army, Prime Minister Borden and his cabinet were unwilling to further deplete Canada's human resources by creating a Canadian air force. Nor were they willing to commit Canada to the heavy financial burden involved.

Despite their government's resistance to creating a Canadian air force, young Canadians still managed to enlist in both the RFC and the RNAS.

In the early years of the war, this was accomplished by inveigling a transfer from the Canadian Expeditionary Force and taking pilot training with the RFC in England. But many would-be pilots were unwilling to risk joining the army and face the horrors of trench warfare, when it was uncertain they could obtain a transfer to the RFC.

Another route lay in first obtaining a pilot's licence and then joining the RFC or RNAS in Canada. Both services had recruiting offices in the Dominion but entry required they hold a valid pilot's licence. These were issued by the Aero Club of America and were known as the FAI certificate or Fédération Aéronautique Internationale (FAI). When the war broke out in August of 1914, only eight Canadians are known to have held these certificates.

Canada's first aviation school had been established by the ubiquitous J.A.D. McCurdy, the pilot of the Silver Dart and a prime mover in Canada's first airplane manufacturing plant. McCurdy had a long association with American aircraft designer Glen Curtiss, the two being active in the early flight experiments at Baddeck Bay, Nova Scotia. McCurdy's job with Curtiss was to obtain orders for Curtiss aircraft from the British War Office.

In the spring of 1915, the British admiralty placed an order for aircraft with Curtiss, stipulating that fifty of these should be produced in Canada. With the orders for the aircraft in hand, Curtiss and McCurdy set up Curtiss Aeroplanes and Motors, Ltd. in Toronto with McCurdy as managing director.

At about the same time, an agreement was reached between Prime Minister Borden and the Imperial War Office that Naval Service Headquarters could recruit pilots in Canada to serve with the RNAS. Armed with an FAI, RNAS recruits were accepted as probationary sub-lieutenants, an inducement not offered by the RFC. Only when they had successfully completed a thorough RFC training program, lasting six to eight months, would RFC cadets become second lieutenants. Moreover, their rate of pay was below that of an RNAS sub-lieutenant.

Correctly anticipating that Canadians would be lining up to join the RNAS, McCurdy established a school at Long Branch, on the shores of Lake Ontario, eight miles west of Toronto. The site covered 100 acres and included three hangars, a landing strip, and three Curtiss F flying-boats.

Other than a few makeshift, farmers' field–type landing strips, Long Branch was Canada's first airfield.*

McCurdy's school began flight training on 10 May 1915 with twenty pupils, and graduated its first class on 11 July. Almost all of these graduates went into the RNAS; only a few joined the RFC. By mid November of 1915, an estimated 250 candidates were waiting to take certificate training. That so many signed up is all the more remarkable when the tuition of 400 dollars is compared to the wage scales of the day. In 1915 a railway mail clerk earned 500 dollars yearly while construction workers earned a princely twenty-five cents an hour.[7] Robert Logan wrote of his financial situation when taking the course:

> I paid $400.00 and a contract was signed in which the School undertook to give me 400 minutes of flying training in the air and would lend me an aeroplane in which I could perform the figure eights and landing tests as specified for qualifying for the International Aviator's Certificate.
>
> This was the procedure followed by all the pupils. We live at our own expense for at least three months … much longer for some pupils. Only a few pupils had homes in Toronto. The flying-boat school, where we were given 200 minutes of flying (all dual) was at Hanlan's Point. The land-plane school was on the firing range at Long Branch, a few miles east of Port Credit. Many of us boarded at the homes of farmers in the vicinity of the rifle range. When I arrived in Toronto I had between six and seven hundred dollars. I had to live on a very tight budget. When I completed the course I borrowed ten dollars (from McCurdy) to take me to Ottawa where I was told to report at the office of the Governor General …. A few of the Toronto men were

---

* Cartierville was our first aerodrome, boasting both a runway and a hangar in 1911. But Long Branch was Canada's first military aerodrome. Located just south of Lakeshore Boulevard and west of Dixie Road, the RFC purchased it and began flying there in late February 1917.[6]

members of wealthy families but the majority of us were decidedly of the earn-your-own-way class.[8]

Although well run and competently staffed, the McCurdy School was too small to meet the demands of the hundreds of enthusiastic young Canadians eager for flying instruction. Many would-be aviators flocked to American flying schools, most of them to the Curtiss School at Hammondsport, New York; the Wright School at Dayton, Ohio; or farther afield to the Stinson School at San Antonio, Texas. The Texas school was run by Marjorie Stinson, a famous aviatrix still in her teens. Her first four pupils were all Canadians. In fact, Canadians quickly constituted more than 50 percent of all the students in American flying schools.

Where there is a strong demand and money to be made, charlatans invariably appear, disguising their true motives with glib but empty promises. Such was the case with the Thomas Brothers Winter School of Aviation at St. Augustine, Florida.

Among the school's first pupils was Alfred W. "Nick" Carter from Fish Creek, Alberta, a student of engineering at Queen's University. A superb physical specimen, Carter had been accepted into the RNAS, pending receipt of his FAI. As all the major American schools were full, Carter along with a friend, T.R. Shearer, opted for the new school at St. Augustine. Having prepaid their four-hundred-dollar tuition fee, they arrived to discover that the school's one and only training airplane was still in crates. They spent the next several days uncrating and assembling the airplane under the direction of a mechanic who, Carter noted, "knew damn all about aircraft."[9]

With the airplane assembled, Carter described their unique training:

> We ran the engine after a lot of hard work pulling the propeller.... But when we revved it up the pistons melted and spat aluminum out the exhaust ports ... Everything was held up until new cast iron pistons arrived and were installed by ourselves.... Finally the machine with the engine running was taken out on the water.... The so-called instructor motor-boated it up and down a number of days, and he claimed it would not get up on the step.

After several days of delay, and modifications to the airplane, including removing the pontoon and installing landing wheels so that it could take off from the beach, the instructor could delay no longer. Carter bullied both the instructor and the owner, even threatening them physically unless training got under way. With obvious reluctance, the instructor agreed to take Carter up for training. Carter described the experience:

> I got into the seat beside Benedict and away we went up the beach. We got into the air and went about a mile, swooping along from side to side, diving and rising, before he got it in a fairly stable attitude close to the ground and he switched it off and plopped in the sand. He was pale as a sheet and shaking. I thought in my complete ignorance that it was great. What actually happened was he got into the air by accident and not knowing how to fly had over controlled like crazy, but was committed until he got it down again near the ground and called the whole thing off.[10]

Benedict made sure he did not get the seaplane airborne again, insisting the students needed to taxi along the water "with the tail up" in order to get "the feel of things." The school folded shortly thereafter when the airplane was wrecked on the beach during "ground manoeuvres." His money gone, an enraged Carter bullied Benedict into a partial refund and returned to Canada.

In Ottawa, the resourceful Albertan contacted his Member of Parliament, R.B. Bennett, who set up interviews for Carter and his friend Tom Shearer with a number of important Canadians, including Major-General Gwatkin and the governor general, all to no avail. Finally, Carter and Shearer, by dogged perseverance, so hounded Canadian officials and the British admiralty that the latter finally accepted them without flying certificates. Moreover, the Canadian government was so happy to see the last of the two Albertans that it paid for their first-class passage to England on the SS *Metagama*. Once in England, both men breezed through their pilot's training.*

These humorous incidents reveal a more serious problem. Private schools lacked the resources to turn out pilots in large enough numbers to meet the demand for pilots. Even the efficient Curtiss School shut down for the winter months. In its two years of existence, the school managed to graduate just 130 licensed pilots. At the other Canadian flying schools, not one student earned a pilot's certificate.

Meanwhile, Canada's minister of militia, the mercurial Sir Sam Hughes, had been won over to the view that Canada should participate in an air-training scheme; no longer was the airplane the creation of the devil, Hughes now saw it as vital to winning the war.

In September 1916, Hughes was in England, where he made an offer to the War Office to raise and train Royal Flying Corps squadrons in Canada and place them at the disposal of the imperial government. In doing so, Hughes reversed the policy of the Canadian government without consulting Sir Robert Borden. Although he concealed his offer from the prime minister, news that he had made some sort of aviation commitment soon reached the long-suffering Borden.

Hughes's propensity for making decisions without consulting his cabinet colleagues had already caused the government much embarrassment. Now he had reversed a government policy on a matter critical to the government's war policy. Borden had patiently endured Hughes's erratic behaviour for years but his minister's unilateral action on the air matter finally exhausted the prime minister's tolerance. He asked for Hughes's resignation.

Before firing his minister of militia, Borden and his cabinet moved to circumvent the damage caused by Hughes. The prime minister made

---

* Nick Carter became an ace with seventeen kills and was awarded the DSC. He remained in the RAF after the war, rising to the rank of air marshal. He was later awarded the OBE and MBE. Retiring in 1953, he returned to Canada where he died in 1986 at the age of ninety-two. Tom Shearer was killed in a flying accident in 1917.

an offer to the British authorities. Canada would advance the money for an aircraft factory while the British would be responsible for the training school.

The War Office received the Canadian offer with a distinct lack of enthusiasm, realizing that the Canadian scheme would put the burden of cost on Britain. Moreover, there was concern among members of the Air Board and the War Office at establishing a school in Canada under the control of imperial officers. They were keenly aware of Hughes's belligerent demands for Canadian autonomy in military matters and believed he would interfere with the running of a British school in Canada. Borden assured them that Hughes would not be a problem but, quite properly, did not mention he had already asked for his minister's resignation.

Lord Sydenham of the Air Board could not understand Borden's position. Canada was a self-governing dominion. How could it accept an imperial military presence in Canada when those troops would not be subject to the control of the Canadian government? The British had withdrawn the last of their garrisons from Canada more than forty years earlier. Sydenham wondered if it was now possible for Britain to exercise command over British troops on Canadian soil under any circumstance. He regarded Canadians as a notoriously unruly people and concluded that, in their own country, Canadians would be *even* more difficult to subject to British discipline than they were in England.

While more deferential than Americans, Canada's pioneer environment had infected Canadians with what the British ruling class regarded as the disease of democracy. Lord Sydenham had accurately foreseen the problems that would arise when British officers in Canada attempted to impose British discipline on Canadian soldiers. The problems would be far worse when the more egalitarian Americans joined the IRFC and trained in Canada.

Brigadier-General Sefton Brancker, director of military aeronautics, chafed at the delays in the negotiations between Borden and Lord Sydenham. A Canadian training establishment had been under discussion for eighteen months and nothing had been accomplished. While the generals and politicians discussed and manoeuvred, the situation in Europe grew steadily more desperate. Brancker pressured his superior, Major General Sir David Henderson, to move ahead with the Canadian plan, pointing out there was no longer any space in England where they could train the extra squadrons needed and that Canada was the only alternative. His arguments won over Henderson.

The Air Board accepted the recommendations of Generals Henderson and Brancker. Shortly thereafter the Treasury Office was won over, convinced that, despite the heavy cost, the emergency in Europe required that the Canadian project go ahead at England's expense.

To head up the Canadian project, Brancker needed a younger, more flexible officer who could adjust to the harsh weather, and the ruder, rougher Canadian society. He chose a stocky, ruggedly handsome, thirty-four-year-old bachelor, Major Cuthbert G. Hoare, a career soldier who had spent the bulk of his service years in central India and had shown a distinct propensity for bending rules to get the job done. Hoare had been serving as commander of number 14 Wing in France when he was summoned to headquarters where he met Brancker on New Year's Day. He was told of the dire need for a training school in Canada, that he would be given a free hand to set it up and command it, and that he was to select his staff and to proceed to Canada at once.

Although there were undersea cables across the Atlantic, unreliability of transport resulting from Germany's submarine warfare meant that the commander of the IRFC in Canada would be largely on his own. He would need excellent judgment, an ability to deal diplomatically and skilfully with colonial officials, and the nerve and confidence to make decisions without advice from senior officials. The commanding officer's ability would be critical to the success or failure of the IRFC training scheme in Canada and, as a consequence, to the war effort in Europe.

# CHAPTER THREE
## COMMANDER ABOVE THE LAW

> What is so ... impressive about him is the free-wheeling verve with which he brushed aside impediments insuperable to more orthodox men. International boundaries, national policies, and the hidebound ways of bureaucracies meant little to him; he ran over all of them wearing velvet boots.
> — *S.F. Wise*[1]

Cuthbert Gurney Hoare was born into the landed gentry of East Anglia. The Hoare, Barclay, and Gurney families were all involved in either banking or stockbroking. In early twentieth-century England, the class system was still rooted in land and family. Traditionally, land holdings carried greater distinction than success in commerce. Consequently, although their money came from banking, the Hoares lived in the style of rural squires. Cuthbert Hoare grew to maturity as a country gentleman.

After graduating from Harrow, Hoare attended Sandhurst, England's most exclusive military academy. As he gave priority to a hunting competition and missed writing an exam, his academic career fared badly; Hoare flunked out of Sandhurst at the bottom of his class.

Shortly after Hoare reached his eighteenth birthday, England declared war on the Boers of South Africa. He immediately enlisted in the Worcestershire Regiment and, in 1901, was commissioned as a second lieutenant. He planned on joining the mounted cavalry in South Africa with the hope of seeing some real action. When his youth and lack of combat experience frustrated this ambition, he promptly transferred to the Indian Army and was posted to Burma.

Hoare spent the rest of the decade in India with the Central India Horse, an elite British imperial unit. During those years, his principal recreation was polo and big-game hunting. Ever in search of adventure, Hoare took some pride in having bagged seven tigers.

His involvement with flying came about accidentally when a fellow officer, Captain Duncan Pitcher, decided to build an airplane and enlisted Lieutenant Hoare as the project's handyman.

Their attempts to build an airplane, while unsuccessful, fuelled a deep interest in aeronautics. When Hoare and Pitcher heard that a private school in Bristol was training pilots at Salisbury Plain, they took three months' leave and left for England. On 29 August 1911, they were among the first British citizens to obtain a pilot's licence.

While in London, Hoare read in *The Times* that the Central India Horse had been ordered to Persia to protect the consuls and British citizens from the chaos that had broken out in the southern area of that country. He left that night via Brindisi and arrived in India just as his regiment was departing. Hoare noted that they arrived "just in time, as after Pitch and myself no other officers ever got to Persia."[2] As his letter indicates, Persia proved a disappointment:

> After landing at Bushire, where we swam our horses to the beach about one mile as ships could get no nearer, we proceeded to Shiraz. In those days Persia was still medieval and not developed. There were no roads and we scrambled up to Shiraz over several passes up to 8,000 feet, by what was merely a terrible rough mule track, on foot.... There was no real reason for our ever going there. The consul at Shiraz was a bit jittery! We spent 1913 in a grand climate.... Very few incidents but we had one British officer killed and two or three other ranks [killed].[3]

Upon his return from Persia, Hoare went on a special course at England's Central Flying School. The course had been created to prepare Captain Hoare and three others to set up a small experimental air force in India.

His initial task was to accelerate the manufacture of airplanes at the Vickers plant. His disrespect for proper procedures helped him bypass the required inspections. A conventional officer would probably have failed, but Hoare connived to get the machines rushed to India.

In the spring of 1914, he travelled to the sub-continent where he joined the first Indian air force at Sitapur. When the war broke out that August, Captain Hoare and the other three members of the Indian Air Force were recalled to fly with the Royal Flying Corps. To this point, the young officer had lived a Kipling-esque life, all high, romantic adventure in exotic climes. But the romance of the Belle Époque era would be quickly demolished by the horrors of the Great War.

In April of 1915, Hoare was posted to France and placed in command of Seven Squadron. He saw combat and earned a mention in dispatches. Already past the optimum age for combat flying, he was promoted to major in 1916 and sent to the Somme to command 14 Wing. As the commanding officer (CO) he was prevented from flying in combat but faced the painful task of sending inexperienced young pilots on missions — with the knowledge that many would not return. At the terrible slaughter of the Somme, a front-line pilot's survival time seldom exceeded a few weeks. It was an experience that would influence Hoare's decisions when he was later sent to Canada. He remained for the final battle of the Somme, which lasted into November of 1916.

During the five months of the campaign, total casualties for all sides reached more than a million men. Almost daily, newspapers were filled with pages of those killed or missing in action. It was the Somme that burned the horror of trench warfare into the consciousness of western civilization.

In late December, Hoare received orders to return to England. He was apprehensive, fearing he would be posted to some dull administrative position. He could not have imagined where his superiors were going to send him.

Hoare's administrative abilities had brought him to the attention of several senior RFC officers. One of those recommending Major Hoare "as the man for Canada" was Lieutenant-Colonel C.J. Percy Burke, nicknamed "Preggy Percy," short for "Pregnant Percy." The nickname resulted from his immense girth and pear-like profile.

Burke had been in Canada as the RFC recruiting officer in November and December of 1915. Upon his return to England, Burke had written an extensive report on the suitability of setting up a training establishment in Canada. Subsequently, Burke got into a dispute with his senior officers and was transferred out of the RFC to his original regiment, the Royal Irish. His recommendation of Hoare as the man for Canada was not the decisive factor in the latter's appointment. The officer who made that decision was Brigadier-General Sir Sefton Brancker; he had conceived the idea of a pilot training plan in Canada two years earlier and was aware of Hoare's tendency to skirt regulations when necessary to get things done.

On New Year's Day 1917, he summoned Major Hoare and six other officers to a meeting at the War Office, nicknamed "Dastardly House" by the junior officers. He informed Hoare of his new job as CO of a training program to be established in Canada. The newly minted acting lieutenant-colonel's instructions were to sail for Canada within a week. Upon his arrival he was to form a pilot training organization of twenty squadrons. The Canadian government would help him. The Imperial Munitions Board, or IMB, would arrange the supply of aircraft, engines, equipment, land, and buildings.

According to Major Dermott Allen, who was present at the meeting, Hoare was permitted £1 million sterling as a start, and could get more when he needed it. Hoare remembers he was given a credit of £20 million. He would spend a great deal more than £20 million sterling, which at that time translated into roughly $96 million in U.S. dollars.

Brancker further advised Hoare that he could expect no help from Britain for supplies but was to find everything as best he could in Canada. He was given no further orders. When Hoare asked, where he should proceed first, Brancker replied that the decision was up to him.

Initially, the Canada scheme did not enthuse the thirty-four-year-old acting lieutenant-colonel but, upon further consideration, Hoare decided that they intended to let him run the show his way and came to the conclusion that it might be "an experience, providing they really mean to give me a free hand."[4] Although a veteran of Europe, Persia, and India, Hoare had never travelled to North America. To him, Canada and the United States were simply colours on a map.

Brancker had placed Hoare in a unique position. Canada was almost an autonomous nation, only matters of foreign policy were the prerogative of the imperial power. In all other respects the Canadian government was fully independent, making and enforcing its own laws and deciding public policy. Although the Dominion did not have formal control of foreign policy, in practice, when foreign affairs affected its interests, Canada often asserted those interests over Britain's priorities.

Hoare would be in charge of a military establishment, operating in Canada with Canadian recruits, yet completely independent of the Canadian government and its parliament. He was formally responsible only to the governor general, at that time an appointee of the British government. As commanding officer of the Imperial Royal Flying Corps in Canada, he had the power to enlist, promote, and discharge soldiers as well as airmen and airwomen. He could also grant and cancel temporary commissions and could appoint or reduce warrant officers. At the time of his appointment, as CO of the Royal Flying Corps in Canada, Hoare was merely an *acting* lieutenant-colonel.

An assessment of Hoare was later made by Major Allen. As the officer working most closely with the CO, Allen was in a unique position to know both the strengths and weaknesses of his dynamic superior. Here is what Allen had to say of the man who would run the IRFC in Canada with virtually unrestricted authority:

> This was ... the man still in his early thirties who was to tackle and carry through one of the most responsible missions allotted to any one of those officers who helped to make the RFC and RNAS. Hoare's position was unique in that he was for all practical purposes, completely his own master with the North Atlantic between him and his nearest effective superior authority (War Office).... Most important of all he had, in practice, full financial powers through the medium of the Imperial Munitions Board.
>
> Hoare was a man of great moral courage, determination, and drive. He was never afraid to make a decision and he made it quickly. His approach towards

his seniors and equals in rank was pleasant and tactful.

Towards his juniors he was apt to be somewhat intimidating until he got to know them well. He was very demanding of his staff who he drove hard. His hours of sleep were under the average, he was an early riser and throughout the day his mind never seemed to rest. He had a habit, maddening to his staff, of starting to "talk shop" and give instructions at ten o'clock at night when everybody except himself was dead tired and about to go to bed. It was unfortunate that he seldom spontaneously said a word of praise or encouragement informally or formally. Formal congratulatory messages or orders were almost always suggested to him, and in fairness he invariably accepted the suggestion. From all he expected zeal, honourable conduct, hard work and efficiency. With officers who did not come up to his standards he dealt drastically and more than one found himself on board a trooper bound for the United Kingdom designated as "temperamentally unsuited for dealing with Canadians."

In regard to "other ranks" he saw to it they were properly housed, fed, and looked after as regards working conditions and amenities. Quite correctly he expected Commanding Officers of Units to see to this sort of thing, but was quick to follow up and remedy shortcomings, noted on inspections. One point upon which he was insistent was respect for his "office." He was in no way a vain man, but he insisted that all ranks should salute him properly when he drove in his open car in the streets. He was quick to notice any officers or soldier who obviously had seen him and failed to salute. His car was stopped and his driver ... had to double back and take the name of the officer and provide a "Charge." Apart from any question of respect of the "King's Commission" Hoare did this to enhance the prestige of the Royal Flying Corps in the eyes of the Canadian troops and civilian population. To the purely civilian mind this may seem petty, but the hard fact remains that, nowhere through the world and irrespective of nationality, do the men of any good and efficient military body fail to greet their officers with some form of salute.[5]

The new CO of the IRFC in Canada was fortunate in Brancker's selection of the officers who constituted the advance team to Canada. Of the six key officers, only two would report directly to Hoare. One of these was his brother, Lieutenant-Colonel Gurney Hoare, who had been seconded to the RFC from the South African Army, Ordinance Division. Four years older than his brother, Gurney Hoare was a fully trained chemist who had taken the long course in ordinance at Woolwich. His duties with the IRFC were twofold; he was liaison officer to the IMB as well as the officer commanding the Aircraft Equipment Branch. This latter responsibility required that he estimate, in advance, the operation's requirements for material, technical and non-technical, and arrange for its procurement and distribution.

The third man in the executive triumvirate was Major Allen, who was initially in charge of all air organization, including administration, training, and personnel. As the organization of the IRFC grew increasingly complex, the twenty-six-year-old evolved into Hoare's chief staff officer.

The son of a barrister who practised law in both Ireland and India, Allen had an outstanding academic career, graduating from schools in England, Ireland, Switzerland, and Germany, where he earned a scholarship to the Sorbonne. A graduate of RMC Sandhurst, his father had insisted he join the Royal Irish Fusiliers where he gained a working knowledge of military administration and law. In addition, he qualified as a military interpreter in both French and German. Ironically, the multilingual Allen had a slight stutter, which earned him the nickname "Balmy." Despite his handicap, Allen's abilities, charm, and good humour earned him the respect and affection of those who dealt with him.[6]

When the Royal Flying Corps was formed in 1912, Allen applied and gained selection to the first course at the Central Flying School. He qualified and was posted to number 3 Squadron as a flying officer in January 1913.

In March 1916, Captain Allen was sent to Edinburgh to start up the Turnhouse Aerodrome from bare fields and to form an RFC training squadron. A few months later, he was promoted to the rank of major and squadron commander. Organizationally gifted, he completed the task of laying out the runways, erecting the hangars, the living quarters, and the ancillary buildings with seeming ease. He had the entire operation, including the training of pilots, running smoothly when he was summoned to the meeting with General Brancker and Lieutenant-Colonel Hoare. Allen proved to be the perfect man for the task in Canada, working smoothly in tandem with his hard-driving CO.

Only one of the original six officers selected as key staff was a Canadian, Lieutenant John K. Aird, who had flown with the RFC since early 1916. His father, Sir John Aird, was general manager of the Canadian Bank of Commerce, but was better known to the Canadian government for his vigorous promotion of a Canadian air force. Only with considerable difficulty had Prime Minister Borden been able to resist Sir John's strenuous lobbying.

To avoid the disaster of a German submarine destroying the entire project, it was decided to send the advance party to Canada on four separate ships. The entire party of 14 officers, 76 other ranks, and 156 motor vehicles left England between the ninth and eighteenth of January. Hoare and his group left for Canada on the tenth.

Hoare was accompanied by three of his senior officers; Major Allen, Major Strubell, and Lieutenant-Colonel Methven. The latter had been a successful businessman prior to the outbreak of the war. Hoare gave him the task of setting up and administering the stores depot. Strubell was in charge of recruiting and records.

Hoare held daily meetings with these officers during which they worked out a timetable for aerodrome construction, flying training, cadet recruitment, and, indeed, every aspect of what was to be a semi-autonomous military establishment. As Allen later observed, they not only adhered to this timetable, in many instances, they were able to better it.

Two important decisions directly affecting RFC (Canada) were made prior to Hoare's appointment as commanding officer. The previous October, the Canadian government and the Imperial War Office agreed on an arrangement to guarantee a steady supply of training aircraft. At that time, the only significant manufacturer of aircraft in Canada was Curtiss Aeroplanes and Motors, Ltd. A branch operation of the American-owned Curtiss Aeroplanes, it manufactured from a small facility leased from the John Inglis Company on Strachan Avenue in Toronto.

After lengthy negotiations, the Canadian government agreed to loan $1 million to the IMB to be used to purchase the assets of Curtiss Aeroplanes and Motors. The IMB would run the facility until the war's end, after which the company would be turned over to the Canadian government. The War Office guaranteed sufficient orders to keep the plant operating for the duration of the war.

The IMB had been set up by the British Ministry of Munitions to act as its Canadian agent for the procurement of munitions and war supplies for the empire, including the letting of contracts and supervising the quality of the supplies. Although nominally controlled from London, the majority of its management and staff were Canadian.

It followed from the decision to purchase the Curtiss plant together with its skilled workforce, tools, and machinery, that a Curtiss-designed airplane would be selected as the IRFC's training machine. Glen Curtiss had designed and built numerous aircraft, but the Royal Flying Corps considered the JN-3 the most suitable. The redesign of the JN-3 to bring it up to IRFC standards was placed under the direction of F.G. Ericson, the plant's chief engineer. The redesigned aircraft was known as the JN-4 (Canadian), but was affectionately nicknamed the "Jenny" or the "Canuck" by all who flew her. It was flight-tested by Bert Acosta and accepted by the IMB and the IRFC on 1 January 1917.

Unfortunately, the Strachan plant did not manufacture the Curtiss OX-5, the water-cooled eight-cylinder engine used in the JN-4. These would have to be obtained from the Curtiss plant in Buffalo. As the United States was still a neutral country, a supply of engines from the Buffalo facility could not be guaranteed. Should the United States enter the conflict, they might require Curtiss to produce engines solely for the American military. It was a risk the IRFC had no choice but to accept.

Aside from the type of training airplane and the selection of a factory by the IMB, Hoare was to decide virtually everything related to the IRFC. During the ocean crossing, he and his advisers made several key decisions. Hoare had read Burke's report recommending Winnipeg as the best location for the IRFC's headquarters. Although Montreal was Canada's largest and most industrialized city, Hoare ignored both cities and opted for Toronto, the deciding factors being the location of the Curtiss plant in that city combined with the shorter winters of southern Ontario.

Hoare and his officers arrived in Saint John, New Brunswick, on 19 January. Proceeding by train to Ottawa, he met with senior officials of the Militia Department, the IMB, and others. He also met with Major-General Gwatkin, chief of the Canadian Army. Gwatkin, a former British staff officer, had been seconded to help Canada organize its militia in 1911. The first encounter between Gwatkin and Hoare did not go well.

Prime Minister Borden had promised Britain an army of half a million men from a nation with a population of less than 8 million. Moreover, there was no enthusiasm for military service in Quebec, nor in many parts of the prairies, particularly among the farm population. Nor were union chiefs enthused, calling for the conscription of wealth before the conscription of manpower. Fortunes were being made by capitalists supplying the war effort while ordinary men were being asked to serve in foul trenches for little more than a dollar a day. Enlistments had been steadily dropping and Borden faced the prospect of creating deep divisions within Canada over the issue of conscription. The alternative was to keep Canadian soldiers in the brutal trenches without fresh soldiers to replace the mounting casualties.

As chief of staff, Gwatkin was keenly aware of the government's problem. When he met Hoare, he asked how many men the colonel would require. Hoare replied he would need five hundred for a start. Gwatkin told Hoare he couldn't get five hundred in six months, and added, "The best thing you can do young man is to turn round, go straight home and tell them you've been sent on a fool's errand."

Somewhat nettled, Hoare responded, "The time to go home is after I have tried, not before."[7] On that dissonant note, the two men parted.

In spite of their initial disagreement, Hoare obtained assurances that the Militia Department would lend all possible assistance to RFC

(Canada). This included recruiting, accommodation, administration, and the use of government land for aerodromes.

From Ottawa, Hoare proceeded by train to Toronto, arriving on 25 January. Offices for headquarters were quickly arranged at the Imperial Oil Company's building at 56 Church Street in downtown Toronto, the same building that housed the IMB.

In a memorandum on the development of the RFC in Canada, Hoare listed his immediate priorities:

1. Barracks for the men (officers and NCOs mostly from England).
2. Barracks for the Recruits Depot (Enlisted men).
3. Offices for the administrative staff.
4. Buildings for quartermaster and technical stores.
5. Selection of aerodromes.
6. Formation of Cadet Wing.
7. Estimates of requirements for first six months.
8. Building requirements of aerodromes in detail. (No engineering officers had been sent by England.)
9. Selection and purchase of mechanical transport.
10. Recruiting campaign (methods, etc.) on a large scale.
11. R.E. Section. (An engineering section had to be established.)
12. Classes of instruction (had to be set up) for mechanics.

It was a daunting list and Hoare lost no time in dealing with it. The day after his arrival in Toronto, he left for Camp Borden.

Southern Ontario was experiencing its worst winter in five years; rural areas were under two to three feet of snow, frozen hard by temperatures consistently below zero Fahrenheit, and sometimes as low as -30° Celsius. Under such conditions, it was impractical to examine the topography and topsoil of prospective aerodrome locations. But time was critical. Hoare could not wait for spring to select the location of what would be Canada's first military aerodrome.

Hoare and Methven made the trip to Borden accompanied by three

*RFC Canada hangars and aerodrome, Camp Borden, Ontario, 1917 (looking south). Courtesy of Library and Archives Canada/Department of National Defence PA022776.*

Canadians: Major General W.A. Logie, and two of his officers. Logie was commander of both Camp Borden and Military District No. 2. He and his officers were there to answer any questions about the site that the Canadian government was offering to the IRFC rent-free.

When the party reached Angus they discovered the unusually heavy snows had forced the railway to close the branch line to Borden for the remainder of the winter. Hoare and his party had to break trail by sleigh, taking nearly two hours to travel the remaining five miles to the camp.

There were problems with the site. Borden had been built on what local residents called the "Sandy Plains," or "Big Sandy." Although the sandy soil drained well, it was littered with stumps, which posed a challenge but could be overcome. More difficult to solve was the area's reputation for sand storms; a dangerous problem for untrained flyers in open-cockpit airplanes with only the most rudimentary of flight instruments.

Offsetting these difficulties was the time that would be saved by accessing the facilities already installed at a cost of some $2 million. These facilities included roads, two railway sidings (Grand Trunk and CPR), a water and sanitation system, and an electrical power plant. All these had been put in place to accommodate the 32,000 Canadian troops camped at Borden the previous year. The Canadian government owned approximately 17,000 acres at Borden and offered the IRFC 1,000 acres rent-free. Hoare planned an establishment of five squadrons (approximately ninety airplanes) and 1,500 men, including officers, cadets, and enlisted men.

Deciding that he could not wait for spring to properly examine the site, Hoare accepted the advice of General Logie and his colonels. Returning to Toronto the following day, he wrote General Gwatkin, requesting that the Militia Department provide accommodation in the Toronto area for one thousand recruits. He also wanted clothing and regimental necessities for these men. Most importantly, he wanted the help of the militia in the recruiting campaign that he planned to launch immediately. He hoped the militia's medical officers would examine candidates for the IRFC at their various recruitment centres across the country. This would save valuable time and considerable expense. The Canadian Militia did not disappoint; on 30 January, Gwatkin acknowledged that these requests would be met.

Meanwhile, the directors of the IMB were moving decisively on other matters. On 26 January, an aviation department of the IMB was formed under the direction of Frank Baillie, a hard-driving businessman who had donated his services to the board. Baillie was also the manager of the fledgling Canadian Aviation Company and recognized the need to expand that operation to meet the IRFC's need for training machines. Concurrent with the establishing of an aviation department, Baillie let out contracts for the building of a new factory on nine acres of land on Dufferin Street in Toronto. Despite the severe winter, the contractors were at work on the site within two days.

During the same week, the IMB, acting on Hoare's advice, concluded a deal whereby the IRFC arranged to use the Curtiss aerodrome at Long Branch. Although Long Branch was too small for a military aerodrome, it was available and would serve as an interim base until Borden was in operation.

On 30 January, just four days after Hoare's inspection trip to Camp Borden, the Aviation Department of the IMB signed contracts with Robert Low, a director of the Ottawa construction firm of Bate, McMahon, and Company. Low, an honorary colonel, had the reputation of never being a day late in completing a contract. He had helped build the Valcartier camp, and had built Camp Borden and several other military establishments in Canada.

Low wasted no time. Within a few days, the spur line from Angus had been reopened and Low had 400 men working day and night. They cleared the stumps in below-zero weather using teams of horses and sleighs. At night they used arc lamps so the work could continue. Two weeks later Low had 1,700 men and 100 teams of horses at the site, with shifts working around the clock. Most of the workers were enemy aliens who could not leave the work site without permission from the chief constable of the county. Low was made chief constable, pro-tem, so the workers had no choice but to stay on the job regardless of the extreme cold.*

Destumping was a simple but labourious process. Each stump was removed by a team of horses worked by a teamster and two labourers. A sleigh would then arrive with a load of earth that would be dumped in the snow beside the hole. When the snow melted the hole was filled in. Several hundred acres were destumped in this fashion.

While the land was being cleared, decisions for the various buildings needed by the new aerodrome were made by Methven and Captain Denton. The Canadian Militia provided the services of an engineer, who worked out the detailed engineering specifications.

Six weeks after construction began, Low had all fifteen of the new hangars erected and had completed most of the accommodation for the cadets and enlisted men. Each of the hangars was 120 feet by 66 feet and

---

* Born at East Saginaw, Michigan, in 1874, Low spent his early childhood years in his father's native country of Scotland. He learned the construction business working for his father in Canada and the United States. As minister of militia, Sam Hughes appointed the hard-driving contractor an honorary colonel.

had large sliding doors at each end. Eighty-nine years later, the hangars were designated as historic structures. Although intended for temporary use and thrown up in a great hurry, eight hangars are still standing; one is a museum and one is used as an administration building.

On 16 March, with the ground still under heavy snow, the IRFC moved some HQ staff to the new aerodrome at Borden, then known as Camp Hoare. Twelve days later, the first batch of IRFC cadets began arriving for training.

Two years earlier, Burke had expressed the view that good pilot material could be found in Canada but not good officers. Burke's views on Canada reflected his upbringing in a class-dominated society. He saw Canadians as lacking in sophistication and good manners and concluded they were unfit to be officers. Canadian pilots, he thought, should be appointed flight sergeants, rather than commissioned officers.

Hoare's assessment of Canadians reflected his pragmatism. He was impressed by the efficiency of Canadian officials and businessmen, noting that Baillie and his chief engineer were highly efficient and business-like in their methods. Commenting in a more general way, he observed that "work appears to be put through here at a speed which is unknown in England."[8]

Despite the quick start, Hoare had serious doubts that his staff could recruit sufficient cadets to supply Britain's needs. He had attended a convention of some two hundred Canadian military officers where it was generally agreed that recruitment in Canada had ceased, that the only way in which further recruits could be obtained was by the introduction of conscription.[9] Canada had a small population spread thinly over a vast geographic area. Hoare anticipated he would have difficulty finding enough cadets to supply ten squadrons. Britain's success in the air war required him to obtain twenty.

Moreover, there was an unexpected complication to the recruiting drive. Initially, it was not pilot-trainees who were the hardest to recruit but ground crew. Until RFC (Canada) recruited sufficient mechanics, pilot training could not get underway on a large scale. It was a problem that taxed all of Hoare's skills and ingenuity.

# CHAPTER FOUR
## KEEPING FLYERS IN THE AIR

> As regards recruiting.... There is undoubtedly a great
> shortage of men, and rates of pay in civil life are
> very high. It is ... clear that there will be a very great
> difficulty, and this subject will prove the weakest
> point in the ... scheme.
> — *Hoare to director, Air Organization*[1]

As soon as flying facilities were available at Long Branch, the IRFC began
recruiting mechanics. This responsibility rested with Major T.F.G. Strubell
who was in charge of overall recruiting. By early February, recruiting
offices had been set up in Toronto and Hamilton and arrangements had
been made with the Toronto Board of Education to set up a recruits'
depot at the Givens Street Public School. The loyalty of Toronto's civic
leaders was demonstrated by the Board's granting the premises of the
Givens school to the IRFC at no charge. Shortly thereafter the Board
made the newly built Crawford Street School available, also at no cost.
Only minor alterations were needed to make the buildings suitable as
barracks for the enlisted men.

Initially, the recruitment of mechanics presented the IRFC with
more difficulties than any other challenge. Hoare had been instructed
to create twenty squadrons and estimated they would require some
6,000 mechanics. But finding them presented a formidable task as
highly skilled mechanics were being paid top wages in the booming war
factories. The starting wage offered by the IRFC to a skilled mechanic
was a mere $1.60 a day. Industry was paying between forty and sixty
cents an hour. For a typical ten-hour day, industry was paying three to
four times the wages offered by the IRFC.

In early February, Strubell and Lieutenant B.V. Grealy began a campaign to enlist three thousand tradesmen. The campaign involved an expensive advertising budget, consisting of large posters of striking design placed on billboards, large display ads in key newspapers,* classified ads for trades in various newspapers under the want ads, and written news items designed to attract interest in trade positions with the IRFC.[2]

Enlistment was for the duration of the war and applications were accepted from men nineteen to forty-five years of age, single or married. The press release advised applicants they would be expected to serve both in Canada and overseas. In practice, the IRFC never intended to post any of their mechanics overseas.

To test prospective applicants, the IRFC had taken over the old riding school at the Toronto Armouries where they had set up a number of workshops. Press releases specifically advised applicants that no unskilled men would be accepted, but bright youths who demonstrated talent and could be readily taught, could be taken on as Class 3 mechanics at $1.10 a day and taught a trade. To facilitate testing, a model workshop was

Imperial Royal Flying Corps recruiting poster, circa 1917. Courtesy of Library and Archives Canada/Imperial Royal Flying Corps Toronto, W.S. Johnston [1917?], AMICUS No. 32906224.

* The ad placed in *The Toronto Star* on 14 February 1917 took up nearly half the page.

built on a heavy truck, designed so that testing could be carried on in the truck, which could be moved from town to town.[3]

Prospective mechanics were to apply at the Hamilton Recruiting Office, which also had testing workshops, or at the Toronto Armouries. Later, recruiting offices for testing trades were set up in Winnipeg, Vancouver, and Montreal. The IRFC was assisted by volunteer civilian committees set up in cities with populations of 10,000 or more. Over 1,000 civilian volunteers were involved in recruiting. Their primary purpose was to find prospective cadets, but they also interviewed prospective mechanics. They took the applications and, if they met the basic requirements, made arrangements for the men to travel to the appropriate testing centres. In Saskatchewan alone there were nine of these committees operating in as many centres.[4]

The committees were usually staffed by the city's more prominent citizens. For example, in Belleville, Ontario, a mid-sized city of 12,000 residents, the committee consisted of Judge Wills; W.B. Deacon, a prominent shirt manufacturer; Colonel W.N. Ponton, lawyer and substantial landowner; H.F. Ketcheson, proprietor of an insurance agency; W.H. Morton, publisher of the daily newspaper; A.G. Davie, editor of that newspaper; and the chairman of the group, A.R. Walker, chief librarian.[5] Having such luminaries on these committees added status to the Imperial Royal Flying Corps and was intended to encourage the better class of young men to enlist.

The IRFC needed all the lustre it could muster as the enlisted men signed up for the duration of the war and were technically liable for overseas service, a powerful disincentive for married men. Nor were they attracted by the remuneration. Rates of pay ranged from $1.10 per day for unskilled third-class mechanics to a $1.60 for first-class mechanics. Sergeants earned $2.00 a day and warrant officers earned $2.80. A press release accurately stated there was a shortage of sergeants and that a really skilled mechanic could advance quickly to that rank.[6]

The term "mechanic" was highly elastic and, aside from the usual welders, millwrights, cabinet makers, carpenters, electricians, and blacksmiths, included male clerks, and servants. In total, the IRFC designated twenty-three occupations as trades.[7]

Major Allen helped launch the campaign with a speech before a large audience at the University of Toronto physics building. He told the assemblage there was a great need for "studious fellows with a knowledge of mechanics, petrol engines, and a sufficient scientific knowledge to make equipment officers." These officers would be required to look after all sorts of skilled tradesmen engaged in the making of equipment.

Allen had attracted his audience by promising to talk about Canadian flyers, which he claimed were second to none. Knowing that many Canadians mistakenly believed admission to the IRFC required them to pay for their flying lessons, he set out to explain what was really required:

> The type of fellow wanted as a pilot is the clean bred chap with lots of the devil in him, a fellow who has ridden horses hard across country, or nearly broken his neck motoring, or on the ice playing hockey. There is plenty of sport to be found in aviation.[8]

The major pointed out that acceptance did not require university graduation or a pilot certificate. However, matriculation was necessary. In a country where only a small percentage of adults had more than an elementary school education, this requirement presented a significant barrier.

Applicants were required to be between the ages of eighteen and thirty with preference given to those under twenty-five. Few considered it surprising that the Imperial Royal Flying Corps required applicants to be of *pure European ancestry*, as well as British subjects. Racism was deeply ingrained in Western culture, particularly amongst Anglo-Saxons. Canadians were subjects of the great British Empire, which spanned the world. A separate Canadian citizenship would not be created for another thirty years.

Two weeks after the campaign began, Strubell had more than a thousand cadet applications to process. But, as Hoare had anticipated, the recruitment of mechanics went slowly. After one month, the lack of applicants forced the closure of the office in Hamilton. All trade testing was consolidated in Toronto with training taking place at Lippincott Technical School.

In mid-March, Hoare wrote to General Charlton in London, confiding, "Recruitment [of mechanics] has caused me more anxiety than anything else."[9]

The trade problem was primarily monetary. The first thing an applicant asked was "How much is the pay?" and "How much will my wife get?"[10] By the end of the first year, of the more than 13,000 interviewed, nearly half had refused to join because the inducements offered were insufficient.

To reduce costs and speed up recruiting, the Department of Militia and Defence made available their medical boards to examine those applying to the IRFC. This saved the force a great deal of time and money. Unfortunately, the boards had been trained to accept only those whose physical condition was absolutely perfect (category A). This created an unnecessary barrier to the hiring of mechanics whose jobs did not require the physical condition of a pilot or infantryman. The British had developed a system of categories from A to E so Hoare's recruiting officers had to educate the medical boards scattered across Canada in the more flexible British system.[11]

The problems the IRFC experienced with the Canadian Medical Boards suggests they took a far different approach than their counterparts in Britain. Lester B. "Mike" Pearson transferred to the RFC from the Canadian Expeditionary Force while in England. In the following passage, he wryly describes his medical exam:

> Recruits were asked if they could ride a horse, sail a boat or handle a motorcycle. If they were accomplished at any of these gentlemanly pursuits, they were reckoned able to solo in two hours.
>
> The medical examination consisted of picking out strands of differently coloured wools to test for colour blindness and a motion test in which the recruit was spun around several times on a typing chair to see if his eye movements stabilized within 30 seconds. A 15 minute interview followed, to sort out the dim, the lame and the halt. "There is a type of facial expression one gets acquainted with when carrying out this sort of

interview," a medical officer reported. "It consists of a furtive look as if always expecting something unpleasant to happen in marked contrast with the straight, decided expression of the crack fighter pilot."[12]

Sometimes, the lure of flying induced men to sign up as mechanics in the hope they could later transfer to the Air Corps. One of these was Joe Goold, a twenty-two-year-old Ohio River boat pilot from Kentucky. When Goold heard the IRFC was recruiting pilot candidates, he wrote inquiring as to his eligibility. He was told his application had been received but there were so many, it would take some time before they could deal with his. After a long delay, he wrote again. Finally, he wrote a third time asking that, if he joined as a mechanic, would he have a good chance of transferring to the cadets? When the reply was in the affirmative, Goold set off immediately for Toronto where he signed up at the Givens Street recruiting centre.[13]

The IRFC needed mechanics for some twenty-three trades, but fitters (engine mechanics) and riggers (those who repaired the rest of the airplane) were the most sought after. Goold was sent to Borden, where he learned airplane and engine maintenance.

Goold was determined to fly and made several applications to transfer, all to no avail. The IRFC needed mechanics and that was what he remained. When the opportunity permitted, he managed to convince a few instructors to take him up and give him some experience handling the controls.

How many would-be-pilots were similarly seduced into the ranks of IRFC mechanics can not be estimated, but, given Goold's response to his letter of inquiry, the numbers were probably considerable.

Always quick to react to problems, Hoare decided early on that the billboard campaign for recruits was too expensive to continue. It was dropped in March, but Hoare had already formulated a more effective and less costly scheme.

A National Service Registration Act had been passed earlier in the war by the Canadian government as part of a war mobilization scheme. Under this plan, men were asked if they would serve the war effort anywhere in Canada as civilians. Those tradesmen who responded in the affirmative numbered approximately ten thousand. Hoare's persuasive powers led the director of National Service to send pamphlets to these men in an attempt to persuade them to join the IRFC as mechanics. Over a six-month period some 860 such men joined the force.[14] While their numbers helped to relieve the shortage, other more radical measures were needed to reach the target of 3,000 mechanics.

One of the reasons so few were interested in serving as mechanics with the Flying Corps was the growing resistance to serving in Europe. This resistance existed among a substantial percentage of the population. Although the IRFC had no intention of sending their mechanics to Europe, it could not advertise this. To do so would make the mens' families ineligible to receive support from the Canadian Patriotic Fund, which paid the family of a man volunteering to serve overseas the sum of twenty dollars monthly for his spouse plus an additional five dollars monthly for each child. It took some effort for Hoare and Allen to persuade the Canadian Patriotic Fund to provide benefits to mechanics in the IRFC and, even then, only partial success was achieved. The Fund finally agreed to pay the benefit but only to the families of those members of the Flying Corps fit for overseas service.

For those not eligible for assistance from the Patriotic Fund, the IRFC was asking them to put their families in positions of poverty. It is hardly surprising that few married men were willing to join the Flying Corps as mechanics.

To more effectively tap into Canada's sparse and wide-flung manpower resources, the IRFC opened recruiting offices in Winnipeg, Montreal, and Vancouver. Each office was staffed by an officer trained at HQ in Toronto and was assisted by non-coms and enlisted men from England. At these recruiting centres applicants, if they passed an oral test, were sent to Toronto for final testing.

From the nucleus of mechanics who had joined the force early on, the Flying Corps appointed most as sergeant-instructors. Fortunately, the majority of Canadians and Americans who joined had been raised on farms and had grown up using tools and machines. Like pioneers everywhere, they were quick to learn practical skills. As Hoare reported to London in May of 1917, "We get few good tradesmen but the men pick up the work fairly quick."[15]

There was another source of labour which a less imaginative and traditional CO might have overlooked or disdained. Women were just beginning to receive recognition as more than an inferior sub-species being regarded as weaker, more emotional, and less able to do the jobs done by men. They had the right to vote in only two provinces and no voting rights in Canadian general elections. (This changed in the election of December 1917, but was limited to relatives of men serving overseas.) Women could not run for office to Parliament or provincial legislatures, nor could they be appointed to the Senate.

After the war, when women were hired as bus drivers in London, England, the male drivers threatened to go on strike. Much the same attitude prevailed in Canada. Writing of the Imperial Royal Flying Corps' decision to hire women transport drivers in Toronto, Allen noted it was done, "despite local criticism."[16]

Initially, women were hired as "civilian subordinates" (an IRFC term) to perform clerical work at HQ. It was thought they could be used only in unskilled and office routines. It soon became evident that they could be trained — in the words of the RAF historian — for "lighter mechanical work." The shortage of male mechanics provided the impetus

*An engine repair crew at Camp Leaside. Courtesy of Deseronto Archives.*

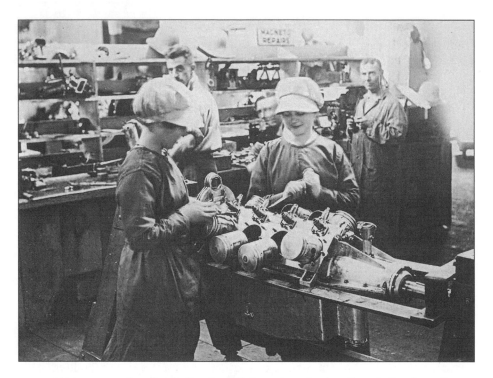

*Women overhauling a Curtiss OX-5 engine, Engine Repair Section, Camp Mohawk. Courtesy of Library and Archives Canada/ Department of National Defence PA-022784.*

for expanding women's roles and a separate section was formed to handle the recruiting and administration of women mechanics.

Sixty-five years after her service at the Deseronto Camp, Eleanor Jukes of Matawatchan wrote of her experience:

> My parents moved from Napanee to Deseronto ... so my sister and I could get work.... We worked at engine repair shop down by the Bay. Our job was to take engines apart, clean and wash in large tanks of cleaning fluid, replace any worn or broken parts. We cleaned and replaced broken or bent pistons, valves, rings, and springs. We ground valves by hand. We wore green full coveralls with caps and got $2.10 a day and paid our board out of that. We had curfew same as the

air force. We were watched while on the street by M.P.'s same as the boys.[17]

In describing these tasks as "light mechanical work" the RAF historian betrayed a common perception of women as less capable than men. For the first half of the twentieth century these attitudes dominated the work place. Women's rates of pay were generally not more than fifty percent of those paid to men. The IRFC broke new ground in pay scales, offering women the same low wages paid to their male counterparts.

The work of female transport drivers was virtually identical to their male equivalents. Writing of his experience as a transport driver with the IRFC, Hugh McWilliams of Guelph noted:

> The Motor Transport Girls were at Leaside, Ontario, we drove from 4:30 a.m. until 11:30 a.m. They drove from 9 a.m. to 4 p.m. The officers were all billeted downtown and had to be collected and returned. The 4:30 a.m. was for early flying. We drove Tender Ambulance and Packard trucks turn about. We were all over the province collecting crashes.[18]

The only difference in the drivers' work was the time they started their shifts — neither sex worked less hours, and both sexes performed the same duties.

By hiring women in such positions, Hoare and the IRFC were breaking the social mores of the time. More than a few eyebrows were raised at this invasion of females into workplaces regarded as the exclusive preserve of men.

As the war progressed, women were enlisted in the IRFC in increasing numbers until, by the summer of 1918, a total of 1,200 had been enlisted. Of these, 135 were employed at technical trades at the Repair Parks, while another 600 were employed as mechanics at the various wings and depots.[19]

At the conclusion of the war, the number of women employed by RAF (Canada) were distributed as follows:

*Central Stores Depot and Barracks at St. Clair Avenue and Weston Road, Toronto, summer of 1917. Courtesy of Library and Archives Canada/ Department of National Defence PA-22827.*

| | |
|---|---:|
| In HQ offices in various cities | 115 |
| Paymaster's Department, Victoria Street, Toronto | 36 |
| Recruits Depot, Jesse Ketchum School, Toronto | 18 |
| No. 4 School of Military Aeronautics, University of Toronto | 90 |
| Cadet Wing, Long Branch | 9 |
| Armament School, Hamilton | 14 |
| Aeroplane Repair Park, Toronto | 134 |
| Stores Depot, Toronto | 180 |
| Motor Transport Section, Toronto | 50 |
| Engineer Section, Toronto | 3 |
| School of Aerial Fighting, Beamsville | 91 |
| 42nd Wing, Deseronto | 230 |
| 43rd Wing, Leaside | 161 |

**TOTAL   1,196** [20]

Hoare and his staff officers were acutely aware of the need to create a positive public image, one that would help recruiting and generate support from the general public. The biggest mass entertainment event in Toronto was the Canadian National Exhibition held every year in late August. In 1917 the IRFC arranged for a squad of flyers to do a regular fly-past each afternoon during the Exhibition. In addition, the IRFC provided a large tent where two airplanes were on display. Experts from Camp Leaside were on hand to explain the workings of the craft to visitors while a workshop was set up in the tent where skilled mechanics could be viewed in action, repairing airplanes and manufacturing parts. This was just one of the ways by which Strubell and B.V. Grealy tried to attract mechanics into the IRFC.[21]

That same summer, Hoare demonstrated his keen awareness of public relations. The City of Toronto, in one of its many patriotic gestures towards the IRFC, donated the money to pay for the production of three airplanes. Toronto's mayor, Tommy Church, who spent a good deal of time at the "chummery," was a good friend to Hoare and many of his staff officers. The mayor suggested that one of the aircraft be named in honour of the newly promoted General Hoare. Hoare graciously declined, suggesting that the three airplanes be named Toronto, Queen City, and Mayor Church. It was finally decided that neither man would accept the honour, both agreeing the aircraft should be named after Canada's newest hero, Captain William Avery Bishop. Both men played to Toronto's civic pride, burgeoning nationalism, and pride in Canada's new hero.

Although a conformist in his private and social life as well as in his dealings with subordinates, Hoare was first and foremost a pragmatist, he did what it took to get the task accomplished. That he could be ruthless as well as pragmatic was evident when, in the spring of 1918, Hoare faced a major exodus by mechanics from the ranks of the IRFC. Had the threat not been scuppered by his clever — but devious — tactics, the entire training program could have been derailed.

The British Parliament passed an act creating a new force out of the former Royal Flying Corps and Royal Naval Air Service. It came into effect on 1 April 1918. Unfortunately, the act creating the Royal Air Force made no provisión for the special conditions under which the IRFC had been operating in Canada.

The IRFC was a branch of the British Army and, as such, used army designations while the new service had a different nomenclature for rank, which included wing commander and squadron leader. Similarly, the Royal Naval Air Service was a branch of the Royal Navy and differed in many ways from the RFC.

But the problem lay not in the nomenclature of the two old services to which their flight arms had been attached, but in the new law's provision that no one could be transferred from the navy or army to the new service without his consent. He was allowed, if he wished, to remain in his parent service. This posed no problem for the British military establishment but, in Canada, members of the IRFC had not joined the British army or navy and therefore when discharged by the IRFC were free to leave the service altogether. In other words, they were under no legal compulsion to accept a transfer to the newly created RAF. This gave the IRFC's now highly trained but poorly paid mechanics an opportunity to return to civilian life where their new skills were much in demand and earned top wages.

The scope of the problem was quickly revealed by the large number of mechanics and fitters who applied for discharge rather than transfer to RAF (Canada). A total of 1,635 or 27 percent of total strength chose not to apply for transfer to the RAF.[22] As the IRFC would cease to exist as of 1 April 1918, these men would have to be discharged onto civvy street. The service could not function properly without them. As they had done so often in the past, Hoare and Allen put their heads together and came up with a plan to head the stampede back into uniform. For the plan to work they had to have the co-operation of the chief of the Canadian general staff, Major-General Gwatkin. A consistent ally of the IRFC and Hoare, Gwatkin did not disappoint.

The previous year, Canada had passed a conscription law requiring able-bodied men to join the army. The list of those requesting a discharge from the IRFC were carefully scanned and some twenty applicants chosen. They were all men whose age and medical condition qualified them for active service overseas. These men were then ostentatiously paraded on the drill ground in civilian clothes at the recruits' depot. They were formally paid up and given their discharge papers, only to be served then and there with their call-up papers by the Canadian military. They were then handed over to a waiting escort of military police "for despatch with a draft for overseas leaving Toronto that night."[23]

The campaign did not stop there. Under orders of Gwatkin, press releases were sent to the various military districts designed to convince mechanics in the IRFC that discharge led to the worst imaginable option — ending up in the infantry. Virtually everyone had heard of the horrors of trench warfare; infantrymen lived in damp to semi-flooded trenches, relieved only by suicidal charges across no man's land in the face of withering machine-gun fire. The press release was headed with the misleading title, "MEN LEAVING RAF MAY CHOOSE OWN UNIT." As this excerpt illustrates, the heading was a masterpiece of irony:

> Members of the Royal Air Force who seek their discharge, instead of their transfer from the R.F.C. will have the opportunity to choose the unit in the C.E.F. ... stated Col. H.C. Bickford, O.C. Toronto Military District, to *The Star*. "There is a serious qualification to this," Col. Bickford explained.... "Recruiting is closed at present for the artillery and the cavalry, so there is nothing for them to choose but the infantry. They may volunteer for the infantry, and if they don't they will be called out anyway. The infantry needs them, and they will be given a most hearty welcome to the C.E.F." said the Colonel.[24]

Commenting on the near crisis five decades after the event, Allen noted:

> The "grape vine" circulated the news with the result that a number of applications for discharge were withdrawn. In point of fact few men claimed their discharge which redounds to the credit of the men as a whole, especially when one remembers the far higher

pay Canadian industry was offering at the time for the very same type of work our men were doing in RAF Canada. This incident supports our contention as to the fine spirit in the units.... High morale such as prevailed stems from good leadership at the top, and this Hoare had in abundance.[25]

To the credit of Hoare, Allen, Strubell, and Lieutenant Grealy, the seemingly insurmountable challenge of recruiting the required 3,000 tradesmen was not only met but greatly exceeded. By war's end, the team had recruited more than 7,000 men for the mechanical section of the IRFC and its successor RAF (Canada). In addition, another 734 women were employed as mechanics in the Force.[26]

While Hoare and Allen were willing to recruit women as mechanics, it seems never to have occurred to them to recruit women to fly airplanes. Given that Air Canada did not hire its first woman pilot until 1977, this is hardly surprising.

Ultimately, the shortage of mechanics was solved because of loyalty to Britain, curiosity about airplanes and, for women, the chance to earn as much as men, do men's work and, for many, to prove they could perform well at tasks at which men thought them incompetent.

As for pilots, initially there had been more applicants than the Imperial Royal Flying Corps could process; that quickly changed. As the war progressed the supply of potential pilots began drying up. As with mechanics earlier, Hoare, Allen, and Stubbel now faced a shortage of pilot-cadets. The shortage threatened to cripple the IRFC and seriously undermine the Allied war effort. Hoare had to muster all his diplomatic and people skills to scrape through the crisis. That he succeeded was due to his unorthodoxy, persuasiveness, and willingness to break diplomatic rules while ignoring the laws of our giant neighbour to the south.

# CHAPTER FIVE
## TRAINING PILOTS DANGEROUSLY

The "boy airman" is the most wonderful of all the wonderful combatants in this war. Those in authority like to catch him young, for his "nerve" is better, and he comes into training an absolute stranger to fear.
 — *Editorial*, The Evening Telegram, *St. John's, Newfoundland*[1]

To be adequately prepared pilots need a certain level of theoretical training. To provide this, Hoare hoped to set up a school of aeronautics at the university, for cadets who had completed their basic training at Long Branch. An appointment was made for Allen and Hoare to meet with Sir Robert Falconer, president of the University of Toronto.

The CO had to use every ounce of his considerable charm to thaw the glacial Sir Robert, but, gradually, the austere university president was won over. In a few weeks, the IRFC had the use of several classrooms and residences at the university. Canada's first school of aeronautics was then placed under the command of Second Lieutenant Brian Peck.

As England had not yet supplied instructors, Second Lieutenant Peck, a Canadian,* was placed in charge of a staff consisting of just one drill instructor and one clerk.[2] Woefully under-equipped and overworked, Peck and his meagre staff managed somehow to instruct the cadets in

---

* Peck served with the Canadian Expeditionary Force in Europe for two years before transferring to the RFC, where he flew on the Western front. His father owned the Peck Rolling Mills, later absorbed into the Dominion Steel and Coal Co. Peck had been educated at Lower Canada College and McGill University. A member of an elite Montreal family, Peck was dashing, efficient, and charming.

the basics of military law, artillery observation, rigging, engines, and the theory of flight. For practical instruction, they had just one ancient Curtiss airframe, one Curtiss airplane engine, and one auto engine. They had no choice but to make do with sparse and inadequate training materials, including a total lack of manuals. These were finally sent over from England in mid-June, four months after flight training commenced in Canada.

Although the IRFC had not received any machine guns for instructing the cadets on gunnery, an arrangement was subsequently made with the O.C. School of Musketry, Military District No. 2, by which the cadets took a course in machine gunnery from Canadian Militia NCOs at Hart House. Although it was very basic, the militia was able to provide actual range practice. In this early stage of training, the length of time a cadet spent at the Cadet Wing was determined by the demands of the flying units at Long Branch and the speed with which each individual could absorb the fundamentals of the course. The first class of fifty cadets absorbed the entire syllabus in just three weeks. After digesting this compendium of raw information, the cadets moved on to the practical skills of flying an airplane.[3]

Although training in gunnery was badly neglected in the early months of the training plan, this deficiency was no fault of Hoare and his officers, who did the best they could with no help from England. The Canadian Militia provided machine guns, ammunition, and army instructors, while the University of Toronto supplied a firing range. The cadets learned the mechanics of the guns and fired a limited number of rounds at stationary targets. Then on 24 April 1917, three weeks after the first flying began at Borden, Hoare received the badly needed instructors from England. The next day he wrote to the director of Air Organization in London, updating his superior on the training situation in Canada:

> One Flying Officer (Observer), 5 Flying Officers, 10 E.O.'s [Equipment Officers], 116 other ranks, and Cooper [Aerial Gunnery] arrived yesterday. This will put me in a far stronger position. They appear to be exactly what I want, and I think now I shall be able to carry on without

further assistance as far as E.O.'s are concerned. I have a
fairly good staff of Canadians coming in. My difficulty
has been having no one to train them.[4]

Among this group of men were the IRFC's first aerial gunnery instructors.
The corps selected a number of their best mechanics to receive special
instruction from the new arrivals in order to qualify them as additional
gunnery instructors. No time was wasted and, on 1 May, the School
of Aerial Gunnery came into existence. Commanded by Captain S.W.
Cooper, the school's first course provided each of the eighteen cadets with
an opportunity to fire a mere forty rounds from one of the two machine
guns available. The course expanded quickly to three weeks and the
firing to one hundred rounds of ammunition. A succinct assessment of
the gunnery instruction was provided by U.S. Naval cadet, L.L. Smart:

> The cadets got in very little aerial machine gun firing but
> there was no shortage of machine gun instruction on
> the ground. The Canadian training, provided by skilled
> non-coms, was thorough and it was good. Many pilots
> can credit their lives with this.[5]

By early spring, basic cadet training had grown to six weeks. A staff officer
described the training of a cadet from his enlistment to his completion of
aeronautical school:

> When a recruit arrives here from one of our Interviewing
> Committees, he is medically examined, once again, and
> paraded for final interview, if accepted he is sworn in at
> once and dispatched to Cadet Wing where he undergoes
> a three week course in drill and is trained as a soldier. After
> this, he is sent to the ... School of Military Aeronautics
> [at the University of Toronto] where he undergoes
> instruction in engines, care and maintenance, map
> reading, cross country flying, and in fact all branches of
> Aeronautics from the theoretical standpoint. He should

*Machine-gun practice at Camp Mohawk, Deseronto,* circa *1918. Courtesy of the Crossman Collection.*

be able to detect from the sound of an engine whether it is running well or not. It is necessary for him to be expert in the assembling and trueing of the machine. He also learns the first principals of the theory of flight and wireless telegraphy; he must be able to read twelve words a minute from the buzzer [Morse-Continental code].[6]

Herbert Andrews provides a cadet's view of the training. Before enlisting, Andrews successfully completed three years at the University of Saskatchewan. The son of a medical doctor in Regina, Andrews kept a diary in which he recorded his views of the training program:

I reported at Burwash Hall where I was given three blankets and a cot for the night.... In the morning we had breakfast (some swell feed?) in Burwash Hall dining room which does not appeal to me as a university dining room, no chairs, but benches minus the backs; big black tables without tablecloths and dishes heavy enough to break stones.... We were on course No. 13 which was the first of the six week courses ... The work was very interesting: we got lectures on everything connected with life and work with the IRFC, from mess etiquette to oiling engines. I found artillery observations especially interesting with the relief map of sections of France in behind Ypres.... There was a 15 minute recess both morning and afternoon. They sure kept us on the move, the pace was pretty stiff, nothing is repeated and if you miss it once, its gone. As for taking notes, it had varsity beaten a mile. I never took so many or so fast in my life.[7]

Hoare and his staff were moving on several fronts. While Baillie and the IMB were overseeing the construction of a new airplane factory, production of JN-4s continued at the old plant on Strachan Street. On 22 February, the first Jenny was completed, a second was ready two days later. The two airplanes were then sent to the sheds at the Long Branch Aerodrome for flight testing.

On 24 February, a brisk sunny morning, Hoare and Allen travelled to Long Branch to view the two new Jennies undergoing testing. Later that Saturday, Hoare was enjoying a late lunch when he exclaimed, "We have two aeroplanes and there are some cadets kicking their heels at the Depot. Why the hell are we not flying?" He then turned to Allen and said, "I want flying started by Monday." Allen pointed out that their schedule did not call for flying instruction for several weeks. "By Monday, I said," was Hoare's retort.[8]

England had sent no instructors, leaving Hoare and Allen to find Canadians to fill the posts. A Torontonian, Lieutenant John Aird, was placed in charge of the hastily assembled squadron and, the following Monday, a few cadets began flight instruction. As Hoare had not received his squadron numbers from London, it was designated as Squadron X.

With flying started, Hoare cabled London asking that the cadres for the First Wing be expedited. A cadre consisted of two officers with flying experience at the front, plus a half dozen NCOs, as well as men from the skilled trades. The cadres were the nucleus used to train units created from officers and enlisted men recruited in Canada.

But the cadres had not arrived and Hoare had to rely solely on Canadian pilots to magically transform themselves into instructors. One of these was Second Lieutenant A.S. Bouttell who served until the end of the war. Bouttell commented acerbically on the experience:

> When I joined the RFC in February 1917, I was posted to X Squadron at Long Branch … which at that time was just in the process of getting a camp organized. We had two JN-4 Curtiss Aircraft. The flying was inclined to be hazardous due to the roughness of the field and we had several minor accidents. At that time we were listed as instructional staff with little or no practical experience in flying instruction.[9]

Originally, the British military had not intended that the IRFC do more than teach cadets the basics of flying before sending them to England where they would learn advanced theory, and master the operation of sophisticated fighter aircraft as well as the difficult manoeuvres of aerial combat. In mid-February, Hoare recommended that a complete training plan be instituted in Canada, arguing that once all twenty training squadrons were in operation, their capacity for such basic instruction would quickly outstrip the intake of cadets. In order to complete the cadets' advanced flight training, he requested the IRFC be provided with an advanced training aircraft. If they were supplied, Hoare stated the cadets could be posted to operational squadrons in Europe immediately upon completing their training in Canada.

On 21 March the War Office cabled Hoare, asking if he could dispense with the men who would comprise the last five of the twenty nucleus flights he had been promised from England. He replied, stating that he would make do with the fourteen from England and would make his own arrangements in Canada for the remainder. The War Office also agreed with Hoare's recommendation that the IRFC complete the higher training of the cadets and on 31 March 1917 the director of Air Organization instructed Hoare to proceed with it. But the War Office waffled on his request for an advanced training aircraft, finally rejecting it some months later.

Hoare and his staff were now expected to provide the entire range of training then being carried out in England and do it without an advanced training aircraft and with far fewer instructors from England. The War Office assumed that graduates of the IRFC would need only a few hours' instruction in the warplanes of the front-line squadrons to which they would be posted. This was comparable to sending a Second World War pilot directly from Tiger Moths to Spitfires, skipping the advanced training in Harvards.*

While these arrangements were being made with the War Office in England, Bob Low was driving construction forward at Borden with surprising speed. Moving with equal speed, Hoare kept his officers busy investigating sites for a second aerodrome. Many enterprising businessmen and municipal officials wanted the IRFC to build its next aerodrome near their town or, even better, on their land. The IMB and IRFC were spending vast amounts of money and enterprising Canadians wanted some of it pointed in their direction. Hoare sent one officer to examine possible locations in New Brunswick, and another to British Columbia. Most requests he turned down outright. In early March, he wrote to the Directorate of Air Organization summarizing the situation:

> I sent Filley to New Brunswick to inspect various sites … but the country is a wilderness and quite unsuitable, besides being very cold.
>
> I have not had very favourable reports so far about British Columbia; land is very expensive and … has nothing to commend it but its milder climate, this is

---

* As a consequence of the imperial decision to deny the IRFC an advanced training aircraft, the graduates sent to England from Canada needed at least two months' further training before being posted to service squadrons on the continent. The decision of the War Office was finally reversed but came too late to impact on the air war.

somewhat set off by the amount of rain … I shall have to go into this very carefully as there is a decided doubt about flying being practicable at all during December, January, and February here, and March is a bad month.

I have looked at a site for the second five squadrons at Deseronto … It has several considerable advantages … so far as I can see, with the snow on the ground, the actual aerodrome would require very little work … and there is a suitable building to accommodate a whole Wing fairly close by. It will be a cheap proposition compared to Borden, and of course will not have to be carried out under the extreme conditions that we have had the last two months. Further, there are excellent communications by land and water from here [Deseronto] to Toronto and Buffalo.[10]

By the last weekend of March, the snow was off the ground and Hoare travelled to Deseronto and thoroughly inspected the site. What he saw

*Camp Rathbun in the summer of 1917. Note that the officers' quarters in the right foreground have verandas on two storeys. The tents in the background are for the cadets. Courtesy of Hastings County Historical Society.*

convinced him of its suitability. Deseronto was to be the IRFC's second wing. Earlier, he had started negotiations for two sites in the Toronto area as well as commencing negotiations to lease land near Vancouver.

The Deseronto Wing would be divided between Camp Mohawk, a three-squadron aerodrome to be built on 350 acres of land on the Indian reserve (Tyendinaga Territory), and a smaller, two-squadron aerodrome to be built on land provided by the Rathbun family. Camp Rathbun was located three miles east of Camp Mohawk, and a short distance north of the Town of Deseronto. Until fairly recently, the Rathbun family had operated a large industrial complex from the town. For a nominal rent, the IRFC leased several unused Rathbun buildings, which were then converted into Wing headquarters. The buildings included a repair shop, blacksmith shop, stores, and offices. An additional fifty buildings had to be erected, water and sewer lines installed, and central heating systems provided for both camps.

The contract for the Deseronto Camps was awarded to Low's company in mid-April, with construction getting underway immediately. Before the end of the month, Low had 1,500 men working at Deseronto. Almost overnight, the dusty streets of the drowsy town were crowded with workers and contractors, increasing its population by more than 50 percent. At night, the construction workers had few diversions. For recreation, there was just one theatre (Naylor's), a pool hall, and two hotels. The one Chinese laundry did a booming business; as one wag observed, "It really cleaned up."

Meanwhile, Low pushed ahead with Camp Borden, which was completed on 2 June. In just four months, his team, assisted by a British Royal Engineer (RE) officer, had cleared 850 acres of stumps, levelled and sown it with grass seed, built 4.75 miles of asphalt road, laid 4.3 miles of water mains, 4,900 feet of sewers, and installed heating and incinerating units, electric lights, power systems, underground gasoline tanks, and erected fifty-seven buildings. In addition, the Grand Trunk and Canadian Pacific railways had laid more than a mile of additional rail sidings. A telephone system had been installed, hooking up the camp with Toronto and other centres.

The fifty-seven buildings included an airplane repair shop, a machine shop, a cooper and blacksmith shop, a hospital, a mechanical-transport repair shop, garages, a dope (glue) shop, a mess building, and quarters for officers, cadets, and mechanics. All this was accomplished without modern power equipment, using only horses and manpower. Equally impressive was the fact that it was completed during the coldest winter of the previous five years.

Independent of Low's company, the corps built themselves some extra amenities, including a 40 x 100-foot swimming pool, a nine-hole golf course, a baseball field, a tennis court, and a quarter-mile track around a football field. From the very beginning, athletics was an integral part of life in the Imperial Royal Flying Corps.

While Borden was being built, the IRFC was moving on several instructional fronts. Previous to April 1917, there had been very little instruction in the use of wireless as a means of communication between pilots and ground forces. In April, Lieutenants J.W. Askham and Dexter, together with fourteen wireless operators, were posted to Canada from England to give instruction to all wings of the IRFC. Askham, the officer in charge, wrote a summary of this training from the time of his team's arrival until the end of the war.

> It was not until April 1917, that serious thought was given to Wireless Training. Previous to this only Buzzing Instruction was being carried out at the Cadet Wing, then situated at the University of Toronto. Even this training was seriously handicapped for want of instructors and equipment. About this time, Lieut. Askham, Lieut. Dexter and 14 Wireless Operators were posted to Canada, bringing sufficient wireless equipment for one Wing.
>
> It was decided that higher training in Wireless should be given at Borden, elementary training at Long Branch, Cadet Wing, and Deseronto. Wireless equipment was entirely insufficient to carry on successful training at these places, but it was so divided that each place had some equipment, allowing training to be commenced. Arrangements had to be made to procure powder, electric exploders, field telephones, and other items in Toronto.[11]

From this nucleus of trained instructors, the IRFC managed to recruit 135 wireless operators from Canadian sources. Many were lured away from high-paying railway jobs to act as low-paid instructors with the IRFC. That the Force was able to recruit these men speaks volumes to the loyalty, patriotism, and idealism of many Canadians. It also speaks to the success of Allied propaganda, which painted the Germans and their allies as monsters out to destroy democracy and civilized society. The recruiting was sufficiently successful that by 30 April 1917, a section for telegraphy had been set up at Borden under the command of Askham to teach advanced wireless.

Sending and receiving in Morse code from an aircraft was primitive in the extreme. A pilot had to work his transmitting equipment, mounted outside his airplane's cockpit, with his left hand, while manoeuvring the airplane with his other hand and right foot.

In his letter of 25 November 1973, (Ret.) Captain Askham states, "We started off with 2 officers and 14 men, and at the end of 1918 had 5 officers, 14 NCOs & 135 men in the Wireless Section."

A major function of front-line pilots was to send messages to their ground forces, giving the location and number of the enemy's troops, guns, fortifications, and movements. Naturally, the enemy forces tried to prevent this. As a consequence, the pilot was often under fire while transmitting. He had no time to ponder or consider what he was doing — transmitting had to be as automatic as his handling of the aircraft.

While he could send Morse code messages, noise and vibration prevented the pilot from receiving them. Ground support used either an Aldis lamp or a system known as Popham Panneau, which used ground strips to form small, symmetrical, rectangular figures capable of rapid variation. Using this method, simple messages could be conveyed to the pilot quickly and reliably. Complex messages were a challenge.

To achieve the necessary fluency in telegraphy, the program of instruction brought the young cadets into almost daily contact with its operation. There would be no significant period of time when the cadet was not practising his sending skills. The object of this constant practice was to continuously improve the cadet's sending and receiving until they became second nature. When a cadet joined, he was first sent to the recruits school where he was introduced to Morse code and received a small amount of instruction and practice. From there he transferred to the Cadet Wing, where wireless transmission became a regular part of his daily routine. He was required to send six words per minute before graduating to the next stage. After six weeks' instruction at the Cadet Wing and the successful completion of his exams, including transmitting six words per minute, the cadet moved on to the School of Military Aeronautics. There was a heavy emphasis on theory at this school, but the cadet continued to practise his Morse code.

In Europe, Allied pilot casualties continued to mount and the pilot shortage worsened. As a result, the Air Board turned to Hoare once again, requesting he get along with fewer trained personnel from the United Kingdom. They also asked if he could add to the instruction given in Canada by including more advanced training in aerial observation, gunnery, and photography. They also requested that, if possible, he form a new school where cadets would receive increased ground training after passing through the Cadet Wing and before being posted to one of the flight training squadrons. A few specialists would be sent from Britain to assist in this new training but the IRFC would have to come up with many more experienced ground tradesmen in Canada than had originally been planned. In other words, Hoare and his dedicated crew were again asked to do a great deal more with a great deal less. Never one to duck a challenge, Colonel Hoare responded as expected and the Canadian training plan went into overdrive.

Under the guidance of Captain Peck and his successor, Major Harcourt, and again with the slimmest of resources, something approximating an interim School of Military Aeronautics became part of the Cadet Wing's syllabus. By the end of April 1917, these cadets were being sent on to Borden for further ground instruction on gunnery, photography, artillery observation, and other skills before proceeding to flight training. Hoare and his officers had managed to comply with the Imperial Board's request before the Board had even sent the promised instructors. Finally, on 11 June 1917, nine officers and thirty-eight instructors arrived in Canada.

The University of Toronto had already made Burwash Hall and the East Residence available to the Cadet Wing. At great inconvenience to professors and staff, the University made the following additional buildings and facilities available: the South residence, the School of Practical Science, the medical building, the thermodynamics building, a portion of Convocation Hall, and the dining halls at Victoria University and Wycliffe College. These buildings and the British instructors made possible the first School of Military Aeronautics in Canada. Known as the School of Military Aeronautics No. 4, it came into official existence on 1 July 1917.

In November, Wycliffe College agreed to turn over its eastern wing to the IRFC. In addition to the dining hall already in use by the airmen, the east wing included lecture rooms, faculty room, offices, a convocation hall, and seventy dormitories. These dormitories provided accommodation for 250 cadets; privacy was not a priority for the military. Nevertheless, the College Council thought it necessary to build a separate entrance on the west side of the college for the university students. They then sealed off all connecting corridors, effectively separating the cadets from the undergraduates.[12]

In September of 1917, the school added to its training facilities at U of T by taking over a small portion of the new Canadian airplane factory. Here, members of the flying units received instruction on the theory and construction of aircraft in an environment where they could witness the actual building of the machines in which they would be training. During the three courses at the school, each of which lasted eighteen days, the cadets learned aerial navigation, map reading, machine guns, engines, rigging, wireless, artillery observation, instruments, and bombs. By the following April, instructors recruited in Canada expanded the school's staff to 236. During this period, cadet numbers swelled from 150 to 900, a sixfold increase.[13]

There were other skills cadets had to learn before graduating from the School of Military Aeronautics. They had to master heliograph reading, sending messages by mirror, reading ground strips and markings (Popham Panneau), reading signals sent by puffs of smoke, operating field telephones, and putting these skills to use for artillery co-operation with

Allied ground forces. To develop this skill, a hangar was converted into a training centre by hanging a bucket about twenty feet in the air above a large map painted to resemble an actual battle terrain. The cadet sat in the bucket while an instructor simulated artillery bursts, using a simple switching system to turn on and off small electric bulbs on the map. The cadet had to instantly note these "bursts" and signal their position to the instructor in Morse code, giving their co-ordinates so that Allied artillery could seek and destroy the enemy batteries. This training was one of the last steps before graduation from the aeronautical school; it had evolved into a highly sophisticated training institution. The differences from the initial school operated by Lieutenant Peck just months earlier were as quantum physics to simple addition.

Before the School of Military Aeronautics came into existence, Camp Borden was in full operation; the first cadets arrived for training on 28 March with flying beginning two days later. By the middle of April, Camp Hoare was in full operation with its designated complement of five squadrons (numbers 78 to 82). It was frequently described as the finest aerodrome in North America, some said in the world. The view of the cadets living and working at the aerodrome was rather less sanguine.

W.C. Gibbard of Calgary recalled the mess as a "delightful and enormous hall. It had a huge fireplace which filled one end, with RFC wings carved in stone ... about six feet wide over it."[14]

While Gibbard recalled the mess building favourably, he failed to comment on the food or living conditions. Alan McLeod of Stonewall, Manitoba, wrote letters home full of complaints about both. The son of a country doctor, young McLeod had been eager to join, signing up the moment he turned eighteen. His letters resonate plaintively across the decades. On 19 June 1917 he wrote:

> I arrived at Camp Borden yesterday. It is an awful hole. I guess I'll get used to it but its lonely here, just a mass of sand and tents ... we are sleeping in tents without floors, there are lots of us in a tent, we have no dressers or wash stands, we have to walk about 1/4 mile to the building to get washed ... we have to get up at 3:45 a.m.

and there is no time to spare till noon and we just have
2 hour for dinner, then in the afternoon after dinner, we
work till 4:30 then have a lunch and fly till 8:15, then
we have supper and after supper, there are lectures from
9–10:30, then we go to bed. We have lots of drill and have
to polish our buttons and boots or get Cain. We can have
a week-end pass once a month ... I just hate this place.[15]

Cadet Alexander Tolchan from Albuquerque, New Mexico, echoed
McLeod's opinion of the food, complaining bitterly about the soggy
bread, sow belly, and stewed tomatoes served for breakfast. Whenever
possible, Tolchan ate breakfast off the base.

Three weeks later McLeod wrote again. At this point his anger with
mess food, IRFC discipline, and the kitchen supervisor's larceny was
taking him in the direction of revolt:

We had chicken bones for dinner, remember I said
bones ... we have rotten meals here, absolutely junk,
we can hardly eat them and we pay $1.50 a day mess,
we held an indignation meeting to-night and we're
going to have something done about it, the steward is
making a rake off.

I applied for leave this week-end and the O.C.
nearly took my head off for asking. He seemed to think
I shouldn't have it, but my opinion didn't coincide with
his. He said I couldn't get leave for a month yet; if they
don't give it to me soon, I'll take it — some fellows do
that and they don't say much.[16]

For the hard-to-recruit mechanics, the routine was easier and the food more
appetizing. Joe Goold was posted to Borden early in the summer of 1917.
His experience suggests Borden consisted of two utterly different camps:

I was shipped to Borden [from Long Branch] and
attached to ... HQ as an Airman. Not much to do but

watch the flying and keep some records … I was put on aeroplane and engine maintenance with the rank of Corporal with No. 78 Squadron…. The summer passed with many leaves of absence to Toronto, etc. I had my violin sent up to me and we formed a small orchestra. We played in the big ball where Vernon and Irene Castle danced new steps of theirs in the spotlight. Vernon was a Flight Lieutenant down at Deseronto with the 43rd Wing…. Oh yes, I got to know girls in Barrie, Toronto, and even Beamsville…. We had lots of fun and the work, if you could call it work, was never dull or arduous.[17]

The flying that Goold observed at Borden was unlike anything known today. It was highly individualistic and almost totally unregulated. Most squadrons adopted a crest or emblem. At the Rathbun Camp, number 90 Canadian Training Squadron (CTS) adopted the skull and crossbones, whereas 85 CTS decided on a black cat, 79 CTS chose a Scotch terrier, and 81 CTS surprised everyone by choosing the fleur-de-lis. These symbols were painted prominently on various parts of the airplanes, including the rudder, fin, and fuselage, usually directly below the rear cockpit. Many aircraft also displayed in large print the name of the town or city that had donated money for the aircraft. What was most unusual for a military service was the practice of a few instructors, notably Vernon Castle and Jack Coats, of painting their individual crest on their aeroplanes. The castle painted on the famous dancer's airplane rudder resembled a chess piece.

As for restrictions and rules dealing with the dangerous business of flying, cadet flyers were restricted only by what rules (if any) were laid down by their trainers or superior officers. The government had no organization to regulate flying, and no laws or regulations had been created for safety. Not surprisingly, accidents were frequent.

Nine days after flying began at Camp Borden, the IRFC suffered its first fatality. Second Lieutenant G.C. Husband was instructing twenty-one-year-old Flight Cadet Harold Talbot, who had arrived at Borden just a few days earlier. Talbot had been up with Husband two or three times on training flights and the instructor decided his student was ready to land the plane. Talbot took over the controls while Husband, in the rear seat, was poised to take them if his student misjudged. Turning into his final approach, Talbot banked into the turn too steeply and spun the airplane into the ground. Husband received minor cuts, but Talbot suffered broken ribs, a fractured skull, and internal injuries. He died at the Barrie hospital twelve hours later without regaining consciousness.

Talbot's family came from Dorchester, Ontario, where his father was postmaster. Harold Talbot was a superb student, winning an Oxford County Scholarship to the Western University of London (now known as the University of Western Ontario). He subsequently took a B.A. in political science at Queen's University, graduating with first-class honours in the spring of 1917. A well-balanced youth who excelled at both sports and academics, Talbot won the Orator of the Year award in 1915–1916, and served as captain of the Queen's championship soccer team.[18] He was preparing to study law when he heard of the IRFC's need for pilot cadets.

His instructor, Second Lieutenant Husband, survived the crash because he was seated in the rear seat. The JN-4 usually crashed nose into the ground, driving the heavy engine back onto the person in the front seat. As instructors were in short supply, IRFC policy was for instructors to sit in the safer rear seat.

Working around airplanes could be a risky business even when not in the air. Camp Borden's second fatality occurred only nine days after Talbot's death. Cadet Perrault of Montreal had just finished a training flight and was alighting from his machine when he saw a shovel that had been left carelessly on the ground. He stooped to pick it up, was struck by the airplane's still-whirling propeller, and died instantly.

The high level of accidents contributed to other problems. For every trainee killed, many more aircraft were destroyed in non-fatal accidents. C.H. Andrews kept a diary in which he described the day's crashes. On 21 October 1917 he wrote:

> Just as I got down, 84 had another crash, a washout (plane destroyed), but the cadet was not dangerously hurt. A mechanic got a broken wrist and arm swinging a prop. By

this time everyone's wind was up, so we washed out for the day. Result of the days work: 17 crashes, (three complete washouts), one killed, 5 in hospital. Very cheering.[19]

Although few days were so disastrous, crashes were an everyday occurrence. In an entry made during the same month, Andrews wrote:

Today was an eventful one on aerodrome, there were seven crashes and a couple of tail skids broken. It was a marvel that no one was even hurt. They were piled up all over the field on ears, noses, and sides. Three or four turned over on landing and two collided. Our squadron had three put out of commission and just at dusk, Bidrin the little Frenchman, pulled off the crash of the day. He went up on his second solo and coming down he nosed straight at Mother Earth at a pretty steep angle and neglected to pull her nose up. The machine was smashed to bits but Frenchie stepped out of the debris smiling and sore because he scratched one ankle. He is the luckiest guy in the place but decidedly unpopular right now on account of washing out our last remaining stick machine.

The main concern of an aspiring pilot was the successful completion of five hours of solo flying and the execution of a minimum of thirty landings The main hurdle was obtaining an airplane that was airworthy. In a letter to his father written on 23 June 1917, McLeod lamented the sorry state of aircraft supply at Camp Borden:

Our squadron No. 79 is rather behind the rest. We have the worst machines and the least in proportion to the number of cadets and yesterday four of the machines crashed and there are only 4 machines now for 25 of us so we can't get much flying in.... This morning is the first morning since I've been here that I haven't been up before 4 o'clock ... I slept till six, and it was sure great, tomorrow (Sunday) we have to get up at 3:45 just the same, it is hard luck. I wish they would treat us better.

The large number of crashes was considered normal by the training hierarchy. They took a laissez-faire attitude to flight training, allowing any cadet who had soloed to take to the air wherever an aircraft was available, regardless of the weather. This policy prevailed despite the fact that the JN-4 had none of the sophisticated instruments used by contemporary pilots to deal with poor visibility, turbulent air, or thunderstorms. This permissive policy contributed to the high incidence of crashes and aggravated the shortage of training aircraft. In a letter to his father on 22 June 1917, McLeod describes a situation that would never have occurred had there been reasonable restrictions on flights during bad weather:

I had a rather exciting time this morning, about 4:30 ...
I went for flight with three others, the air looked rather
misty but we didn't think anything of it, but as soon as
we got about 100 feet off the ground, we couldn't see a
thing, it was all mist, you could only tell by feel whether
you were going up or down or side slipping or how you
were going. As soon as I saw this I thought I would go
to the aerodrome and land but I couldn't find it. I flew
around for about 2 hours and at last through a spot in
the mist I saw land, but not very clearly. I wasn't going to
float around so I came and landed and when I got down
I found I was only about 2 miles from the aerodrome so
I just ran the machine in. I was sure thankful to get to
the ground. One of the other fellows landed in a field
about 20 miles away, another fellow crashed his machine
in a swamp and isn't back yet, the other fellow landed in
another field about 10 miles away.... I was the luckiest
one of the bunch. Gee I was scared.

As every pilot who has flown a small aircraft knows, flying blind can be disconcerting and frightening. But a modern pilot has a radio, gyrocompass, altimeter, a gauge displaying the horizontal and vertical planes of the airplane, plus a directional finding system. All these aids are invaluable to the flyer in locating the airplane's position and preventing it from crashing into the side of a hill or building. Cadets in the IRFC had only gauges for oil pressure and fuel, an airspeed indicator, a tachometer, and an altimeter. Only the altimeter was of any assistance to the pilot flying blind. Allowing these inexperienced cadets to fly airplanes with little equipment and in conditions of poor visibility was akin to playing Russian roulette with three bullets in the chambers. The miracle of McLeod's flight is that only one of the four aircraft was wrecked.

The shortage of serviceable aircraft was further aggravated by IRFC training methods, which strove to get the cadet flying on his own with a minimum of dual instruction, a major contributor to airplane smash-ups. Even McLeod, a gifted pilot, was unable to avoid crashing. On 11 June 1917, he wrote his parents describing his smash-up:

> I like it here fine, the flying is great. They didn't give us enough instruction and as a result we broke a few machines by making bad landings. I had a crash yesterday. I didn't know the wind had changed and I came down with it instead of against it and smashed the plane up. But the O.C. just laughed and said, "that was a fine landing." They never care if you have a smash, if you didn't they would think there was something seriously wrong. It is impossible to hurt yourself when making a landing. You may smash the machine but you can't get hurt. The only way you can get hurt is to fall from the air and you can't fall unless you try stunts and I tell you I am mighty careful. I got lost yesterday. I was up for a long time and I couldn't find the aerodrome.... I am going to get some more instruction. They gave me my solo with the least [instruction] of the bunch.

From the earliest days of flying, aerodromes, no matter how small, have been equipped with windsocks. These socks are large enough that, in reasonable visibility, a pilot can see the sock from a height of 1,000 feet or more, making it easy to determine the direction of the wind. Apparently there was no windsock at Borden on the day McLeod had his first crash. Moreover, cadets often flew without maps, which were not yet available in any quantity. It is hardly surprising so many airmen got lost or crashed.

In fairness to the IRFC, aerial mapping was in its infancy and, in the early months of the training program, maps were in short supply. In order to find Toronto or IRFC landing fields, cadets were instructed to follow rail or hydro lines, both easy visual guides. To reach Toronto or Camp Borden they generally followed the rail line. Still, these aids were not much help in conditions of poor visibility. As a consequence, a great many pilots became lost and were sometimes forced to land on dangerous terrain.

With so many crashes in the training program, producing sufficient airplanes to keep the pilots in the air became a major challenge. Moreover, it was a problem over which Hoare and his officers had little control. The challenge had to be met by a group of Canadian civilians at Canadian Aeroplanes Limited and, in particular, by Frank Baillie, its dynamic, hard-driving president, and by F.G. Ericson, its chief engineer. Neither of these men had any wartime experience, but both were deeply committed to the IRFC and to winning the war.

# CHAPTER SIX
## CANADA'S FIRST AIRPLANE FACTORY

I consider the JN-4 as built in Toronto the best
training machine in existence.
— *Charles A. Lindbergh*[1]

The Imperial Munitions Board was set up in 1916 to oversee wartime production in Canada. Although staffed primarily by Canadians, it did not answer directly to the Canadian government, but rather to the British Ministry of Munitions in London. In October of that year, the Canadian government agreed to provide up to $1 million for an aircraft plant to be under the management of the IMB. In conjunction with this arrangement, the British government would handle all aspects of the IRFC recruiting and training of pilot-cadets in Canada and further guaranteed sufficient orders to keep the aircraft plant operating for the duration of the war, after which the plant would revert to Canadian ownership.

The IMB set up Canadian Aeroplanes Ltd. and appointed Frank Baillie as president. An entrepreneur who moved as quickly and decisively as Hoare, within days of his appointment Baillie had arranged the purchase of the assets of the only producing airplane factory in Canada, Curtiss Aeroplane and Motors Ltd. The assets included a small factory on Strachan Avenue in Toronto and, more importantly, the rights to the JN-3 airplane, and was tooled and staffed by competent engineers and tradesmen. As the manufacture and design of aircraft was still in its infancy, the knowledge and expertise of these men was invaluable.

At the time of his appointment, the forty-one-year-old Baillie had already achieved more than most executives manage in a lifetime. He had risen from bank clerk to general manager of the Metropolitan Bank at the age of twenty-seven, making him the youngest general manager of a bank in Canadian history. He subsequently formed various companies, including the brokerage firm of Baillie, Wood and Croft, as well as the Canadian Cartage Company of Hamilton. He was also president of the Burlington Steel Company and had recently been appointed director of aviation for Canada by the IMB. In October of 1916, he organized Canadian Aeroplanes Ltd. and hired its executives, including its chief engineer, F.G. Ericson.[2] It was Ericson who oversaw the design changes to the American JN 3, which were to make the Canadian version such an outstanding training aircraft.

The JN-4, or Canuck, as she was affectionately known, was a two-seater bi-plane powered by the OX-5, an eight-cylinder, water-cooled engine of ninety horsepower, manufactured in Hammondsport, New York. The Canuck's cruising speed was 60 miles per hour (mph), its stall speed 45 mph, and its maximum speed between 75 and 80 mph.*

With a wingspan of forty-three feet, seven inches, the Canuck was large for a training aircraft. The cowling around the two cockpits was made of aluminum fastened with copper screws, giving it a modern look. Other than that, the airplane was constructed almost entirely of wood, wire, and cloth. It was sometimes fondly described as a collection of wood, wire, and bolts, flying through the air in formation.

The conversion of the JN-3 to the JN 4 Canadian was accomplished by changes to make it sturdier and therefore better suited to the rough handling of unskilled cadets. The wheel control was converted to a joystick, making it the first aircraft in North America to boast this innovation. The undercarriage was strengthened and the tail skid redesigned for rougher handling. The tail design was streamlined and the rudder, elevators, and fin were converted from wood construction to metal tubing. In addition, ailerons were added to the lower wings for increased lateral control.[3]

The aircraft was built primarily of wood — mostly ash and spruce — covered with expensive Irish linen, all held together with piano wire.

---

* Its specifications were as follows: wingspan upper — 43 feet 7 3/8 inches; wingspan lower — 34 feet 8 5/16 inches; fuselage — 27 feet 2 inches; propeller — 8 feet 3 inches; fuel tank — 20 U.S. gallons; oil tank — 4 U.S. gallons; cruising range — approximately 200 miles; permissible gross weight with a two-man crew — 1,920 pounds.

However, German submarine warfare in the North Atlantic threatened imports from Ireland. Aware of the expertise available in the Canadian fabric industry, Baillie set out to find a replacement for the fabric in Canada. The problem was overcome when Canadian Aeroplanes found a high-quality cotton manufactured at the Wobasco cotton plant in Trois-Rivières, Quebec. Much less costly than Irish linen, when treated with a waterproof and windproof solution with a celluloid-like finish, it proved just as reliable.[4]

Baillie tried to avoid importing components for the Canuck, preferring to obtain them in Canada where politics and submarines were less likely to interfere with supplies. However, there was no experienced aero-engine manufacturer in Canada and he was forced to turn to the OX-5 engine built by Curtiss in the United States. This was a concern to Baillie as it was against American law for its corporations or citizens to sell articles of war to nations at war. In early 1917, the United States was still neutral.

Baillie found Canadian manufacturers for the instruments, which consisted of a simple airspeed indicator, an altimeter, oil pressure gauge, tachometer, and two lights and switches to control the panel and lights.

The only instrument differing significantly from those on today's small aircraft was the tachometer. Manufactured by the Stewart-Warner plant in Belleville, Ontario, it was known as the Stewart-Warner K-2 Tachometer. Adapted from an early automobile speedometer, it was mounted vertically behind the instrument panel and read through a slot in the panel. All instruments were lighted by two dry-cell batteries.[5]

The redesigned version of the JN-4A was flight-tested at Long Branch by American test pilot, Bert Acosta, on New Year's Day, 1917. Fortunately, for the success of the IRFC, chief engineer Ericson and his engineers had designed a winner. The Canuck was easier to fly than both the JN-3 and the American-built JN-4A or Buffalo.[6] Perhaps its greatest quality as a training aircraft were its crash features. In most accidents, the plane simply collapsed around the pilot. It was commonplace for a pilot to walk away uninjured from a totally wrecked aircraft.

As it took some months for Canadian Aeroplanes to achieve full production, RFC Canada was forced in the early stages to obtain its aircraft from the Curtiss plant in Buffalo. In the view of many, the

Buffalo was more difficult to fly. Roger Vee trained on both the Canuck and the Buffalo and noted that, "The Canadian Curtiss had practically no dihedral ... The Buffalo ... had five or six degrees [dihedral is the wing angle to the horizontal]. The Canadian Curtiss was the easier machine to land."[7] For the beginning pilot, landing an aircraft was, and remains, the most difficult manoeuvre to master safely. Unlike mistakes at higher altitudes, low-altitude errors seldom give the pilot time to recover.

Unfortunately, the Buffalo had an even more dangerous flaw. Cadets complained it had a tendency to get into spins. Getting out of a spin is part of basic flying but, in early 1917, spins were not fully understood, and, when a pilot followed his natural instincts and pulled the airplane's nose up, he kept the wings stalled, which accelerated the spin. The result was often fatal. As Hoare noted in a report to the director of air in London:

> Callaghan was most unfortunately killed in a smash this week. The machine got into a spin at about 500 [feet] and the pilot failed to get out. The Buffalo machines have proved bad in this respect, it is a common and usually groundless complaint of pilots that machines have a tendency to spin, these [the Buffalo] however actually do have if badly handled.[8]

With the choice of aircraft decided, Baillie made his next major decision without waiting for the arrival of Hoare and his staff. The plant on Strachan Street was clearly too small to produce the airplanes needed for a training plan as ambitious as that visualized by Sir Sefton Brancker. On 17 January, Baillie arranged for the construction of a much larger factory at the corner of Dufferin and Lappin.

Taking up 235,000 square feet, or nearly five-and-a-half acres, the plant was scheduled for completion for 1 June. Despite the severe winter, construction began in early February. By 1 May, equipment and staff were being moved into the new building. A month later, the factory was fully complete. Hoare was to learn that the IMB always met its deadlines.

On 25 January 1917, Hoare arrived for the first time in the City of Toronto. Baillie was one of several people with whom he had discussions.

Both men were quick to make decisions and both demanded total commitment from their staff. It was inevitable that two such strong personalities would clash, but the initial meetings went favourably. Hoare decided on the spot to establish the HQ of RFC Canada in the Imperial Oil building on Church Street, the same building where the IMB and Baillie had their offices.

In his memorandum of November 1917, Hoare, summarizing the achievements of RFC Canada in its first year, stated that, "The remarkable development of this factory under the management of Mr. F.W. Baillie … has been one of the chief factors in enabling the rapid development of Aviation in Canada.[9]

When Hoare and Baillie first crossed swords is not recorded but Major Allen observed one such encounter. In April of 1917, the new Canadian Aeroplane factory was not yet on stream and only a few airplanes were being sent from Buffalo. As a consequence, the IRFC faced a severe shortage of airplanes at Borden, where cadets were arriving in large numbers. In the trenchant opinion of Baillie, this shortage was exacerbated by the inspectors from the Aeronautical Inspection Department. These inspectors were rejecting large numbers of aircraft components as unfit for use. Baillie's dual positions as president of Canadian Aeroplanes, as well as director of aviation for Canada, increased his power and influence and could have created serious problems for Hoare and Allen, both of whom were firm believers in the inspection system. In mid-April, Allen reported to Charlton on the shortage of airplanes:

> As reported in the last semi-official letter, the same difficulties continue to exist. Machines are coming through incomplete, and deficient of various parts….Today there are actually only 3 machines serviceable at Borden.[10]

Commenting on the problem forty-five years later, Allen observed:

> I have seldom seen a man so explosive as the late Sir Frank Baillie, when he heard that A.I.D. Inspector at Canadian Aeroplanes had rejected a batch of components. General

Hoare politely and firmly told him "just where to get off." In a very short time, there was no greater upholder of the independent inspection of the A.I.D. than Sir Frank.[11]

There were two reasons for the airplane shortage. One lay in the training methods of RFC (Canada), which followed the British practice of getting the cadet flying on his own as quickly as possible. As a result, many cadets smashed up their airplanes either in heavy landings or as a result of banking too steeply on turns or other incorrect flying procedures. In July 1917 alone, some twenty-eight airplanes were completely demolished. By the end of September the number of complete write-offs were: thirty-two (Borden), twenty-six (Deseronto), and thirteen for the Toronto camps — a total of seventy-one aircraft completely destroyed.[12]

In May, RFC (Canada) established an engine repair park in Toronto for the purpose of salvaging damaged engines as well as rebuilding those which had accumulated 400 hours of use. In August, the park relocated to larger premises, expanding its operations to include the entire airplane. By November 1918, the total strength of this unit numbered 125. As a result, a great many severely damaged airplanes were rebuilt, helping to keep cadets in the air and minimizing the loss of training time. In addition, maintenance operations were set up at Borden and Deseronto for machines not too badly damaged as well as for regular maintenance work on both engines and airframes.[13]

The other cause originated at the Curtiss Hammondsport plant, which manufactured the OX-5 engine. Deliveries of the engines began in March but only about 30 percent were serviceable. The problem originated in the metal used in the bearings and some time was wasted finding a replacement. In the meantime, RFC (Canada) had to make do with the Buffalo, plus the small percentage of Canucks with satisfactory engines. Progress in meeting this problem was rapid and, by mid-July, Hoare reported that, "The engines are beyond all praise, and are the most reliable of any type I have experienced. I have one engine that has run 150 hours without a top overhaul and is as good as ever."[14]

Hoare's optimism proved Pollyannaish. Although the Official Injury Reports tend to conceal it, the OX-5 engine was a leading cause of accidents. The lack of reporting was due to the nature of engine failure. When an engine began losing speed, the pilot usually had time to find a safe field for landing and bring the plane down safely. When engine failure resulted in death, it was usually impossible to determine the cause of the accident and the problem went unrecorded. Moreover, engine failures were so common many training officers simply didn't bother to record them.* For example, in May of 1918, official reports show three accidents caused by defective engines with two resulting in fatalities. During that same month, there were at least double that number.

Cadets were aware of the engine's defects. The letters of Alan McLeod and the diary of C.H. Andrews testify to their unreliability. On 31 July 1917, McLeod wrote home observing sardonically that, "Our Curtiss engines only run when they feel like it."

While Ericson and the engineers at Canadian Aeroplanes were solving the problems of aircraft production, the IMB was constructing two new camps north of Toronto. The North Toronto Wing consisted of a camp at Leaside and one at Armour Heights, about five miles north of Toronto's city limits. The abundance of flat countryside to the north of these camps made them ideal for artillery observation and bombing training. The Armour Heights camp was opened on 15 June 1917. Flying at Leaside began three weeks later.

Canadian Aeroplanes moved into high production with surprising speed and, by early June, barely a month after their new plant was occupied, Hoare was able to report that, "We have an admirable factory here and can turn out machines sufficient for any numbers, and shall be thoroughly well equipped by the autumn."[16]

Only the highest quality of woods could be used in airframe construction. Under the stress of flight, particularly when performing

---

* The following were not reported in the ORs: on 6 May, Cadet Weeding's engine stalled at 1,500 feet, forcing a crash landing that destroyed the airplane; three days later, an unidentified aviator flying out of Borden was forced to land when his engine failed; on 21 May, Cadet Rawley's engine quit, forcing him to land and seriously damaging the airplane. The first two pilots escaped serious injury, but Rawley was not expected to survive.[15]

*Armour Heights, fire house and equipment, Toronto, 1917. Courtesy of
Library and Archives Canada/ Department of National Defence PA- 022951.*

stunts, defective wires or wood members could snap with disastrous
results. The shortage of high-quality spruce reached critical proportions
in the fall of 1917. In early October, Hoare was complaining to London
that he doubted they could find sufficient spruce for the factory in all
of B.C. In response to this crisis, Baillie and the IMB formed a special
department in Vancouver for the sole purpose of buying the high-quality
wood required. Obtaining sufficient quantities of high-grade spruce
was a continuing problem but the IMB's new department in Vancouver
met the challenge. Canadian Aeroplanes was so successful that it soon
outstripped the needs of the training establishment in Canada.

On 6 April 1917, the United States entered the war on the side of
Britain and France. Soon afterward, the U.S. entered into a co-operative
pilot training scheme with RFC (Canada). Hoare was concerned that
the supply of OX-5 engines being manufactured in Hammondsport,
New York, might now dry up. To meet the needs of the growing U.S. Air
Services, America could quite legitimately commandeer all the engines

the plant produced. Fortunately, Hoare had cultivated excellent relations with American officials who agreed that Canadian Aeroplanes would receive a minimum of 50 percent of the engines produced by Curtiss up to a hundred monthly and not less than ninety in any one month should production fall below 180.[17]

Canadian Aeroplanes became so proficient at manufacturing the Canuck that, by the fall of 1917, they had a surplus. This created a financial problem for the company, which was in danger of having to lay off large numbers of trained workers. Fortunately, Hoare obtained an order from the Americans for ninety Canucks plus spares, which kept the factory on Dufferin Street at full production. His personal relations with the Americans together with the superior qualities of the Canuck helped Hoare obtain further orders until, by the end of the reciprocal training scheme, the United States had purchased a total of 680 machines.

Initially, plans called for the production of fifteen aircraft weekly and, in its first months of production, Canadian Aeroplanes usually met the target. However, by December, the factory was turning out, including spares, the equivalent of five aircraft a day or thirty airplanes a week. Each aircraft cost $7,625, including $2,375 for the engine.

All this was accomplished with a staff that averaged about 2,000 employees, many of them women. At peak production in 1918, the factory was producing an average of 200 Canucks a month. During its nineteen months of operation, the plant produced the equivalent of 2,871 JN-4s made up of 1,260 airplanes plus parts equivalent to another 1,611 aircraft.

In 1918, Canadian Aeroplanes received an order from the United States Navy to produce thirty F-5 Flying Boats. With a wingspan of 102 feet and a total flying weight averaging 14,000 pounds and powered by two 400 hp Liberty engines, it was then the largest aircraft ever designed and built in North America. The order was obtained despite stiff competition from two American aircraft builders. Canadian Aeroplanes completed their prototype three weeks ahead of the competition and so impressed the U.S. Navy that the admiral in charge of procurement wrote, "On account of the excellent workmanship of Canadian Aeroplanes shown in the construction of navy flying boats, the bureau is glad to recommend the facilities of your plant."[18]

In early autumn of 1918, the Allies assumed the war in Europe would drag on for at least another year. Canadian Aeroplanes had demonstrated their engineering capabilities with the successful building of the F-5 Flying Boats. As a consequence, by late spring of 1918, the reputation of the company for workmanship, ingenuity, and high standards of engineering led the Air Board in London to place an order with Canadian Aeroplanes for 500 Avro 504K aircraft to be put into service with RAF (Canada) as an advanced trainer. These were the airplanes Hoare had asked for eighteen months earlier. Some delay resulted from the need to make minor design changes so that some parts would be interchangeable with the Canuck and also to replace materials not readily available in Canada. Two of these airplanes were produced, the first being delivered to the Rathbun Camp in Deseronto, the second to Beamsville.[19] Production was just getting underway when the armistice was declared. In addition to the two complete Avro 504Ks produced by the company, another hundred machines had been fabricated and were ready for assembly when hostilities ceased and production stopped.

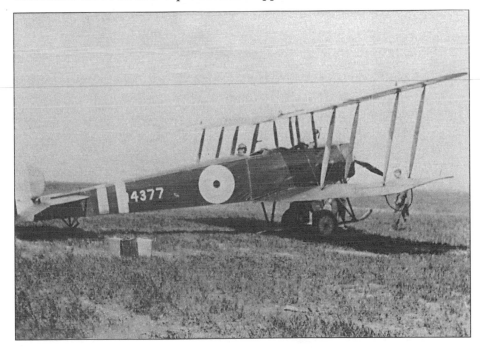

*An Avro 504K. Courtesy of Crossman Collection.*

After the war, British-built Avro 504Ks became the primary training aircraft for the short-lived Canadian Air Force and later for the RCAF. Relatively advanced for the time, the Avro 504K was powered by a 130-hp Le Clerget rotary engine and could obtain a top speed in excess of 100 miles per hour. It remained the primary training airplane for the RCAF until the 1930s.

Aside from backyard mechanic-inventors who put together aircraft of dubious quality, Canadian Aeroplanes was the first aircraft manufacturing company in Canada. It produced aircraft of high quality, overcoming many obstacles in the process and establishing an enviable reputation for both production and engineering standards. It can rightly be regarded as the genesis of an important Canadian industry later exemplified by the Avro Arrow and, more recently, the Bombardier Company of Montreal.

Although Baillie and his crew had risen to the challenge of producing sufficient training airplanes, Hoare and his staff officers faced a different challenge. Canada was a vast and thinly populated country with a total population of less than 8 million. Moreover, most of its young men had been recruited over the two and a half years of the Great War. Hoare had already been told by the Canadian military that he would be lucky to find 500 men in the entire country who could qualify as flight cadets. Where could he possibly find the 200 cadets needed every month to supply the vast training machine of IRFC?

# CHAPTER SEVEN
## FINDING FLYERS

Owing to the great distances between towns and the scattered population, almost all applications had to be dealt with by correspondence, either from headquarters or out stations. Transportation had then to be given to bring a man at least three hundred miles for a medical board, after which, if successful in passing the oral tests, etc., he was transported to Toronto. This journey in the case of a man enlisting in Vancouver occupied four days, coming 2,500 miles. Sleeping accommodation had to be provided and also meals on route. None of these difficulties were encountered in England.[1]

— *Lieutenant-Colonel C.G. Hoare, Officer Commanding*

Shortly after the IRFC arrived in Canada, Major Strubell, the officer in charge of recruiting, was overwhelmed with applications from men eager to train as pilots. Although the recruiting of flight cadets had not started, advertising for mechanics in mid-February got the IRFC some publicity. It was enough to cause a flood of applications from young men eager to join so they could learn to fly and serve in what was perceived as a gallant and exciting air war. By the end of the month over 1,000 applications had been received from all parts of the Dominion. Strubell had few staff and was not equipped to deal with such a deluge of applicants.

Neither Hoare nor Strubell were misled by this initial abundance of applicants. They knew that a majority would not meet the standards required for air crew. As statistics would later show, only about one third of applicants would make the cut and some of these would not graduate. Nor did they expect the rush of applications to continue. Upon his arrival in Ottawa, Hoare had met with Gwatkin, chief of the Canadian general staff, who said he was on a fool's errand and would not be able to recruit 500 men in six months. Later, at a meeting of 200 Canadian Militia officers, this shortage was confirmed. The officers told him they were unanimous in their view that recruitment had ceased and nothing short of a conscription act would make it possible to obtain further men.[2]

By 1917, the war had been maiming and killing soldiers for two and a half years. Any illusions that warfare was glamorous had evaporated, replaced with the realization that modern warfare was unimaginably horrific. Moreover, jobs in Canada were plentiful and well-paying, while hard-pressed farmers and their sons, who were needed to supply vast amounts of food stuffs to the front, were finally reaping the benefits of years of labour. Moreover, the wages of a foot soldier were totally inadequate to support a family at home.

Nor was the war popular in francophone Quebec, which effectively meant that one third of Canada's small population was impervious to all blandishments to volunteer for overseas service. Even the romantic lure of flying failed to instil enthusiasm amongst the francophones in la Belle Provence. Recruiting was most successful in Ontario and British Columbia, where the population was predominantly Anglo-Saxon. In the prairies, where a third of the population came from central Europe, there was little loyalty to Britain or her Empire. There was also increasing resistance amongst organized labour, which was demanding that wealth be conscripted for the war effort before they would accept the conscription of men.*

But Hoare had advantages not possessed by the militia. First and foremost was the romance of flying. Men travelled from as far as Argentina in the hope they could meet IRFC standards. Aviation was particularly

---

* Quebec, with a population equal to 80 percent of Ontario's, supplied 564 air crew to the RAF and RNAS, whereas Ontario supplied 3,005. With only 16 percent of Ontario's population, B.C. supplied 686 air crew. Based on the 1911 census, B.C. supplied more air crew per capita than any other province.[4]

popular among the British settlers in the western provinces where many young men abandoned farms, family, and good jobs to travel across the country in hopes they would be accepted.

William C. Gibbard exemplified this zeal. He had homesteaded between Maple Creek, Saskatchewan, and the Saskatchewan River and had built up a large investment in farm equipment and buildings. Nevertheless, he wrote that, "The desire to join the RFC had afflicted me." He sold off the results of several years' labour and took a train east to Toronto. He later wrote of his life as a cadet. "We lived for flying and were in despair when shortages of machines, sickness, orderly duty, etc., grounded us. Outside social activity was non-existent and was not desired. No time for anything that did not further our aviating."[3]

Hoare also planned to exploit a source of elite manpower not legally available to the Canadian Militia. The Canadian Militia was under strict orders not to offer enticements to Americans to enlist in its service. In 1818, the American congress had passed the Foreign Enlistment Act, making it a criminal offence to recruit Americans on American soil for service against a friendly state. Later, the United States had extended the act by making it an offence to offer inducements that would entice Americans to go abroad to enlist. Prime Minister Borden had initially discouraged any enlistment by Americans into the CEF but, as the war dragged on, was assured by London that Britain welcomed American volunteers. Facing a manpower crisis in Canada, he reversed his position. After 1915, the Canadian government, although not actively recruiting U.S. citizens, readily accepted American volunteers who crossed into Canada. After that, thousands of adventurous Americans joined the CEF.

In the summer of 1916, Canada's meddling governor general, the Duke of Connaught, believing this to be a breach of British Imperial Policy, complained bitterly to Borden about this practice. The prime minister replied that Canada possessed complete powers of self-government and adamantly resisted the governor general's intrusions into Canadian affairs. When the Duke attempted to interpose his authority as a field marshal in His Majesty's Forces, Borden replied icily that the matter did not call so much for the exercise of military skill as for the considerations of international law. As an experienced lawyer, Borden knew his ground. Nevertheless, the prime minister put a stop to the worst abuses of Canadian recruiting practices. In November, Connaught was replaced as governor general by the Duke of Devonshire, who refrained from interfering with Borden's decisions.[5]

Initially, Hoare was unaware of the restrictions applying to recruiting in the United States. He fully intended to recruit Americans into the IRFC, even planning to recruit on American soil. He believed he could set up recruiting offices in the U.S. as long as he appeared to be recruiting British citizens who were residing in that country. If Americans showed up at the recruiting offices, the IRFC would sign them on.

In April, Hoare reported to Charlton that he was relying on the States. In his letter to his superior he wrote, "My general impression is, as I told you last week, that I can get good material from the States, especially as I am certain their early attempts at Schools [military flying schools] will be a failure there, and the keen ones will come to us."[6]

In the meantime, Hoare and Strubell continued to work on recruiting in Canada. On 24 April, Hoare wrote Sir Robert Falconer, principal at the University of Toronto, requesting that he advise the coming spring's graduates of the opportunities afforded them in the IRFC and suggesting many would be eager to join.[7] In an earlier meeting with Hoare and Allen, Sir Robert had been won over to the IRFC cause and willingly cooperated with the request.

A few weeks later, Allen, acting on behalf of his CO, wrote Sir Robert that, "I not only want Cadets for immediate service, but also wish to have the names of men who will join some time in the future."[8] The idea was to develop a list of prospects that could be drawn upon when they reached the age of eighteen.

The IRFC had come into being with a great rush. By the end of March 1917, the first flying had commenced at Camp Borden; Camp Mohawk was in operation a month later. Up to this point, there had been no need to search for cadets but, with two training camps coming on stream, student pilots would be needed in large numbers. The initial estimate had been that the IRFC could train 600 cadets by the end of year. A high casualty rate and the demands of the air war created a need for a great many more.[9]

Once cadet recruitment got fully under way, Strubell lacked the manpower to deal with the large number of applications. To solve this problem, he utilized the services of the Aero Club formed in December 1916 by William Hamilton Merritt. The club set up committees of prominent local citizens in the major regional centres of Toronto, Montreal, Charlottetown, Winnipeg, Regina, Calgary, and Vancouver. These committees were empowered to interview applicants and, if satisfactory, have them examined by the local medical board whose services were generously made available by the Department of Militia. If these examinations and interviews proved satisfac-

### Aerial Warriors

MASTERY of the air prevents the loss of thousands of allied troops. The more aeroplanes, we can maintain at the front the greater becomes the security of our men in the trenches, and the more effective our artillery fire.

For our aerial warriors are the eyes of the army, guarding our troops from surprise tactics of the enemy, laying bare his deadly guns and directing our own guns with unfailing accuracy.

At the same time they clear the air of Hun machines—thus "putting out the eyes" of the enemy batteries.

Young men from 18 to 30, strong, keen and courageous, men of fair education, and eager for accomplishment, will find the opportunities in the Imperial Air Service very attractive. While training for their commissions cadets receive $1.10 per day. Class 1, men under the M.S. Act are eligible. Those wishing to enroll as cadets should either write or apply in person to one of the following addresses :

*Imperial*
### Royal Flying Corps

*Recruiting poster, circa 1917. Courtesy of Library and Archives Canada, AMICUS No. 32906224.*

tory, the board could send the applicants on to Toronto for final testing and approval. These committees operated under IRFC medical standards and, while they did not actively promote recruiting, provided the IRFC with a much-needed recruiting organization in the vast Canadian hinterland.

Later that summer, the demand for cadets rose to 300 per month; then, in early fall, it reached 400 per month and by mid-fall 500 per month. Only a few months earlier, in May, the IRFC had estimated it would need just 600 cadets for the balance of the year. Clearly drastic measures were needed if the IRFC was to find sufficient manpower for the escalating demands of the war.

From the very beginning, the IRFC used imaginative methods to recruit. Early in March 1917, Hoare advised Charlton that, "I am considering giving squadrons city names to stimulate recruiting and create rivalry. Toronto has easily supplied a squadron already. The local municipality [Toronto] take a keen interest and voted us $2,500.00 this week towards recruiting expenses."[10] Hoare was anxious to reward and encourage this support.

Hoare knew how to manipulate public opinion. With Canada about to implement conscription he wanted to assure the public that flying was safe. As part of that strategy he invited Colonel Merritt to make the first flight from the aerodrome at Armour Heights. A few months later, Merritt, now chairman of the IRFC Cadet Committee, made a statement to the press that was widely reported in Ontario. His intention was clearly to encourage enlistment: "There is an opening now existing for 500 young men as flying officers in the Imperial Royal Flying Corps in Canada ... it presents an opportunity for young Canadians of quality who wish to help their country and secure a most valuable education without cost to themselves, a chance they may never have again." He went on to deny "the feeling in some quarters that flying was a particularly hazardous undertaking." It was reported, "He recently had an opportunity of deciding it and viewed Toronto from an altitude of 3,000 feet. It is doubtful, he believes, whether there are not more accidents proportionally among chauffeur beginners."[11]

On 12 October 1917, the IRFC took over the recruitment offices manned by the Aero Club of Canada. This was part of a plan to enlarge the civilian committee organization and form committees in every Canadian town with a population of 10,000 or more. In communities of less than 10,000 at least one important citizen was sought out to form a recruiting committee. For administration purposes the Dominion was divided up into five recruiting districts, each with an HQ office in one of the following cities: Halifax, Montreal, Toronto, Winnipeg, and Vancouver. Each district office was under the command of a resident IRFC officer who answered directly to headquarters.

There was also a second or field officer whose job was to visit the various committees in the district and provide assistance and instruction. He was also instructed to promote the IRFC amongst the local populace. Visiting small towns in his smart uniform, the officer attracted the attention of the press and readily granted interviews, providing effective advertising for IRFC's manpower needs at a low cost. In all about a thousand volunteers made up the approximately 350 civilian committees established across Canada.[12]

During October, Hoare was instructed by the War Office in London to form a fifth wing as soon as possible. With enlistment declining, Hoare decided to lower standards and make the tests easier. This shift was also evident in press releases and newspaper ads which stressed that cadets did not need a university education but merely "a fair education." Later press releases changed this to "ordinary intelligence and education."[13]

The order to form a fifth wing put a great deal of pressure on Hoare, who turned to the Canadian Militia for help, advising Gwatkin, "I cannot see how we can obtain the Cadets … unless you help us further."[14] Despite a shortage of recruits in the Canadian Army, Gwatkin co-operated fully, the only restriction being that the loss of those men who wished to volunteer for transfer would not interfere with the organization or efficiency of the units concerned. Many militia men volunteered until, by the end of the war, some 5,900 cadets had been directly recruited from the Canadian Army into the RFC/RAF in Canada.[15]

Fortunately, at the time of the crisis, Americans of the highest quality were joining the Flying Corps and their numbers were increasing. How they and other nationalities became aware of the IRFC in places as distant as Hawaii and Argentina can be attributed to the novelty of flight and particularly to the novelty of the air war. Never before had there been battles such as these. For adventurous young men eager to participate in this glamorous combat, learning how the IRFC would train them to be participants in this great adventure was equally newsworthy.

The impact on young Americans was exactly what Hoare had hoped. On 19 September 1917, the *Vancouver Sun* reported that many cadets were being sent east to train for the aviation corps. Among a group of twenty cadets were seven Canadians from Vancouver, ten Americans from Los Angeles, and three from Honolulu. In other words, more than half of this group were Americans. This example was not an anomaly. S.F. Wise estimates that as many as one third of the pilots sent overseas by the RFC/RAF were American.[16] Once the United States entered the war the number of Americans volunteering for the IRFC declined.

The American entry into the war on 6 April 1917 meant that American manpower would be required by American military units. The influx of American recruits into Canada would almost certainly be stopped by U.S. authorities. The following month, Hoare received word that Americans were now barred from enlisting in the IRFC. In a letter to Charlton dated 11 May, he stated, "This shall likely make it very difficult to obtain the numbers we shall require. I was counting on as many as I required from the States and from what I hear, they would have been easily obtainable." But Hoare was not certain that Americans were absolutely vital, stating in the same letter, "I don't know really how the cadet question now stands but should do so in the course of the next 6 weeks."[17]

In mid-April, Hoare was ordered to go to Washington to meet with senior officials and discuss flight training. Both London and Washington were clearly unsure where these discussions would lead and Hoare was given no specific instructions At that point he did not have a specific plan in mind, nor did he believe that American cadets were absolutely crucial to the operation in Canada. This is evident in his communication to Charlton at the Air Directorate.

On 20 April, he cabled Charlton reporting the progress of his visit, "I ... established, I think, very cordial relations with their war department." This proved a gross understatement. Hoare was a consummate diplomat and clearly charmed them all, laying the groundwork for an advantageous relationship.

Among his achievements was an arrangement with the American general, G.O. General Squire, in which the latter agreed to allow the IRFC to continue quietly recruiting Americans and to do so from an office in New York City. It was an entirely personal deal and directly contrary to official American policy. Nor was there any guarantee as to how long the arrangement would last but, for the moment, the problem of an adequate supply of cadets for the IRFC had been solved. Hoare summed up the situation in a cable to Charlton on 15 June:

I have established an R.F.C. Recruiting Staff in N.Y. … and will see that any good material is not lost to the Corps.

The Cadet question is not so acute as it was. Strubell tells me he thinks he has 250 for certain this month and I am busy working quietly in the States. Denton and Bonnell are there, the latter nominally on leave; on his return Filley is going to Boston and I shall put in a day or so there on my return hitting off the University celebrations, I shall thus have an opportunity of meeting a large number of the best sort of people. Filley tells me he is certain that we can get good results. I have had a batch of Kingston boys in [RMC], they will make absolutely first class Officers and are quite as smart as Sandhurst boys in pre-war days. More are coming.

Generally speaking, I am very satisfied with the material I am getting, and I think the system of Interviewing Committees which are now spread all over the country, is going to work admirably and advertise our needs … and the supply of Cadets is adequate … [18]

Later that month, Hoare paid a visit to the New York recruiting office on Broadway Avenue and found it a poor location. He obtained free offices on Fifth Avenue from the Benson and Hedges Tobacco Company. The new location was immediately more successful in attracting recruits. Hoare supplied the office with recruiting staff from Canada and posted two IRFC officers there, believing their smart uniforms would attract potential recruits to the office where the officers could not only answer questions on the intriguing subject of aircraft and flying but could do so from first-hand experience. The New York office would end up supplying the greatest number of American recruits. [19]

In spite of Hoare's successes, recruiting problems continued, as the summer wore on the demand for recruits again threatened to outstrip the supply. In an interview with *The Toronto Daily Star* in mid-August, Allen stated the IRFC had an immediate need for 500 cadets and then an additional 200 a month just to keep up to strength. He also reiterated that cadets didn't need a university education but needed only "a fair education."[20] It had become increasingly clear to Hoare that Canada could not provide sufficient university students and graduates to supply the Plan's needs for officer cadets. Moreover, Hoare himself had dropped out of Sandhurst. He was doubtless less impressed than his fellow officers with the need for a university degree.

The terrible casualties and the problems of finding suitable cadets affected the IRFC's standards on more levels than education. It was generally agreed that the best pilots were those between the ages of eighteen and twenty-five, with the absolute age limit being thirty. Even that limit was sometimes ignored. In one case, Hoare and his recruiting team were so impressed they accepted a thirty-four-year-old. This was so unusual Hoare felt compelled to explain his action to the Air Board, writing on 12 September, he rationalized:

> I have, in a few cases, taken really likely cadets over 25. I have one whom I think I ought to mention as his case may be questioned some day. He is a Romanian British subject aged 34, by name PAPINI. I have met him several times in N.Y. He seems an excellent fellow, young for his age, a light-weight and the keenest cadet I have struck. He has repeatedly turned up, even as far as coming to Toronto and I think he is worth taking a chance on.[21]

Bending the rules with the Americans, lowering the standards on age and education, all these were barely enough to meet the IRFC's recruiting needs. On 28 September, Hoare articulated his problems to the Air Board in London:

> I cannot say definitely that the supply of Cadets will or will not be sufficient. The situation is this — The British Recruiting Mission has given a written undertaking not to recruit American subjects; that I can do so is entirely

duc to personal influence at Washington, and though I
think I can carry it through, I cannot possibly give you a
definite assurance. Though recently there has been a boom
in Canadian cadets, they are still not sufficient. We have
453 in the Cadet Wing, of which 100 are Americans.[22]

Hoare did not realize the boom in Canadian cadets would continue. There
were two causes for this improvement. On 28 August 1917, the Military
Service Act of Canada became law. It required that all able-bodied
males between the ages of 18 and 45 register for military service. As a
consequence, many young men who had hoped to finish their university
studies before going to war now faced the possibility of being called up
by the army and sent to Europe to endure the horrors and drudgery of
trench warfare. A more attractive alternative lay with the Imperial Royal
Flying Corps in Canada. If they could qualify for the IRFC, they might
get to fight a more romantic type of warfare. Neither choice offered great
odds for survival, but to many, if not most, the war in the air was far more
attractive than life in the trenches.

The other factor contributing to the increase in Canadian cadets was
a result of the demographic makeup of the population. Families were
generally large, often numbering more than ten; this was particularly true
in rural areas where children went to work on the family farm at an early
age. Consequently, as the war continued, more and more young men
reached the fighting age of eighteen. It was these young men who were so
desired by the IRFC. From the fall onwards, the supply of healthy young
Canadian males combined with the continuing, although declining,
supply of Americans was sufficient for Hoare to create a fourth Wing in
the spring of 1918.

Hoare's arrangement whereby he had quietly enlisted Americans for
the IRFC finally came to the attention of the U.S. Congress and State
Department. In early February 1918, he was forced to end the practice
of signing up Americans in the United States. However, some Americans
continued to join the IRFC. It was not until the end of July 1918 that the
governor general closed down the British recruiting office in New York.
By then, the RFC/RAF in Canada had enjoyed an extraordinarily long

run and benefited enormously from the young Americans who joined the RAF in Canada.*

Fortunately, when recruiting finally ended in the U.S., the supply of fit young Canadians was sufficient to keep the Plan in full operation. In fact, by June 1918, RAF (Canada) had more cadets than it could handle. The surplus volunteers were placed on a reserve list to be called up as needed. Another 457 trainees, who had finished their ground instruction, were sent to England to complete their flight training.[23]

During the twenty-one months the RFC/RAF recruited in Canada, some 35,000 young men applied to join the service; of these 9,200 were accepted. The fears there would not be enough manpower reserves to justify the high cost of a large training operation proved unfounded, in large part due to Hoare's willingness to bend the rules, but also because both Canadians and Americans had an unbounded enthusiasm and aptitude for flying.

---

* On 1 April 1918, the Royal Flying Corps, along with the RNAS (part of the navy), was absorbed into the new Royal Air Force, which in Canada was sometimes called the Imperial RAF (IRAF).

# CHAPTER EIGHT
## THE MAKING OF A FIGHTER PILOT

No madcap cavalier of the age of chivalry ever had
such wild moments as the air fighters experience
in the ordinary run of things. Seated in a plunging
spider's web of wire, wood and canvass, the cavalier
of the air hunts his game ... A machine gun duel
ten thousand feet above the earth is more fantastic
than any incident in romance. The wildest dreams
of fiction are the facts of the present war in the air.
— *Editorial*, Vancouver Sun[1]

The early training of pilots in Canada was incomplete and costly, both
in terms of training accidents and in fatalities on the Western Front. The
deficiency in early training was demonstrated by the first graduating
class sent overseas by the IRFC. The eighteen cadets sent to England for
final training left Canada in May 1917. They had no training in either
deflection shooting or aerial fighting. This deficiency was partially
remedied when they reached England. Nevertheless, of the eighteen who
survived the training and got to England, fifteen had met the enemy by
year's end. Of these fifteen, five had been killed, three were missing in
action, three were seriously wounded, and two were prisoners of war.
Only two survived the combat unscathed.[2]

Fortunately, by late summer of 1917, the basic elements needed to train
pilots were largely in place. Once a recruit had passed his medical and been
accepted into the IRFC, he was sent to the Givens Street depot, where he was
clothed and received a kit-bag containing toothbrush, change of underwear,
spare shirt, razor, shaving brush, and various odds and ends. William
Lambert remembers that they received two pairs of underwear consisting of

*First graduating class at Camp Borden, May 1917. Courtesy of Library and Archives Canada/Department of National Defence RE-19011.*

"long drawers and a long tailed undershirt — all wool, and very heavy! I had never worn anything like that in my life … even in winters … [previously] I never wore anything but cotton shorts and shirts. When that underwear touched the bare skin, you started to scratch and never stopped."[3]

The clothing issue was completed by a greatcoat, a sturdy set of boots, and thick socks; all heavy. Lambert complained that the drill sergeants had the eyes of eagles. If they saw just a speck of dirt on the uniform or, if the brass buttons were not polished sufficiently to serve as mirrors for shaving, the poor cadet had the book thrown at him. From his first day, the cadet learned that life in the military was very different from the comforts of civvy street.

At the depot, the cadet was given an introduction to military life that could last as long as two weeks. The introduction included drill, personal hygiene, physical fitness, and military discipline.*

---

\* Initially, barracks were created for cadets at the Givens Street School. As the influx of cadets increased and additional barracks were required, Crawford

He also obtained an initiation into the mysteries of telegraph sending and receiving. From there he was transported to the Cadet Wing at Long Branch where he gave up the comforts of a crowded barracks to live under canvas.

The Cadet Wing put the aspiring airman through an eight-week program intended to bring him to prime physical condition through a regime of military drill, physical exercise, and athletics. His earlier introduction to the Flying Corps was broadened to include the basics of military discipline and law, aerial navigation, the use of the Aldis signal lamp, and the improvement of his wireless skills to send and receive at the rate of eight words per minute.

Vivian Voss (aka Roger Vee), a South African who had been studying at Johns Hopkins University, came to Canada in May 1917 and described the daily routine of the Cadet Wing at Long Branch where the cadets were billeted in tents:

> Réveillé sounded at six-thirty and we had to be on breakfast parade at seven-fifteen, properly shaved and with our boots and buttons shining.... After breakfast we had physical training for forty minutes, and then a wing parade at which we were inspected by our officers. After this we had lectures and drill until 12:30, when we stopped for lunch. At 1:30 we began again, lectures or drill till 5 p.m. We were free then till dinner at 6:30. After dinner we were nominally free till 10:30 p.m. But each evening we had to copy out, in ink, into large note-books, the notes taken during the day. This usually kept us busy till "lights out" at 11 p.m.[4]

Voss failed to mention that the cadets did their bathing and shaving in chilly Lake Ontario. Known as the "bathing parade," it was a regular routine

---

Street School was added. In November 1917, cadet operations were consolidated at the newly built Jesse Ketchum School. The schools were made available at no cost by the Toronto School Board.

and about as popular as the medical inspections for social diseases.

From Long Branch the cadets went to the relatively comfortable surroundings of the Aeronautical School at the University of Toronto. Until July, the school remained part of the Cadet Wing under the leadership of Captain Brian Peck of Montreal, who, as Hoare observed, did an outstanding job:

> The school has of course been going for some time, admirably organized by Peck (2/Lieut). I think he deserves every credit; there are not many officers of this rank who almost entirely unaided and starting with no staff other than a borrowed NCO from the Canadians, could have developed what he has done.[5]

Cadets came into the school in groups of 150 with two weeks intervening between groups. Here they learned the theory of flight, meteorology, astronomy, engines, rigging, wireless, artillery observation, instruments, bombs, and machine guns. The instructors knew their subjects, but were woefully ignorant of proper teaching methods. Moreover, in the first few months of the course, cadets had little of a concrete nature with which to work. The shipment of airplanes and engines sent over from England for instructional purposes never reached its destination. As often happened, the IRFC was forced to improvise with the resources available in Canada.

Alan McLeod joined the IRFC on his eighteenth birthday. Initially, McLeod was enthusiastic, but quickly grew despondent, complaining in his letters to his parents that the instructors expected too much. A few excerpts from his letters reveal a routine guaranteed to dampen the enthusiasm of all but the most Spartan of warriors:

> *6 May 1917*
> This morning ... [we] transferred to the School of Military Aeronautics. Now we have only 1 hr. a day for drill and the rest of the time it is lectures. This morning we had lectures on wireless — we have to be able to send 18 words per minute and receive 12. We also had lectures

on the different types of engines in aeroplanes and they are certainly different to car engines. I am going to enjoy this — we have to practice wireless at night and need expensive books. One cost me $5 and we only get $3 a week. My uniform will cost a lot — I have to buy a certain kind of walking out boots and special puttees ... a lot of fellows have been discharged — I hope I have the natural ability for machinery to stay in this. I know a lot about a car but its not the same so I'm going to work harder than I ever did before.

*11 May 1917*
I can't say that I like this life exactly, it is simply work from 5:30 a.m. till 11 at night and no time to spare. We are taking up map reading now ... you have to be able to glance down at the ground and know where you are at once ... and I tell you it is pretty hard work and we don't get the time for the work. I haven't had a spare minute to myself except Sunday since I started this course.

*16 May 1917*
I am rather discouraged on this job. I can't understand engines. I have no more mechanical ability than a horse. I pay attention and hear every word of the lecture and I ask questions till the instructor gets mad and all the fellows laugh ... those complicated 12 cylinder engines are like a Chinese puzzle to me. [Rotary engines are quite different from fixed, in-line car engines.]

*20 May 1917*
They teach us engines and photography ... and they have no engines or camera to demonstrate it on, we just have to imagine we have them ... that stuff is hard to understand without actually seeing it, we have been told all about map reading and have been given pages and

pages of notes but we haven't seen a map yet and have no practical work at all.

*[date missing] May 1917*
The thing that keeps me going is the thought of flying which will not come off for 2 months yet. I seldom go anywhere in my time off as it is so far to any of our friends in this big city. The officers are strict — they are all English and never say a kind word from one day's end to the other.

*22 May 1917*
The instructors have no time to explain anything over again and to-day an officer gave us a lecture on bombing and he talked so fast that we couldn't take it down. We were supposed to take it word for word and none of us got half of it, and we have all that stuff on exam next week …
The fellows are all sore and most of them have given up, they are rushing us so fast … of course I'll keep on trying.

Today a sloppy looking Aviation Officer was lecturing us on observing from an aeroplane and he told us about something that we would have to do when we became pilots and then he said, "But I don't expect many of you will ever become pilots" he had a poor idea of encouraging a class, it discouraged a lot of the fellows but it didn't worry me much.[6]

The IRFC lacked trained instructors while those they did have were forced to push the students through in a great rush to satisfy the needs of the flight-training units. McLeod went through during that early period. Writing to his parents on 22 May, he was stinging in his criticism of the quality of instruction:

This isn't like school where a teacher is paid to teach you things & has to do it. These fellows rush through things

here and are not interested in your welfare like a teacher
is. I tell you I find this a lot different than school. You
can have everything explained there and the teacher will
take turns with you but here they don't care two rats for
you but that always is the way with the army.

Only eighteen, McLeod remained deeply homesick during his time at
the Aeronautical School. Despite his pessimism, he was determined and
tenacious and managed to pass the exams. His success may have been
due in part to the shortage of applicants, which by June 1917 had reached
near-crisis proportions. In certain subjects the instructors allowed the
men to rewrite the exam if they failed. Some cadets who were proficient
in telegraphy took the exam for others who were unable to get up to
speed. One student took the telegraphy exam for three cadets.

By mid-summer, instruction had improved considerably. The
American naval cadet, J. Stirling Halstead, thought the training
excellent and commented favourably on the opportunities to take
apart and reassemble several types of airplane engines. Similarly, in
rigging, they had actual airplanes to work with, using crashed JN-4s
for practice. In one instance, Halstead noticed dried blood on the seat
of the airplane they were repairing, a reminder of the dangers involved
in flight training.[7]

Vivian Voss joined the IRFC in the middle of May 1917, shortly after
completing his degree at Johns Hopkins University. He found the physical
training demanding but breezed through aeronautical school, which, in
the short time since Alan McLeod's attendance, had been lengthened and
improved with new equipment and additional instructors. Academically
gifted, Voss saw the course through very different eyes than McLeod:

Actually this theoretical work was interesting and not
difficult. We had instruction on two main types of
machine-guns, the Vickers and the Lewis. The former
was the type used by pilots and the latter by observers. We
were also given practical demonstrations with these guns.
There were lectures also on the Constantinesco Gear, a

most ingenious device for interrupting the automatic firing of a Vickers gun so that it fired only in between the blades of a propeller, even when the latter was revolving at full speed. Again we had to listen to simple discourses on the theory of flight and the construction and rigging of aeroplanes. I remember the general scepticism when we were told that the air pressure on the lower surfaces of the wings was responsible for only one-third of the lifting force, while the remaining two-thirds were due to the suction above the wings.[8]

After four weeks of lectures, the cadets spent one full day writing exams. Eighty percent on each subject was required to pass this section of the course.

Despite homesickness, difficulties with aeronautical theory, and flagging enthusiasm, Cadet McLeod persevered, writing his exams on Thursday, 31 May 1917. In a letter to his parents written four days before the exams, he faced his demons and pondered his options:

> We write our exams next Thursday and then we have from Thursday night until Tuesday night off. About five days and if we pass we'll leave for Deseronto the next day and if not, its good bye to the R.F.C. I don't know what I'll do then, I think I'll join the Cavalry, I fancy it. I may get through my exams but I'm not counting on it at all, and I don't care much for my own sake, if I do fail, I'm fed up on this business and all the fellows feel the same about it, but for your sake I'd like to get through.

McLeod's transfer to flight training in early June took place at a time of rapid growth in the corps. By early May, the Deseronto camp was up and running and handling basic flight training while Camp Borden, known as Camp Hoare, was handling both basic and advanced training. Although not designated as a flying camp, Long Branch was still providing basic flying instruction for the overflow of cadets who could not be accommodated at either Borden or Deseronto. McLeod was one of the pilots posted to Long Branch for initial flight training.

Tall, sturdy, and a gifted athlete, McLeod proved a natural flyer. In early June, after just his second day of dual instruction at Long Branch, he wrote euphorically to his father:

> *6 June 1917*
>
> I was flying for a while this morning ... Gee it was great. I took complete control of the machine, the Lieutenant said that I did really well, so there is some chance that I (will) become an aviator. I feel as much at home in an aeroplane now as I do in a car. Gee its great, travelling 200 miles an hour on a nose dive, its some sensation when you hit the ground ... landing you are travelling about 75 miles an hour but you never realize it unless you saw the speed indicator.

> *7 June 1917*
>
> I had a great flight today, I raced with a train ... I sure think it's the greatest thing out to fly ... its certainly grand, I just love it but it makes you awfully tired ... I'm sure glad I was sent here. The fellows that went to Deseronto have had no flying yet. They have drill nearly all day because they have so many they can't train them.

McLeod had found his milieu. Despite his difficulty with the theory of flight, he flew solo after just five hours of dual instruction. Moreover, he relished his first solo, a reaction which contrasted sharply with that of Vivian Voss, the cautious academic who was terror-stricken on his first solo flight. McLeod wrote of his solo experience:

> *10 June 1917*
>
> I did my solo flight yesterday and made a howling success of it ... did really well, but I made up for it this morning ... for some unknown reason I misjudged the

distance and landed behind the flag instead of in front, I struck hard ground and landed too suddenly. I smashed all the wires on the undercarriage and nearly broke the propeller ... but got away unhurt, hardly any of the fellows get hurt ... I guess I'll try it again this afternoon and make a good landing, this is Sunday but we have to work all the same, but we never work very hard.

*12 June 1917*
The flying is great but they didn't give some of us enough instruction and as a result we broke a few machines by making bad landings. I had a crash yesterday ... and smashed the plane all up, but the C.O. just laughed and said that was a fine landing. They never care if you have a smash ... it is impossible to hurt yourself when making a landing.

The enthusiastic flyer was transferred to Borden on 18 June, describing conditions there in his daily letters:

We sleep in tents without floors but they give us stretchers to sleep on, we have good meals, we eat with the officers, we have a French chef and foreign waiters all dressed in spotless white ... we get up at 3:45, fly till 11 o'clock, then have a lecture from 11 to 12:30. We have an hour for lunch ... then from 1:30 to 4:30 we have lectures, then we have a 2 hour off for afternoon tea and fly till 8:30 ... come and have dinner and lectures again till 10:30, then they let us sleep for a while, some mornings we don't have to get up early for morning flying but not often, those occasions we get up at 6:30.

The afternoon tea break was a source of considerable annoyance to the Americans who preferred coffee and couldn't understand why they should stop flying at 4:30, which was considered an excellent time to be airborne.

Bad landings were frequent but seldom fatal to the pilot, and caused only minor delays in flying activity. In McLeod's case, the airplane was repaired in half an hour and another pilot was flying it that morning. The philosophy dominating the IRFC's training system was to get the pilot flying on his own as quickly as possible. This not only saved on the instructor's time, enabling him to train more pilots, it put the fledgling pilot in situations where he was learning by doing. The British thought this the best method for training pilots. As a result, accidents were a daily occurrence.

Despite the dangers, bright and talented young men were not only willing, but enthusiastic about risking their lives to fly. Even the very wealthy were not deterred. *The Toronto Star* noted that among those Americans who had joined the U.S. Air Services and were in Canada for training was Captain C J Ryan, son of a Standard Oil financier. Others were A.D. Wells, a noted New York financier; W. Stokes, a wealthy Philadelphian and internationally famous polo player; Henry Bangs, a plantation owner from Virginia and nephew of a famous author; E.S. Pou, son of a senator from South Carolina; H. Youngreen, editor of a well known farmers' paper in South Carolina; and, in the tradition of his adventurous father, Kermit Roosevelt, son of ex-president, Teddy Roosevelt.

The youthful Roosevelt had attempted to join the IRFC. Fortunately, the recruiting officer had spotted him and, wisely, brought the matter to the attention of the CO. Hoare appreciated the delicacy of the situation and contacted the U.S. State Department, which henceforward insisted that all recruits for British Forces in the United States should be through the officially recognized British recruiting mission in New York City. Roosevelt did wind up training in Canada, but as part of a large contingent of American cadets.[9]

In one important respect, the IRFC was ahead of its British parent. Hoare had instructions from London to send pilots to Britain after they had received just seven hours of solo flying; he ignored them. Hoare and Allen had seen too many green pilots killed in France where the inexperience of young pilots had made them sitting ducks. To build their callow pilots' confidence and skill, the IRFC endeavoured to give their cadets as much solo flying as possible before sending them overseas.

A cadet was required to fly a minimum number of hours solo and complete a certain number of landings before moving on to more advanced training at Borden. These numbers were gradually increased as the plan matured. In the beginning they were as low as five hours solo and fifteen landings, later rising to ten hours solo and thirty landings. In addition, a cadet had to be able to climb to three thousand feet and land within a circle forty yards in diameter. As power landings were unknown, the task greatly improved the distance judgment of the aspiring pilot, who had to cut his engine to idle and estimate the glide distance to his target, stalling the wings at just the right height and location over the marked circle.

The cadet also had to master both the Lewis and the Vickers machine guns, passing theoretical and practical tests on each. The practical involved getting the gun working after it had jammed which it did frequently. The cadet also practised assembling and disassembling these guns until the process was second nature. This work was handled in the elementary flight training phase. Posting to Squadron 80, which handled air gunnery, did not take place until all other training had been completed.

In order to pass to the next phase, McLeod and his fellow cadets had to achieve a minimum standard in six subject areas. These included wireless, artillery code, sending on silenced key, and Panneau signalling. This involved flying the airplane while reading Panneau strips on the ground from a distance of 100 yards at the rate of four words per minute. Another test involved flying the airplane while correctly sending the map co-ordinates of three different targets by wireless to a ground officer. One error meant failure. The sixth area, called air training, required the cadet to fully let out his aerial and wind it back at least five times while flying the airplane.[10]

Cadets who mastered the six areas and the basics of flying at Deseronto were then sent to Borden for advanced training. Here they practised formation flying, bombing, artillery observation, and aerial machine-gunnery. Of these bombing was the simplest. The pilot judged when he should release the bomb on the target, and, using a mirror which reflected his airplane, sent a signal to an enlisted man on the ground who could determine from the signal whether or not the bomb would have hit the target. No real bombs were used.

*Wireless training at Deseronto. Instructor Corporal Fred Searle is visible in the bottom right stall. Courtesy of Crossman Collection.*

Artillery observation consisted in flying figure eights over a tent containing an enlisted man who received the wireless signals sent by the pilot when he spotted a puff of smoke. The pilot was required to determine the smoke's location and send this information to the man in the tent. The mechanic in the tent controlled when and where the puffs took place.

Alan McLeod did well on this part of the course, writing his parents that the exam was easy and didn't take him long. His confidence had grown steadily, telling his parents that he had got used to getting up early and that he was "some wireless operator now — I can send and receive to beat the band … I have been practising a lot lately."[11]

While there were some deficiencies in training methods, there were other areas, especially photography, where the IRFC had made considerable progress. McLeod passed into this section shortly after it had been thoroughly revamped. Until mid-June 1917, military training in aerial photography did not exist.

Lieutenant E.F. Hall, an experienced British photographer, arrived at Camp Borden at the end of April. When he tried to set up a photography section, he discovered that none of the expected equipment had arrived from England. This was possibly the result of German submarine action, which frequently ruptured Atlantic supply lines. With the support of the IRFC, Hall was able to make arrangements with Eastern Kodak in Rochester who supplied the necessary cameras and related equipment. While the initial lack of equipment caused some delay, two months after his arrival, photography training came formally into existence.

Hall had been sent to Canada along with two NCOs and thirteen enlisted men, all with some experience in military photography. Within a few months of their arrival, their ranks had been augmented by eleven Canadian photographers, lured into IRFC ranks despite the higher pay available in civilian life. These men taught the cadets a wide variety of photography skills, including bomb sights, camera obscura, bachelor mirror (a mirror used by pilots to flash a signal to ground troops), line photographs, use of tilter, how to work the C-type camera, and the use of a dark room.[12]

By 4 July, when McLeod passed into Advanced Flying Training at No. 82 Squadron, the photography section was working smoothly. In addition to honing his flying skills, McLeod was now able to obtain advanced training in photography as well as in cross-country flying, wireless, bomb-dropping, and artillery observation. After the successful completion of these courses, he would be posted to No. 80 Squadron, where he would enter the final phase of training and learn aerial fighting and gunnery.

While learning artillery observation, McLeod was also honing his increasingly proficient wireless skills. The training program wisely applied this skill to actual battlefield problems such as spotting and sending the co-ordinates of an artillery shot. This enabled the artillery gunners to make the necessary adjustments and hit the target. In a letter to his father on 10 July 1917, he explained how it worked:

> Tomorrow morning if the weather is good, I have to go up and do a shoot as it is called. Shots are fired in different places and you have to send down by wireless

where they hit, so the gunner will know where he is firing. We do just the same as is done in France, it is no cinch I tell you.

Before moving on to the School of Aerial Gunnery, the cadet had to complete a total of thirty hours of solo flying, successfully simulate a forced landing, and climb to an altitude of 8,000 feet. Unfortunately, the JN-4 had a tendency to stall in the thin air and fall into a spin. As instructors had little knowledge on getting out of spins, the results were often fatal.

McLeod had shown such promise in mastering the advanced flying course that he was one of only seven cadet-pilots chosen from his squadron by the CO to do nothing but fly. Henceforth, he was excused from all drill and lectures. Shortly thereafter he wrote home advising that he had been doing a lot of instructing and had passed all his instructor's tests. On 5 July, he wrote home recounting his activities and accomplishments:

> I have all my instructors' tests, they were no cinch. I had to make 4 figure eights in the air at a height of 3,000 feet and come down with the Engine off and land in the centre of a circle. You have to do this test 3 times … the next is harder, you have to go up to 10,000 [close to the limit of endurance without oxygen], stay up there awhile, come down with the engine off, in spiral and S turns and land in the centre of a circle. The next test is the cross country test, you have to make a cross country flight of 100 miles and make 3 outside landings. I got them all, so I have been giving new fellows instruction.

The following day the eager pilot broke Camp Borden's record for height, taking a machine, just arrived from the factory, up to 12,300 feet; 300 feet higher than the old record. A few days later, the increasingly confident cadet was transferred to another squadron to do nothing but wireless from the air. The following day he commented, "I have just finished an exam on Artillery Observation. It was easy so it didn't take me long."[13]

Two days later, McLeod was informed by his CO that he had completed all his air wireless and could have two days' leave. After that he would be taking a two-week course in aerial gunnery, which would complete the last phase of his training.

When it was set up in May, the gunnery school could only provide practice in ground shooting. Cadets learned how to load and dismantle the Lewis gun and got limited practice firing at stationary ground targets. Cadets obtained no practice in deflection shooting; almost a necessity if they were to have any chance of shooting down an opponent in a dogfight.*

On 1 July 1917 more equipment arrived from England, including camera guns. These new weapons were designed so that an aspiring fighter pilot could learn deflection shooting. The early camera guns were mounted on the top wing and resembled a machine gun. After the simulated dogfight, the pilots landed and developed their photos which revealed whether they had correctly estimated where their opponent would be when they pulled the camera trigger. Later, moving pictures were developed that provided a much better record of a pilot's shooting progress. Not surprisingly, camera guns proved instantly popular with cadets.

McLeod was fortunate in that he got into the course just as aerial shooting was being introduced into the syllabus. Writing home in early July, he indicated his prowess as a marksman:

> Its not bad firing a machine gun. I put 95 shots out of 100 just near the Bull. I was up tonight in the aeroplane firing with the machine gun at dummy aeroplanes on the ground. I did fairly good shooting.

In the early stages of the aerial gunnery course, one instructor towed a target called a drogue, while another instructor flew a second airplane

---

* Deflection shooting requires the gunner to estimate where his moving target would be when the bullets from his machine gun reached it. He must therefore aim ahead of his target. It requires a comprehension of geometry and an ability to guess the speed of the target. He must also take into account the speed and direction of his aircraft as well as the speed of the bullets his gun is firing.

with the cadet operating a Lewis gun on a moveable mount situated behind the rear seat. As the target crossed his line of fire, the cadet fired a burst at the drogue. The system posed dangers to both the pilot towing the target as well as to the cadet doing the shooting (who had to avoid falling out of the cockpit while aiming and firing).

The cadets also practised deflection shooting with camera guns mounted to fire through the propeller. This gave them practice at flying the airplane and shooting at the same time. In the phase of final training, two pilots would engage in dogfights using camera guns. This training came closest to mimicking actual combat.

Alan McLeod's timing was propitious; had he completed his course three weeks earlier he would have missed the training in camera guns and mock aerial-fighting, both essential to mastering deflection shooting. McLeod began the course in aerial gunnery just two weeks after the introduction of camera guns. He took to the new training enthusiastically, writing home on 20 July 1917:

> Gee, I had lots of fun to-night. I had an air fight with
> another fellow. We both had camera guns, we'd pull the
> trigger, it would take a picture, it was all kinds of sports.
> The pictures haven't been developed yet so I don't know
> how I came out, it seemed all right though.

It was indeed all right. McLeod did so well that, on 31 July, he was made an aerial gunnery instructor. He was also recommended for a commission, which would arrive from England in a few weeks. Yet despite his rapid progress, the young cadet was thoroughly disillusioned with life in the IRFC and threatening insubordination:

> I'm a pilot for Air Gunnery now, it's a rotten job, the
> flying is all right but in our spare time we have to clean
> up the Hangers [sic] and all sorts of stuff. It's rotten.
> There were 8 of us chosen by Major Tilley as Pilots, we
> are the Senior Cadets of the Camp and have charge of all
> the other Cadets & some mechanics.

I guess it was an honour in a way though to be chosen as an Aerial Gunnery Pilot … I take fellows up and they fire the machine gun at dummy aeroplanes [drogues] and I also pilot for the Camera Gun, two machines go up and have a fight in the air. I drive the machine and the other fellow takes the pictures. Last week I used to take the pictures, but I have graduated from that job now … The worst part of the work is that half the time your machine isn't working because these Curtiss engines only run when they feel like it … you have to bum around and see that the mechanics are working on your machine because if you don't watch them they'll quit … In the mornings and at other times, they put us at sweeping out the hangers [sic] and cutting grass … in the scorching hot weather.

I don't know when we're going overseas, we couldn't go when we expected on account of … no boats sailing. Coutts and a bunch of other fellows from here have been sent to different Camps as instructors. I'm sorry they're gone … I guess we'll go across together but goodness knows when.

We're all going to get leave I think but if we don't, we're all going to take 2 weeks, there would be no use [you] telling me not to … all the boys are going to stick together so there will be 30 of us in trouble if any, if they discharge me I won't weep. I'll be mighty glad to get out of the R.F.C., that's the way we all feel … they won't say much after giving us all the training and commissions.[14]

McLeod was showing the effects of living in a pressure cooker for four months with little time to relax. In the end, he got his two weeks' leave and returned home briefly before departing for Europe. His frustration is understandable but, despite the young aviator's many complaints, the IRFC's training program was working well, as McLeod's subsequent career would prove.

Second Lieutenant McLeod reached Europe in the fall of 1917, and when he did return to his hometown of Stonewall, Manitoba, he returned a hero, being one of only three Canadian airmen to receive the Victoria Cross (VC), the Empire's highest honour.

He was gazetted for the VC on 1 May 1918. The citation to his award reveals how well the IRFC had trained this exceptionally courageous and talented young aviator:

> Whilst flying with his observer [Lieutenant A.W. Hammond, MC], attacking hostile formations by bombs and machine gun fire, he was assailed at a height of 5,000 feet by eight enemy triplanes which dived at him from all directions, firing from their front guns. By skilful manoeuvring he enabled his observer to fire bursts at each machine in turn, shooting three of them down out of control. By this time Lieutenant McLeod had received five wounds, and whilst continuing the engagement a bullet penetrated his petrol tank and set the machine on fire. He then climbed out on to the left bottom plane [wing], controlling his machine from the side of the fuselage, and by side-slipping steeply kept the flames to one side, thus enabling the observer to continue firing until the ground was reached. The observer had been wounded six times when the machine crashed in No Man's Land, and 2nd Lieutenant McLeod, notwithstanding his own wounds, dragged him away from the burning wreckage at great personal risk from heavy machine-gun fire from the enemy's lines. This very gallant pilot was again wounded by a bomb whilst engaged in this act of rescue, but he persevered until he had placed Lieutenant Hammond in comparative safety, before falling himself from exhaustion and loss of blood.[15]

Alan McLeod's feat illustrates not only his courage and talent, but also the thoroughness of the training he had undergone.

After a rapid but unsteady beginning, by mid-July the training program had attained maturity. In addition to a School of Military Aeronautics, a Cadet Wing, a School of Aerial Gunnery, a wireless section and a transport section, the IRFC now had three wings comprising fifteen training squadrons. In 1916, Vice-Admiral Kingsmill had stated in a memo that it would be at least a year before pilots were graduated from any school set up in Canada.[16] Hoare and his officers had sent the first batch of twenty-eight pilots overseas in late May 1917, just four months after their arrival in Canada.

McLeod completed his training in less than four months. In England, the training program took eight months. Although more complete in that pilots trained in England were familiar with front-line aircraft, pilots of McLeod's ability could pick up these skills in a few weeks.

Not only was the IRFC training Canadian pilots, they were working in concert with the Americans who were borrowing RFC manuals and training techniques. Moreover, the IRFC was helping to jump-start the training of an American air force by training 1,700 American cadets sent by the United States to Canada. All this had been accomplished by the end of July 1917. Hoare and his small support staff had not arrived until late January. It was an impressive achievement and was a major factor in Hoare's meteoric rise from acting Lieutenant-Colonel to full Brigadier-General on 1 August 1917.

# CHAPTER NINE
## SOCIAL LIFE IN BELLE ÉPOQUE CANADA

In this new experience you may find temptation both in wine and women. You must entirely resist both temptations and, while treating women with perfect courtesy, you should avoid any intimacy. Do your duty bravely. Fear God. Honour the King.[1]
— *Field Marshal Kitchener, addressing Canadian troops, 1915*

Members of the IRFC generally enjoyed an active social life, particularly those stationed in Toronto. When American General Squire visited the IRFC in the spring of 1917, he stayed at the rambling Victorian house rented by Hoare and his staff officers. The home was run by the officers with the help of two batmen and a housekeeper. The atmosphere at the "chummery," as it was called, appealed to Squire. Major Allen spoke three languages fluently and, like Hoare, was knowledgeable on many subjects. Squire himself was a man of wide-ranging interests. After graduating from West Point and while serving in the U.S. Army, he had continued his studies and completed his doctorate. It was at the chummery that Hoare and Squire worked out the deal for the Texas agreement.

On those evenings when he was not travelling, Hoare would sit in the drawing room, nursing a whisky, smoking his pipe, and talking shop until his officers were droopy-eyed and longing for bed. But such relaxing evenings were rare. Hoare, Allen, and other officers were frequently invited to the finest homes where they were entertained by the cream of society. At horse shows and race meets in Toronto, Hoare and Allen were frequent guests of the governor general, Lord Devonshire. Hoare shared Devonshire's interest in farming and country sports and the two men spent hours discussing horses and crops.

At official events, Allen, at twenty-six a highly eligible bachelor, would find himself partnering Lady Dorothy Cavendish, the daughter of Lord and Lady Devonshire, and later the wife of British prime minister Sir Harold McMillan. Allen also enjoyed the company of Dorothy's older sister, Lady Blanche Cavendish, with whom he shared a love of horses, and who he described as a "young woman of good looks and charm."[2] As an educated and cultured officer in his mid-twenties, Allen's pleasure in female companionship was warmly reciprocated.

Hoare and Allen were also the beneficiaries of the hospitality of the lieutenant governor of Ontario, Sir John Hendrie. Officers of the IRFC frequently found themselves at the dinner table of Sir Hendrie and his wife at Government House in Toronto. After dinner they would take turns dancing with the Hendrie daughter.

Tommy Church, mayor of Toronto, was an occasional guest at the chummery. A dapper man in his early forties, Church was a prohibitionist in both politics and theory. In practice, the gregarious politician was a fairly heavy drinker. One evening, Church was swaying gently in his chair at the dinner table, when he pulled himself to his feet and, still swaying, said to Hoare, "Pull down the blinds, General, pull down the blinds, I am a Prohibition Ticket!"[3]

Hoare begrudged the time spent on formal social events but remained charming and usually put the occasions to good use. He took advantage of balls and racing meets to discuss the IRFC's needs with the governor general, the only man in Canada to whom he answered directly.

Hoare, like many of his officers, maintained his standard of living by drawing on family wealth. As a lieutenant-colonel his wages were grossly inadequate to the demands of his position.

Serving in the IRFC involved a degree of financial sacrifice for all ranks. Writing to his parents from the aeronautical school in Toronto, McLeod complained that from his pay of two dollars and ten cents a day, he had to pay a dollar-fifty for his meals, as well as paying for his laundry, stamps, and writing paper. The lack of leave or places to spend his money enabled the frugal youth to save four dollars in just two months. At eighteen, "Buster" McLeod had few youthful vices; he neither smoked, drank, nor gambled. His one vice was a passion for speed; he loved to race cars along the dangerously twisted country roads of Manitoba.

When America entered the war, J. Stirling Halstead left Harvard Law School to join the U.S. Navy. Halstead was one of a group of thirty naval cadets specially selected to take IRFC training in Canada. While stationed at Camp Borden, he noted in his diary that the only recreation indulged in by the cadets at Borden was gambling, which went on in a frenzied fashion night after night, sometimes not ending until it was time to report for early-morning flying. On one occasion, he joined a bridge game observing that:

> There were several tables of poker or bridge in the large living room of the cadets' mess building and a dice game going on in the centre. As the evening wore on, the crowd playing dice became a howling mob. The poker and bridge players were joining in the uproar by

*Men's canteen, Camp Borden. Courtesy of Library and Archives Canada/ Department of National Defence PA-O22778.*

making bets from their tables with the result that those games became chaotic. And so it went on far into the night with early morning flying and everything else completely forgotten. It was even impossible on many nights to find quiet by going to bed because there would be equally noisy games going on in the shower and wash rooms of the barracks.[4]

The cadets had to be up at 3:45 a.m. for early-morning flying. Halstead attributed some of the flying fatalities at Borden to those late-night card and dice games. While gambling fever was common in the American billets, there is no evidence of its abuse amongst the Canadians.

One group of American cadets arrived in Toronto by train only to find no officers or NCOs to meet them. The American Army Signal Corps had apparently neglected to tell the IRFC exactly when the cadets would be arriving. With no one to direct them to their destination, the exuberant Americans improvised a solution. They hired taxis and headed for the King Edward, the best hotel in town, where they settled into a series of all-night poker and craps games. Away from the restraints of kin and country, their celebrating got out of hand; complaints flooded the front desk. After two days and repeated warnings to the cadets to quiet down, the manager of the King Edward called the IRFC imploring them to take the young men away.

The behaviour of the "missing" Americans was the exception, as was the gambling at Camp Borden. Toronto held far more opportunities for social activities than did Borden, which may account for the lack of problems at the recruits camp, Long Branch, or the aeronautical school, all located in or near the Queen city.

The recruits depot was initially based at Givens and Crawford Street Public Schools but, by November 1917, had moved to the more spacious Jesse Ketchum School. Here, the large, high-ceilinged rooms were converted into barracks, supplying warm, and, by the standards of the times, reasonably comfortable accommodation. A recruits depot band was formed and regularly played all units bound for the United States or Texas down to the train station. The band and the camp dog, Bruno, a Saint Bernard, also accompanied the men on their bi-weekly route marches. Three times a week, the band played concerts in the recruit's canteen. As its reputation grew, the band found itself in demand for dances and hockey games.

A large park stood next to the Jesse Ketchum School and was used as a parade and sports ground. In the fall, a portion of the park was converted into a football field. During the winter it was flooded and used as a hockey rink. Outdoor night lighting was provided free by the City Parks commissioner. In addition to the band, the canteen contained three billiard tables, tables for card games, and a reading area. The Jesse Ketchum School supplied the recruits with a comfortable environment, as well as a variety of recreational and social activities.

Life for the officer cadets at Long Branch was less comfortable. In the summer of 1917 and again in 1918, the cadets were billeted in tents. One of the cadets had a flair for writing and, in 1918, began a weekly broadsheet titled the *Cadet Wing Review*. The broadsheet chronicled the social and athletic events at the Long Branch camp, providing a first-hand account of its social and sporting activities.

Cadets' social lives were frustrated by the lack of telephones. Excluding the phones used by the officers and NCOs for official use, there was just one pay phone for the entire camp. The *Cadet Wing Review* reported this single pay phone was so much in demand that there was always a lineup to use it.

During the week, the Long Branch cadets were shaved and shined by 5:45 a.m. and in bed by 9 p.m. Nevertheless, they enjoyed an active social life, partially as a consequence of the camp's proximity to Toronto, but mainly because of the talent and enterprise of the camp inmates. One of these, a Corporal Pierre Caillaux, had been an employee of the Chicago Opera Company. Using a large tent as a theatre, he organized the musical, comedic, and acting abilities of the cadets to put on a series of highly successful Thursday night concerts.

To facilitate weekend visits from wives, family, and lady friends, the Young Women's Christian Association operated a hostess house directly across from the camp. A large curtained reception area, complete with comfortable chairs and chesterfields took up most of the portable building's 1500 square feet. An eight-foot-wide front porch completed the structure. The set-up allowed couples a modicum of privacy but not enough to endanger the YWCA's strict standards of decency.

At the end of the summer, cadets were posted to one of the various flying camps to continue their training. Just prior to departure, a big dance was arranged at the Lake View Hotel in Port Credit.* The following excerpts from the *Cadet Wing Review* capture the flavour of the event:

> The anxiety lest there be a scarcity of enticing feminism was soon dispelled when one glanced around the brightly lighted room filled with smiling cadets and charming Toronto girlhood. The guests arrived early and before eight o'clock the grounds were well filled with a happy throng. Lieutenant Paterson was on hand dressed in mufti [civilian clothes] and it was due to his untiring efforts that the evening was so thoroughly enjoyable. He was everywhere and knew everyone. Quite a difference from the Mr. Paterson we know on parade. About four hundred couples were present including the commanding officer, Captain H.E. Earl, Captain Metcalf [chaplain], Lieutenants Frew and Fletcher. Mr. Frew and Cadet Clifford entertained with several selections on the banjos or ukuleles or something, but everyone seemed to like it and demanded encores.
>
> The wing orchestra maintained their reputation for excellent music, and when the "Good Night Ladies" floated over the assembly happy faces testified to a most enjoyable evening. Eleven o'clock came only too soon, and we had to leave for camp, as the passes read 11:45 pm.
>
> When the [street] cars arrived at the camp, the conductor (who was a kind man) held the car long

---

* The hotel was owned by Joe Burke, whom the Royal Commission On Customs And Excise named as an ale and whisky smuggler with ties to the gangster Rocco Perri. Burke was likely bootlegging when the dance was held.

enough for some fond farewells, as the ladies (God bless
'em) would not see their escorts again for twenty-one
days, for alas, Company D ... had been quarantined.[5]

With the exception of Camp Borden, innocent entertainment appears
to have been the norm. After the disruptions caused by the all-night
gambling sessions at Borden, Halstead found Camp Deseronto almost
too quiet. The evenings would have been boring, he noted, had it not
been for the delightful music of Harry Gordon — an accomplished
pianist with an endless repertoire of tunes — who played continuously
after supper until bedtime. Gordon would play any piece requested by
the cadets, who invariably gathered around the piano for a singalong.

Early morning flying started at 5 a.m., which meant the men were
up by 3:45 a.m., had some bread and jam with tea, and were on the
tarmac before sunrise. As the wind did not come up until later, the air
was usually calm, making for ideal training conditions for the novice
flyers. This regimen was harder for the Americans, who enjoyed a hearty
breakfast with lots of coffee. The tea, bread, and jam, left out for the early-
morning flyers was a subject of much complaint by the Americans.

In keeping with the Ontario Temperance Act, canteens were non-
alcoholic. Here the airmen could buy cigarettes, pop, chocolate bars,
and a popular item — postcards of the camp. Some of the bestselling
postcards were those depicting JN-4s after a crash.

Nor was there a shortage of crashes to photograph. On one particularly
bad day, Regina native Herbert Andrews witnessed his first fatality at
Deseronto. Before the day was out, there were seventeen crashes, one killed,
five in hospital, and three airplanes completely destroyed. In addition, a
mechanic had broken both his wrist and arm in swinging a prop.[6]

If the deceased airman was buried near the camp, a single aircraft
would circle overhead as the flyer was laid to rest. The pilot would then
pass by, slowly tipping his wing, before returning to base.

Both the American, Halstead, and the Canadian, Andrews, were
undergoing basic flying training at Deseronto in October 1917, and
were present for the special Thanksgiving dinner at the mess. Halstead
did not comment, but Andrews noted in his diary that there was a

*Burial of Lieutenant Colin Coleridge, who was awarded an OBE for saving a cadet's life at the risk of his own. He died in a crash five months later. Courtesy of Hastings County Historical Society.*

bountiful supply of duck and Brigadier-General Hoare was present, but the only liquid refreshment was grape juice, with "no kick at all."[7] This latter comment suggests that, at least occasionally, the cadets did find something alcoholic to imbibe. The only source of alcohol would have been the local bootleggers and moonshiners. Sixty to seventy years later a number of Deseronto veterans were interviewed, but none could remember alcohol being available.

When the cadets and other ranks at Deseronto had some leave they usually spent it in Belleville, then a bustling community of 12,000. The city boasted a number of attractions. Among the officers, the Quinte Hotel, with its grand ballroom in the Greek Corinthian style, was the most popular. An elegant hostelry, it was built with the financial support of the Corby family, who had founded the large distillery three miles north of the city. The Corby family sold their interest in 1905 but the connection persisted as William Hume, general manager of the plant, was married to the daughter of the hotel's owners.

On Thanksgiving weekend, Andrews and more than a dozen cadets hopped a train from Deseronto to Belleville, arriving in the city about 9 p.m., they immediately headed for a local dance. In his diary, Andrews describes the place where the dance was held "as not an extra swell affair."[8] There were at least a half-dozen places in Belleville where dances were held at that time. Andrews and four of his friends got a ride home in a Ford sedan, arriving back at camp at four in the morning.

The good citizens of Deseronto did their best to welcome and entertain the IRFC men. Corporal Joe Goold, the one-time Kentucky riverboat pilot, attended many local dances at the White Hall. Formerly a church, the hall had been converted by the Presbyterian congregation to a church hall. It was within walking distance of downtown Deseronto, where Goold lived and worked.

On his first visit, Goold walked to the hall with a bunch of fellow mechanics. On entering the building, they were met by a mature lady, Miss Stoddard, who acted as chaperone to the younger women and introduced them to the men. Goold was pleasantly surprised at how attractive they were but was not particularly interested in any of them. Goold and his buddies were directed to take seats in wooden fold-up chairs, which faced a large stage running across the front of the hall.

The Presbyterian minister, Mr. McCorkindale, took the stage and welcomed the young men to the club, announcing there would be a dance every Wednesday night until the hot weather arrived. After his introduction there was a program of songs, solos, recitations, and skits. Finally, McCorkindale announced that there would be a recitation by Miss Marion Rennie. In his memoirs, Goold describes the young woman and his reaction upon first seeing her:

> She stood there in the middle of the stage waiting for some noise in the rear of the hall to subside … I caught my breath. Truly she looked like a lovely flower. Green party dress with a sort of sash with tassels. A slim white throat, oval face and an adorable dimple in the chin and the most beautiful pink and white complexion.… But loveliest of all was the cloud of golden hair piled on top of her head. I had the queerest feeling as I looked at her.… I took her to be about sixteen. [She was

eighteen.] Probably the Mayor's, or some MP's daughter, I surmised.... I was impressed by her voice; it was so clear and sweet, just like a silver bell.[9]

Goold wanted Marion Rennie for his wife and was not easily deterred. From that first Wednesday night in early May, he was in constant attendance at the weekly church dances and a regular visitor at the Rennie farmhouse. Goold was pleased that Marion was not as young as he had originally thought. He was twenty-three — just five years older than Marion. As a skilled aero-engine mechanic and the holder of a riverboat pilot's licence, his postwar employment prospects were promising. Marion did not discourage his visits, but, for some reason he could not fathom, she refused to commit herself to an engagement.

Eventually, Goold learned that the lovely Marion had promised to wait for a local lad who had been posted overseas. Safe in Canada, Goold could hardly press his case against a competitor who was enduring the horrors of trench warfare. Nevertheless, he waited and persevered in his attentions. Finally, Frank returned from the war and Marion, with many tears, told him she had changed her mind. She and Goold were married in 1921.[10]

It was inevitable that many young women would be attracted to the dashing cadets in their smart uniforms and exciting flying machines. Looking back on his training in Canada, American cadet Russell Greenslade reflected, "Most of us majored in girls. There were lots of them."[11]

In many cases the contacts between the girls and cadets had permanent results. Charlie Hunter crashed his airplane, suffering life-threatening injuries. A painfully slow recovery was followed by several months in the infirmary. One of the nurses tending the severely injured cadet was Sister Scholes, a lively young woman with humour to match. She and Hunter were married in 1923 and lived much of their life in Kelowna, British Columbia.[12]

Although their jobs were not as glamorous as the flyers, many of the mechanics met their future partners in the IRFC. Raphael Hicks was a motor transport driver at HQ where he met fellow worker Maude Tullock. They later married and moved to Baldwinville, in New York State.[13] Unfortunately, not all romances turned out so well.

In July of 1917, Eldra Brennan, an eighteen-year-old lass from St. Catharines, married IRFC Cadet Frederick Kenneth Thomas of Fishkill, New York. A few months later she discovered that Thomas already had a wife back in Fishkill. Eldra was persuaded by her mother and the Police Chief to drop the charges of bigamy so that Thomas could serve the Allied cause. The cadet promised to reform and the magistrate discharged him. Shortly thereafter, he was sent overseas.[14]

The mother's attitude and judge's advice reveal how much the war had changed values and morality. The exigencies of the military took precedence over morality and a young woman's reputation.

War undermines the moral restraints of society, particularly those pertaining to standards pertaining to alcohol, gambling, and sexual mores. The strict Victorian era was followed by the Edwardian, which, led by the wanton example of the King, witnessed a gradual weakening of the old taboos. Led by suffragettes, women were asserting their rights and demanding a more equal status with men. Indirectly, the movement helped free young women from the constraints and supervision of their elders. The advent of the bicycle and the automobile led to a more mobile society, making it even more difficult to supervise the activities of young women. In 1896, Susan B. Anthony said that the bicycle had done more for the emancipation of women than anything else in the world. Views on what was acceptable behaviour had evolved, allowing young women to pursue athletic pursuits such as tennis, canoeing, and cycling. As the ability to chaperone increasing mobile young women declined, parents often had to settle for a stern lecture on morality and pray the girl would put family reputation above youthful passion.

The war itself contributed to the erosion of the old morality. The senseless slaughter of trench warfare bred a deep cynicism towards established authority and its prevailing views on morality and ethics. The atrophy of the old restraints was evidenced by the growth of a militant labour movement, the lost generation of the twenties, and the expatriate authors and artists who fled to Paris, then regarded as the centre of immorality and decadence.

LeRoy Prinz, an American cadet who trained at Long Branch,

Armour Heights, and Borden, commented on availability of girls and on the prostitutes who worked the fringes of Camp Borden:

> Was there any night life in Canada? Whaddya think? There used to be a place called Pa and Ma Vetter's. Nearly every aviator in Canada knew Pa and Ma Vetter … they had three or four of the most beautiful girls in Canada. But nearly everybody went to number 22 Lansdown … off towards Long Branch, and would leave their names and addresses where they could be located in town. Girls? Are you kidding? Well you can't fly all night. When you got to Long Branch, you were along the beach where there were invariably hundreds of pretty gals..... And Camp Borden? The only gals you could find up there were 100 feet off the outside of the field in a woods. Two or three to a tent. They were the busiest bunch you ever saw.[15]

Although the bonds of Victorian morality were weakening, they still prevented most middle-class women from engaging in premarital sex. As a consequence, prostitution flourished around all but the smaller camps. Captain Gordon Bates, in command of the Canadian Militia's base hospital in Toronto, disclosed that there were about 1,900 admissions per year resulting from "social diseases," the euphemism then in use for venereal infections. He also disclosed that 12 percent of all admissions to the Toronto General Hospital were the result of these diseases. In the late summer of 1917, this disclosure led to a dozen organizations meeting at Toronto City Hall to take, "immediate action to wipe out the evil."[16] The organizations predictably included the Women's Christian Temperance Union and the YMCA, but also members of the business community, including the Toronto Board of Trade, and the Rotary Club.

By modern standards, the social activities of both officers and cadets were remarkably wholesome. In rural areas and small towns, the changes wrought by the automobile, the war, and the women's movement barely nudged the old values. The lack of anonymity in smaller communities resulted in a more law-abiding society, one more dominated by community and parental values.

By 1918, there were four Wings in operation of which three, Borden, Deseronto, and Beamsville camps, were located in small, rural communities. In these camps, the old values predominated.

Examples of this can be readily found in the entertainments enjoyed by both sexes. At Deseronto, arriving airmen immediately nicknamed the town, "Deserted." William Webster spent some time there as a machine-gun instructor. At twenty-three, Webster was about the same age as his students. Camp Mohawk did not impress him, he wrote that, "It looked a bit dreary [when he first arrived] and got more dreary as winter came. Deep snow etc."[17]

Like many officers, Webster couldn't wait to escape Deseronto. On weekends, he took advantage of the railway to travel to the city of Belleville, where he found several billiard halls, restaurants, and dance venues. He spent much of his time at the opulent Quinte Hotel where he met members of the local society, including the Spafford family, whose son, Jerry, had returned wounded from the front. Webster stuck up an acquaintance with Jerry and got to meet the two Spafford daughters, both nurses. Although he enjoyed their company, his relationship with the sisters did not progress beyond the social and platonic.

As Webster met more people in Deseronto, his train trips to Belleville became less frequent and his romantic life improved. He even changed his view of winter in the country:

> One family, Baumhour by name, were very good to me
> personally. They allowed their beautiful daughter Viola
> to go sledding in a rented cutter with me and we went all
> over the snow covered fields at full gallop. I rented the
> cutter from a stable in Deseronto as many of the other
> chaps did (but not with Viola).[18]

In a seven-page letter, Webster mentions alcoholic beverages only once. In the letter he describes one of his after-hour students as "Dopey" Dow (of the Montreal brewing family.) Dow was one of many students who hired Webster for extra lessons in the evenings, paying him handsomely for tutorials. Dow had difficulty grasping both the theoretical and the practical but Webster allowed that, "He was a good scout, especially when he went on leave to Montreal. [Quebec was the only province that had not instituted Prohibition.] He brought back hampers of food and a good source of the bubbly."[19] Dow's generosity with food and alcohol did not go unrewarded, he passed his exams without difficulty.

Naylor's was the only theatre and movie house in Deseronto. Silent movies were relatively new and many considered them inferior to live stage shows. Naylor's Theatre was host to a great many top-notch live theatrical performances, featuring a variety of entertainers, including the world-famous Vernon and Irene Castle. Lieutenant Castle was an instructor at Camp Mohawk in the spring of 1917 when his wife made a rare visit to the camp. As she was busy with stage and movie productions, Irene seldom saw her husband while he was in Canada. Despite their brief time together, Vernon Castle could never refuse to perform for a worthy cause. He and Irene put on a dancing and comedic concert at Naylor's Theatre with the proceeds going to provide comforts for the cadets training in Canada.

The theatre's owner, Thomas Naylor, frequently made his premises available for productions put on by cadets, assisted by a few mechanics from the camps. These concerts were in aid of the members of the IRFC and involved many professional entertainers. One group was known as the "Camp Mohawk Pierrots," who performed frequently at Naylor's Theatre as well as an occasional performance at other venues, including Belleville's city hall. A notice in the local newspaper in February of 1918, catches the flavour of the event:

R.F.C. MINSTRELS TO-MORROW NIGHT
*City Hall Should Be Packed to Greet Talented Aviators —*
*Camp Mohawk Pierrot Troops Contain Artists of Renown*

Belleville is in for a treat tomorrow night when the Camp Mohawk Pierrots present their original minstrel show at the City Hall. This will be the first opportunity the people of Belleville have had of seeing this talented organization and will be the last as they are leaving for Toronto on Saturday. Great accounts of the excellence of the entertainment have come from Deseronto where they played last week. Naylor's Opera House was packed to the doors and the unanimous verdict was that it was the best entertainment ever seen in Deseronto. The verdict is not surprising when it is considered that more than half the artists are professional and their training has been in expert hands. Among the artists are ... Niegel Barrie, leading motion picture actor ... J. Bowman, professional performer of sleight of hand and conjuring tricks, T.A. Roberts, exponent of Hawaiian and southern music, and E.J. Edwards, tenor vocalist ... The entire proceeds will be devoted to purchasing comforts for the members of the Royal Flying Corps in Canada and overseas ... and as the price is only 35 cents, it is in the reach of all. The tickets are now on sale at Doyles Drug Store ... The performance begins at 8 o'clock, as it takes nearly three hours to go through the programme. There are no waits whatever. Something doing every minute.[20]

The group performed their "farewell concert" at Naylor's Theatre on 1 April 1918 with a cast that, with the exception of Corporal Bowden who recited "The Shooting of Dan McGrew," was composed entirely of cadets.

As soon as a cadet had completed his basic flying training at Deseronto, he was transferred to Borden or North Toronto for advanced flight training and from there, overseas. As a consequence, there was a high turnover of cadets at all camps. None of the headliners who appeared at City Hall in Belleville six weeks earlier remained in the troupe when it made its farewell appearance in April.

At Long Branch there were weekly sporting activities as well as a cadet band that was constantly in demand. The *Cadet Wing Review* provided a detailed examination of the social life at the camp. The editor's wry humour permeates this passage:

> A very successful dance was held in the mess on August
> 6th last, where steps of all description (unheard of before)
> were shown — one officer who is perfectly ignorant of
> Canadian dancing (or any other kind of dancing for that
> matter) complained that he had his mouth full of hair all
> the time, and suggested some kind of skull cap for the dear
> ladies — there is such a thing as distance Mr. Fletcher.[21]

The Long Branch band was much in demand at the various camps, including Borden, North Toronto, and the School of Military Aeronautics. Of all the camps, Long Branch was undoubtedly the most socially active, holding weekly dances, concerts, skits, and musical performances. It was also the only camp to put out a weekly paper. Long Branch also maintained a busy schedule of athletic events.

There was a negative side to all this social activity, especially at Long Branch, where a special hospital was built to treat the men in the IRFC who had contracted venereal disease. The hospital was fully equipped to treat syphilis and gonorrhea with beds for up to 150 patients.

Commenting on the problem of social diseases, Major Brefney O'Reilly, OC (officer commanding) the Medical Corps, observed from Fort Worth, less than a month after the Canadian units had arrived that:

> The prevention of venereal disease has presented many
> difficulties. Educational lectures are given at frequent
> intervals to the men of every unit by the MO in charge.
> Medical orderlies have been trained to administer
> prophylactic treatment to men who have exposed
> themselves to the possibility of venereal infection.
> The results obtained from this routine method have
> been most satisfactory; of the first 500 treatments
> administered according to specific directions within
> eight hours of exposure, not one has as yet failed. No
> cases of gonorrhea or syphilis up to date have developed
> of the men so treated.[22]

The YWCA was particularly concerned with the moral well-being of the soldiers, and requested permission from the RAF to establish their presence inside the various camps. Hoare stalled them for months but, in the summer of 1918, did allow the YWCA to establish "comfort buildings," where members of the RAF could meet girlfriends, wives, and other members of their family on Sundays.[23] Several ministers in Ontario decried this practice as a violation of the Lord's Day Alliance Act and wrote their MPs to protest it.

On 7 May 1918, the MP for Charlevoix-Montmorency raised the question in the House as to why there were no religious or church parades allowed to the various denominations so that they could perform their religious duties at the camps. The prime minister answered that the House had no authority over the RAF — an increasingly embarrassing situation for the government — but that the matter had been taken up with the officers in charge of the camps.

Previously, Hoare had stalled the establishment of pastors in the camps fearing they would interrupt Sunday training. He had anticipated the move by the churches to pressure various MPs and wisely took preemptive action. He quickly squelched an uproar by advising church officials that he had telegraphed General Gwatkin on 30 April, asking for six ministers of suitable religious denominations to carry out services at the various units. He noted that no religious services were necessary at the School of Military Aeronautics as it was located in the heart of downtown Toronto, within walking distance of several churches. Hoare also stated that cadets were free to attend any religious service they wished and were free from 10:45 a.m. every Sunday.[24] He did not mention that early-morning flying began in the wee hours and was over by 10 a.m.

In mid-May, Hoare met with the National Council of the YMCA to discuss the matter of their admittance to RAF camps. In early June of 1918, he agreed to allow them to establish their presence in the various camps, leaving it to the commanding officers in each camp to work out the details with the YMCA. It was agreed that Camp Borden would be the first camp where this would be carried out.

Although not specifically stated, it was clear that the YMCA would not in any way attempt to interfere with the training program or do anything to slow down the training of the cadets for overseas service.[25] It was made clear that flying and training came first.

While there were many outlets for the youthful energy of the cadets, once they graduated to flight training the focus of that energy usually shifted entirely to flying — an activity which a great many cadets recorded as the most invigorating and stimulating experience of their lives.

However, even flight cadets were enthusiastically urged to participate in athletic activities. Indeed, the Force promoted athletic activity with the enthusiasm of an Olympic coaching team.

# CHAPTER TEN
## THE SINE QUA NON OF ATHLETICS

> There are those among our enemies who sneer at our persistence in sport, even though we are in the midst of war. It would seem ... we are wiser than they, because, beyond a shadow of a doubt, the benefit of athletic endeavour which our commanders are at such pains to encourage among us, showed clearly in the physical excellence and sportsman-like attitude of the thousand or so young fellows who made our field day so attractive.
>
> — *Editor,* Cadet Wing Review

> The men who excel in sports are, as a rule, the men who excel in their work.
>
> — *Brigadier-General C.G. Hoare,*[1] *Long Branch field day, 31 July 1918*

It was a given of the British ruling class that sports built both character and a drive for excellence. During the early decades of the twentieth century, enormous emphasis was placed on sportsmanship as a prerequisite for acceptance as an English gentleman. In the British military there was an implicit understanding that an officer must be both a sportsman and a gentleman. To the British upper classes, the words gentleman and sportsman were synonymous.

This emphasis on sports received a warm reception from both the cadets and the enlisted men of the IRFC. Flight cadets were especially enthusiastic about sports. At an average age of twenty-two, they were in their physical prime. Consequently, there was a continuous stream of organized sporting activities at all training camps, while the enlisted men of the Repair Park and depots were equally active.

Virtually every team and individual sport was emphasized. Boxing was seen as a man-on-man competition, much like the duels fought by fighter pilots in dogfights. But few cadets could meet the high physical and mental standards demanded of the crack fighter pilot. Wartime flying required teamwork between members of flight formations as well as between the pilots and their ground crew. Team sports were therefore equally as important. Activities such as hockey, soccer, baseball, and cricket were all encouraged. All sports helped develop both physical fitness and mental toughness. No sporting activity was discouraged. Even chess clubs were approved, and a library was formed for the more intellectually oriented.

This a priori belief in sports was evident from the very beginnings of the IRFC in Canada. While Camp Borden was under construction, the officers, on their own initiative, built a nine-hole, three-thousand-yard golf course and made it available to all ranks. The course benefited from the volunteer labour of both cadets and officers with the supplies paid for by the IRFC. *The Northern Advance* gave front-page coverage to a competition between members of the Barrie Golf Club and the RAF, noting the latter were "skilful players." At the conclusion of the afternoon match, the hosts treated the flyers to dinner at the Barrie Inn. A return match was arranged at the RAF golf course at Borden.[2] Sports had the added benefit of fostering good community relations.

Enlisted men or mechanics were equally infected with the sports ideology and participated in large numbers. For example, the recruits' depot entered a team in inter-league soccer as did the Repair Park and the mechanical transport depot. Mechanics participated in the teams fielded in the Inter-League Soccer League by the Armament School in Hamilton, and the camps at Long Branch, Beamsville, and North Toronto.

At Long Branch, cadets, officers, and mechanics put together a base soccer league, consisting of five teams, each drawn from one of the four companies, plus a staff team. Some particularly energetic and talented members of these teams also played on the IRFC team, competing against tough competition for the Brigden Cup. The 1917 team made a respectable showing their first year out, trouncing the previous year's champion CNR team in Montreal by a score of three to zero. The upstart RFC team was finally defeated in the playoffs for the Brigden Cup.

The Long Branch camp was particularly active in sporting events. In addition to its soccer teams, the camp participated in the Inter-League Baseball League, which, like soccer, was made up of five teams drawn from the various camps and depots. There were also weekly matches with lots of practices and pick-up games. In boxing, each of the four companies managed to enter a fighter in almost all of the seven weight divisions. Long Branch also entered a team in the Toronto Baseball League. In all, the RAF made up five of the ten teams comprising this league in 1918.

With the exception of Deseronto, all Wings held at least one annual "sports day." For example, on 25 May 1917, a Cadet Wing Sports Day was held at Long Branch with entrants from Burwash Hall, (later the No. 4 Aeronautical School), Deseronto, and Borden.

A second Cadet Sports Day was held at Long Branch on 31 July with some thirty-two events taking place. Twenty-seven of these events were restricted to cadets, with three events for the ladies, one for the officers, and one for the children. No events were held for the enlisted men.

The Camp Borden Wing also competed in the sporting

*Warrant Officer "Streamline" Sharpe as master of ceremonies, Camp Deseronto Sports Day. Courtesy of Deseronto Archives.*

activities sponsored by the Canadian Army Corps stationed nearby. A Kitchener Day was held at Camp Borden on 29 July 1917, in which some 262 soldiers and airmen competed in nine events. Less than three weeks later, the Canadian Army and the IRFC put together a similar sporting event, which they called the Camp Borden Sports Day.

On the same day the IRFC, competing in the provincial soccer league, defeated the previous year's champions for the Shamrock Cup, which went on display at IRFC headquarters.

On 27 June 1918, the newly constructed Beamsville camp organized its first field day, held just two months after the camp opened. Prior to the field day, the camp organized a Victoria Day athletic meet and air show, which was well attended by townspeople and area farmers.

On 1 August 1918, Camp Deseronto held its first field day, an all-day competition arranged by Wing W.O. "Streamline" Sharpe, who stood a pencil-thin six feet, six inches tall.

The highlight of RAF's (Canada) sporting activities came on 17 August 1918, when the first annual sports day was held for all wings and depots of the Force. Entrance to the Island Stadium in Toronto harbour was by invitation only with some 10,000 in attendance. Music was provided by the Long Branch Cadet Band and a band from New York City. There was also squad drill from the various camps and schools.

*Lieutenant Ballough competing in the shot put event on Camp Deseronto Sports Day. Courtesy of Deseronto Archives.*

*Sports day at Camp Deseronto, 1 August 1918. Formerly the headquarters of the Rathbun Company, the three-storey building in the background served as the administrative centre for the Deseronto Wing. Courtesy of Hastings County Historical Society.*

The program featured some thirty-four events with a few unscheduled competitions added, bringing the program to a conclusion as scheduled at 6:15 p.m.

The enlisted men also entered many teams in various sports. Only the best players competed in the provincial soccer league, yet both the Repair Park and the stores depot entered competitive teams. These same depots also entered teams in the Ontario Amateur Lacrosse Association. In the provincial baseball league, teams were entered by the Repair Park and the transport depot. The transport depot also entered a hockey team in the Intermediate Ontario Hockey Association (OHA), as did the Repair Park, which also fielded a baseball team in the Military League.

In that most individual of sports — boxing — mechanics often performed better than the cadets. For example, in a series of seven bouts staged by the Imperial Royal Flying Corps in the Transportation gymnasium on 12 February 1917, the mechanics won four of the five bouts in which they competed, winning three by knockout.

An inter-military competition to determine the Military Athletic Championship for the Toronto District military area was held at the Exhibition grounds on 7 September 1918. Military District No. 3 [the Toronto district] provided its best athletes in ten track and field events as did RAF (Canada). The CEF entered one hundred men in the competition, and only forty from the RAF. The day after the event, *The Toronto Star* reported that, "Outside of the sprints, the RAF contingent pretty well cleaned up the card."[3]

In the fall of 1918, the RAF entered two excellent hockey teams; one in the intermediate OHA league, and another in the senior OHA. Called simply the RAF team, the senior RAF team quickly developed into the chief rival of the highly ranked Dentals team.

The Armistice of 11 November did not immediately end the entry of the RAF team, as demobilization of the troops was expected to take several months. Moreover, once discharged, the men were technically subject to be called back into service for another six months. By late December, however, it had become clear that RAF (Canada) would soon be just a memory. On 20 December 1918, the RAF hockey team officially folded, ending their chance to become the Ontario Senior Hockey League champions.* Its talented players were quickly snapped up by rival teams, including the powerful Dentals.

* As the NHL had cancelled competition for the year, the Ontario Senior Hockey League was arguably the top league in Canada.

# CHAPTER ELEVEN
## HIJINKS ON THE GROUND AND IN THE AIR

Air combat was new; its rules and practice were improvised daily. The acquisition of technical accomplishment above the earth filled them with a particular kind of pride and elation. There were no grey haired officers above them. They were pioneers and frontiersmen.... Unrebuked, they invented a code of chivalry with the German airmen. None would have stooped to attack a disabled enemy plane trying to return to home base. Both sides recognized enemies with whom they had encounters, signalling to them, laughing in challenge.
  — Thornton Wilder[1]

In 1998 two Canadian Forces pilots flew a Sea King Helicopter under the newly constructed bridge linking New Brunswick to Prince Edward Island. The daredevil pilots were suspended from flying duties and subjected to fines. The Canadian Forces and Transport Canada take a dim view of pilots who ignore any of the myriad rules regulating flying.

This was definitely not the case during the First World War. In fact, the Canadian government had no laws or regulations of any kind governing the flying of aircraft. Naturally, adventurous young cadets took advantage of this vacuum and attempted every stunt imaginable. One of the more popular was making unscheduled landings in farmers' fields. Every one of those landings put the pilot at risk.

Poor mess food was the major motivation for these unscheduled landings. Airplanes and aviators were a novelty, providing a welcome diversion from the labours of farm life. Invariably a local farmer and his

*A Rathbun cadet's stunt landing in a Deseronto field didn't turn out the way he anticipated. Courtesy of Deseronto Archives.*

wife would provide the young airman with a hearty farm-fresh breakfast or lunch. If the airman lingered at the dinner table, he invariably found an enraptured audience for his tales of daring-do.

Providing the pilot survived them, forced landings were good preparation for combat in Europe where enemy guns frequently damaged airplanes, forcing flyers to land on less than ideal terrain. Herbert Andrews was in the early stages of pilot training at Camp Mohawk when his airplane developed engine trouble during an early morning flight. He recounts the incident in his diary:

> About half way to Belleville, at 3,000 ft, my engine suddenly dropped to 600 revs and refused to pick up, so I turned around with the wind and looked for a nice soft field … I overshot the field and was about to strike a snake fence when I gave her the gun. The 600 revs were barely enough to lift her over and I landed OK in the next field which fortunately was a good one … I went to a house about 50 yds away and phoned the

squadron office. The natives began to gather in droves and an old gent brought me a breakfast in a tin box. In about half an hour Lt. Coupal in "Kidah" with a mechanic dropped into the next field..... While the mechanic was trying to find out what was wrong, Lt. Coupal went to Belleville in a car to get some gas as my supply was low. While helping the mechanic with the engine I had the prop back fire on me with switch off, and knock me about 10 ft. No damage done. By the time Lt. Coupal got back we had located the trouble; the timing gear ball-race had worn out and allowed the gears to change so that she was firing in the wrong place. Coupal then flew back to the aerodrome for new parts. While he was away I had a swell chicken dinner in a nearby house. About half an hour after he got back, we got her fixed up and I got out of the field clearing an orchard by several feet. The natives were quite sad to see me depart as I invented most marvellous answers to the numerous questions.[2]

Andrews' matter-of-fact recounting of the worn out ball-race illustrates a problem plaguing the IRFC. The aircraft were in constant use and subject to considerable abuse by both students and instructors. Despite regular and frequent maintenance, the JN-4's engine proved unreliable.

Occasionally, a forced landing had fatal consequences. Ken Spafford recalls a pilot who had engine trouble shortly after leaving Camp Mohawk. Heading east towards Belleville, the pilot attempted a forced landing on the McAlpine farm just west of Marysville. Approaching from the east into the prevailing wind, the airplane just missed the house and barn and glided into a pasture. It would have been a perfect landing, but the plane collided with a small tree, the force of the impact snapping one of the wing wires, which whipped across, beheading the hapless pilot.

Most had better luck. Cadet David Plumpton flew to his uncle's farm north of Brighton. In an attempt to swoop close to the barn, he clipped the building's roof and wrecked his airplane. Six mechanics and a large

*Mechanics stand beside Cadet Plumpton's wrecked airplane, which they have just loaded onto an RAF truck near Brighton, Ontario. Courtesy of Shawnee Spencer.*

truck were dispatched to pick up the pieces. Plumpton was unhurt and graduated later that year.

One instructor, more daring than any youthful cadet, was Vernon Castle, the internationally famous dancer. At twenty-nine, he was well past the age of most top stunt pilots, but his natural ability overcame his opsimathy; he was recognized as an outstanding stunt pilot by all who saw him work his magic. After a day of instructing, Castle would relieve the stress and tension of guiding nervous young pilots through their manoeuvres by taking his Canuck to 8,000 feet and performing a series of barrel rolls, loops, and the most difficult of all, Immelmann turns. In the latter manoeuvre, a pilot does half a loop and then rolls half of a complete turn. The mechanics on the ground claimed they could always tell when Castle was flying because his manoeuvres were so graceful. A mechanic from St. Catharines described Castle's flying as, "absolutely beautiful, like he was dancing in the air."[3]

Chasing trains became a routine pastime for the cadets at Borden. One routine was particularly annoying to the passengers and crews of the CPR train running from Toronto to Barrie. The pilot would wait for the train along a section of the line between Baxter and the tiny hamlet of Ivy. When the train appeared, the flyer would swoop down from the rear bumping his wheels on the tops of the passenger cars and then, as he came to the coal tender, gunning the plane up and over the steam engine.

To prevent the train crew from seeing the aircraft's identification numbers, the pilot would drop down in front of the steam engine, until reaching a point where the telegraph poles were spaced wide enough to allow the reckless airman to swing off the tracks and out of sight.[4]

Chasing cattle was rather a tame sport and not appreciated by local farmers. On more than one occasion, angry farmers paid visits to the COs of the various camps, demanding the flyers stop harassing their animals, claiming it reduced their cows' milk production.

Pilots found more sport in chasing milk wagons along city streets. The horses were faster than cattle and the milkman was too busy struggling to control his panicked steed to note the markings of the airplanes. Chasing milk wagons was common practice in towns and villages near flying camps. Eardley Wilmot used to indulge in the practice before earning his wings and becoming an instructor. A natural stunt flyer, he devised a speedy method for delivering his laundry. As the backyard of the Wilmot home bordered on the Bay of Quinte, Wilmot would fly along the bay until reaching the family home, at which point he would swoop up over the backyard, tossing a bag full of laundry as he did so. One of his sisters would retrieve it and have it washed and ironed, ready for him to pick up on his next visit.

By air, the town of Picton was only fifteen minutes from the Mohawk and Rathbun camps. Picton became a popular destination for the cadets as it had a fairground with a bandstand. A favourite stunt was to run the airplane's wheels along the roof of the Crystal Palace, a grandstand with hundreds of glass panes. This delighted the spectators in the stands but created consternation among Fair Board members.

When a JN-4 came into view, scores of youngsters would head for the fairgrounds, each hoping to be the one to get twenty-five cents for watching the aircraft while the pilot went into town. On one occasion, a pilot took Ed Allen up for a spin rather than paying the quarter. The youngster was elated to forego the money for his sudden elevation to local hero, the envy of all his friends.

Allan also remembers the day when local dignitary, Cal Scott, found himself face down in the middle of the fairground, unable to move for several minutes while a gleeful pilot careened his machine around the field just low enough that Scott dare not stand.

Occasionally, stunting had serious consequences. One cadet flew from the Leaside Camp to Oshawa, where he drew much of the population out into the streets to watch his daring manoeuvres. After he had exhausted his repertoire of tricks, the cadet attempted to land on the roof of a downtown factory. He failed; one wing was supported by the roof of the Dominion Bank while the rest of the aircraft wound up tangled in the overhead hydro wires. Oshawa and Whitby were plunged into darkness. Without electricity, commercial and industrial activity ground to a halt.

The humiliated airman was able to climb out of his machine and make his way onto the roof of the bank but, in working his way down, dislodged some bricks which clattered down, striking some curious onlookers. A Mrs. Guy suffered a broken arm. The flyer refused to divulge his name but the local newspaper wrote down the airplane's registration. When the local fireman arrived on the scene to remove the JN-4, the RAF refused to let them proceed. It was not until after 10 p.m. that a crew from the Leaside camp was able to remove the airplane and power returned. The RAF refused to release the pilot's name but an officer issued an apology and authorized the payment of repairs to the damaged property. The culprit was later identified as Cadet Weiss.[5]

Every once in a while, a cadet pushed his luck too far. This happened to a student pilot during a high altitude cross-country flight. Going over the town of Collingwood on Georgian Bay, the cadet spotted a large bridge-type derrick in a shipbuilding yard. All thoughts of his prosaic cross-country assignment evaporated as the young aviator swooped down, guiding his airplane beneath and between the derrick. The stunt caught the attention of the workers, who clapped their approval. The preening youngster repeated the stunt, to even more applause from the fascinated workmen.

Not satisfied with two successful passes under the structure, the intrepid cadet made yet another run at the derrick. This time a wingtip snagged one of the latticed iron uprights and the airplane spun out of control, smashing into the corrugated iron roof of an adjoining building. The craft was totally demolished, but, amazingly, the young pilot suffered only a bad shake-up and minor injuries. His foolish stunting had cost the IRFC another aircraft, and the cadet received a short spell in the camp lock-up.[6]

Not all the cadet stunts were due to youthful exuberance; some were the result of actual criminal intent. Aircraft mechanics had ample opportunity to learn the basics of flying. Two Americans training at Camp Leaside under the Texas agreement were particularly enterprising. Having taught themselves to fly, the mechanics proceeded to steal a JN-4. B.J. Auluffe of Rochester and Oscar Slade of New York City, both twenty-three, hold the dubious distinction of being the first felons to steal an airplane in Canada.

The mechanics flew the Jenny to the United States and, wearing IRFC uniforms, put on exhibition flights, gave lectures, and collected money, ostensibly for the Red Cross, but in reality with themselves as beneficiaries. They were apprehended in Roanoke, Virginia, and brought back under guard by the IRFC. The *Toronto Evening Telegram* reported that the enterprising recruits had collected a large sum of money.[7] The miscreants were court-martialled. Maintaining its policy of secrecy, the RFC did not disclose the trial results.

In 1929, the famous bush pilot Wop May helped the RCMP hunt down the Mountie killer Albert Johnson, better known by his nickname, the Mad Trapper, but airplanes were first used for hunting desperados by IRFC pilots stationed at Deseronto more than a decade earlier. The object of their search was Henri Monette, alias Charles Edouard Girard, described by the press as an arch-conspirator and leader of the dynamite gang in Montreal, which had blown up the mansion of one Montrealer and planned to blow up more.

Monette was the leader of a radical group opposed to the conscription bill introduced by the Unionist Government of Sir Robert Borden. In early August 1917, the group stole a quantity of dynamite from the

Martineau quarry in Montreal, planning to blow up the homes of various prominent politicians and businessmen, including the prime minister and Sir Donald Mann, one of Canada's wealthiest industrialists. All of the intended victims were prominent supporters of the conscription bill. The group also intended to dynamite the offices of the *Montreal Gazette*, *Montreal Star*, *La Patrie*, and *La Presse*.

The plotters succeeded in partially destroying the summer home of Lord Atholstan before being forced into hiding in Montreal and the surrounding countryside. One of the gang was really an undercover operative for the police, and, over the next few weeks, the net was closed and all the plotters save two were captured. Shortly thereafter, Handfield, alias Leduc, was tracked down by the Lachute Police. Rather than surrender, the fugitive drew his pistol and carried on a running gunfight with his pursuers. Finally, surrounded and with no means of escape, Leduc took his own life. This left only the ringleader, Henri Monette, at large.

By now the Sûreté de Québèc, the Ontario Provincial Police, and the Dominion Police were massing their resources to catch the elusive "arch criminal." But Monette had disappeared and, for several weeks, no trace of him was unearthed. Finally, in early September, the notorious plotter and an associate were sighted driving a large grey touring sedan north of Kingston. The Montreal police scoured the area unsuccessfully before requesting the assistance of the IRFC. Several keen airmen were put to work patrolling the territory running north from Napanee, including Yarker, Harrowsmith, Sydenham, and the Perth Road district. The object was to find the car and alert the Montreal detectives.

Reports continued to come in that the criminals were in eastern Ontario. Monette was reported to have left an unpaid garage and hotel bill in Cobourg before disappearing. Unfortunately for the IRFC's dashing image, the elusive Monette was neither captured nor spotted by the force. Had they been more successful, the history of the corps might have assumed legendary proportions. Despite the IRFC's lack of success, this was the first time airplanes had been used to hunt desperados in Canada.[8]

Monette was eventually captured on 18 September by the chief of the Montreal police, aided by Montreal detectives and the chief of the Dominion Police. He was found hiding out in an elementary school at

Point aux Trembles, and maintained that, during the entire period, he had never left Montreal.[9]

Not surprisingly, the fly-boys retained their devil-may-care attitude after armistice was declared and RAF (Canada) was being wound down. Three young pilots were arrested, not for stunts in the air, but for stunts on the ground. A satirical *Star* scribbler captured the atmosphere of the court:

> No more may the members of the RAF "fly" unrestrictedly in their automobiles along the streets of Toronto. Hitherto, they have enjoyed a large measure of exemption from the speed cop: but-never again! Magistrate Ellis has said so ... he fined two of them, Charles F. McHugh and Emile Gagnon, $5.00 without costs each, and remanded W. McCallum until called on. "These people pay their own fines," remarked a captain. "As far as we are concerned, we would like to see them soaked; then they will not come back again, and we won't have to repair the cars so often."[10]

This insouciant attitude to rules and regulations was not just confined to cadets. C.G. Hoare, CO of the training plan, ignored rules when they stood in the way of his goals. Nowhere was this more evident than in his dealings with the Americans.

# CHAPTER TWELVE
## THE DANCERS: VERNON AND IRENE CASTLE

> That these two, years ago, determined the course
> dancing would take, is incontestable. They were
> decisive characters, like Boileau in French poetry
> and Berlin in ragtime; for they understood, absorbed,
> and transformed everything known of dancing up
> to that time and out of it made something beautiful
> and new. Vernon Castle ... was the better of the
> two. In addition to the beauty of his dancing he had
> inventiveness ... but if he were the greater, his finest
> creation was Irene.
>
> — *Gilbert Seldes, theatre critic*[1]

Vernon and Irene Castle appeared to dance onto the world stage overnight. An observer would have been excused for imagining they had been waiting in the wings, deciding when to emerge and let the world in on the secret of their wonderful talent. The reality was much different.

Vernon Castle was born on 2 May 1887, the child of a middle-class family in Norwich, England. At nineteen, he was earning his living as a self-taught magician and conjurer. In 1906, he moved to New York where he embarked on a stage career. It was the age of slapstick and Castle's physical appearance made him a natural comedian. At five foot eleven inches, he was not especially tall but, at a slim 118 pounds, appeared much taller. Drama critics described him as "a soda straw with legs," or as "an attenuated green bean."[2] A large hawk-like nose and irregular features added to his comedic appearance.

Five years later he married Irene Foote, the daughter of a New Rochelle physician. Irene was several years younger but at eighteen was determined to be an actress. Almost as tall as Vernon, she was slim, graceful, and strikingly beautiful. Before they married, Vernon managed to get her a small role in a Broadway production.

As a comedian in stage productions, Castle, while a regular player, was not a star. After six years on the stage, he was still a minor eccentric comic with a putty nose who wound his thin legs around a cane in front of the ladies of the chorus.

Restless and impetuous, Castle was ready for a change. Offered the opportunity to play in a French revue scheduled to open in Paris in the spring, he agreed, as long as Irene received a part. This was arranged and, accompanied by Zowie, their English bulldog, and her parents' long-time servant, Walter Ash, they sailed for France.

As a finale to one of their stage roles, Vernon and Irene decided to introduce French audiences to the new dancing craze then sweeping America. Known as "the Grizzly Bear" or "Texas Tommy," neither of the Castles had ever seen it performed but had read about it in clippings sent to them by Irene's mother. Vernon worked out a routine based on newspaper accounts and his own sense of rhythm, timing, and showmanship. The French audiences went wild, stamping their feet and shouting, "greezly bahr" until the Castles came on stage and performed again.

The Castles' career as dancers took off when they appeared at the Café de Paris. The café was the finest supper club in all of France; only the very rich could afford this elegant establishment whose patrons were the aristocracy of Europe. They became fast friends with the famous proprietor of the café, Louis Barraya, known to his friends as Papa Louis.

As their fame spread, the Castles began receiving invitations to perform at soirées, and would sometimes do three of these a night. Then, at midnight, they would appear at the Café de Paris for their final performance, afterwards partying well into the early hours and joining friends for breakfast at Maxim's. Almost overnight the Castles became the toast of Europe. Upon their return they swept the United States just as quickly.

By 1914, Vernon and Irene had set up Castle House, a highly profitable dancing school, owned a popular restaurant on Broadway — which they named Sans Souci — had written the screenplay for and starred in the film *The Whirl of Life*, based loosely on their careers, were frequently on dance tours, starred in Broadway productions, and still managed to spend some time each summer dancing at The Café de Paris. The money was rolling in almost as fast as Vernon could spend it.

He was a legendary tipper, cab drivers invariably received a tip larger than their fare. He was equally generous to friends. Irene chided him that he would never get the money back but her pleadings fell on deaf ears. Money, said Vernon, was for spending. More thrifty than her husband, Irene took to banking her share of their income. His profligate spending was the cause of frequent quarrels.

Women were another source of contention. Gorgeous young women were constantly chasing down Vernon and throwing themselves at the graceful dancer. But Vernon had something of the innocent child about him, and, after a row, Irene always forgave him. Perhaps her more discreet transgressions made forgiveness easier for, as she later admitted, "When Vernon was busy with his affairs of the heart, I wasn't any brokenhearted blossom left to weep alone."[3]

They were at the peak of their careers, yet Vernon was unhappy. Although he had lived in the United States for a decade, he retained his loyalty and love for England. Moreover, the war was going badly for England and, instead of doing his part, Vernon was living a life of wealth and privilege. Always more concerned with principle than with the practical, he tore up an entertainment contract worth a fortune in order to fulfil his duty to his country.[4]

Vernon began flying lessons in December 1915 and obtained his FAI certificate from the Aero Club of America on 9 February 1916. He left for England and, after completing his training as a military pilot, was posted to France as a second lieutenant.

While in Europe, Vernon wrote his wife almost daily. His letters are full of affection for Irene, but, despite their separation, he was clearly satisfied to be doing what he believed was his duty for England and democracy.

Almost thirty, Castle was well past the optimum age for a fighter pilot, but his natural athletic abilities compensated for the slowing of reflexes that begins in the teens. Castle had taught himself to play the drums, to dance, to clown and act on stage, and to master conjuring tricks. He did all these things exceptionally well. It is not surprising that, in spite of a late start, he made an excellent pilot.

A sensitive man, he was vulnerable to the brutality of war. On one occasion, he was returning from a reconnaissance flight over enemy lines, and was jumped from behind by a German fighter. Castle managed to elude his pursuer and get on his tail. A brief burst from his Lewis gun was all he needed to shoot down his opponent, who crashed just inside the British lines.

Typically, Lieutenant Castle's first concern was the enemy he had shot down. He arranged for the German pilot to get the best surgical care and, when his former opponent was able to walk, attempted to get him into the officers' mess. The German pilot was so grateful that he gave Castle the Iron Cross he had won in combat.

In one of his letters to Irene, Castle mentions that he had been lunching in their old haunt, the Café de Paris. The war had changed everything — the café was not the same — but Papa Louis had refused to let his beloved dancer pay for his meals. Undoubtedly, this saved Lieutenant Castle some embarrassment, as his military pay was less than five dollars a day.

On 10 March 1917, Castle shot down his second German airplane, but, the following day, had half his engine shot away by an opponent. His plane plummeted 1,000 feet, but landed in a pile of wire, which cushioned the fall. The airplane was a total wreck, but Castle escaped with only minor injuries.

This was the second time he had been shot down and survived. A grateful French government awarded the popular aviator-dancer the Croix de Guerre, the highest medal they could bestow on a foreigner. His tour of duty was up and Castle was due for leave. But, the War Office did not send him back to the front, perhaps believing he should be sent to Canada before his luck ran out. Colonel Hoare had already expressed his concerns about recruiting problems in Canada to the Directory of Air Organization. As a famous entertainer, Castle was of more value to the war effort in Canada, where his presence would attract recruits to the IRFC.

With recruitment a priority, Lieutenant Castle was sent home on leave to the United States, where his presence served to publicize the glamorous life of the fighter pilot and encourage young Americans to

*Vernon Castle at the wheel of his Stutz Bearcat during the summer of 1917. Courtesy of Hastings County Historical Society.*

join the IRFC. In early May, Castle was posted to Camp Deseronto as an instructor. After Paris, London, and New York, Deseronto, or "Deserted," as the cadets called it, came as a severe culture shock.

Deseronto folk were as surprised as the famous dancer when he was posted to their small town. He arrived driving a bright yellow Stutz Bearcat, accompanied by two German shepherd police dogs and his Rhesus monkey, Jeffrey.

The IRFC revitalized Deseronto. In the latter half of the nineteenth century it had been a thriving industrial centre for the Rathbun lumber, manufacturing, and rail operations. In the early years of the twentieth century, logging declined dramatically in southern Ontario, undermining the foundation of the Rathbun Company's operations. In the years before the Great War, the company gradually closed down and Deseronto dwindled to a backwater of less than 3,000 residents. A few amenities remained. The airmen and mechanics could patronize Naylor's Theatre, or Fraser's Ice Cream Parlour. A substantial number of young women worked as mechanics on the airplanes, but were barred from such dens of iniquity as Whitton's Pool Room, The Steward House, The Arlington House, or The McVicker House. Not surprisingly, these smoky dens of macho conviviality did a thriving trade from the influx of IRFC airmen and mechanics flocking into the town.

For the townsfolk and the rural residents of the surrounding area, the most interesting entertainment was provided by the aviators themselves. Every Sunday, their chores completed and church attended, local residents flocked along the township roads bordering the aerodromes to watch the pilots in their flimsy airplanes. They would bring picnic lunches, park their Model Ts or buggies in the tall grass along the township road, and spend the afternoon trading crop information and gossip with their neighbours. But mostly, they were there to watch the aviators.

The novelty of flying in those years emerges from a reporter's description of Camp Mohawk, which appeared in the *Napanee Express* under the heading, "Mohawk Camp is Fascinating":

> Just a few short weeks ago … the plains were almost barren of structure but today a veritable city has sprung into existence. Sprung up in the night as it were ….
>
> Touching the right-of-way of the railway is the canvass home of the men. Here, in regulation military style, are hundreds of tents that are the sleeping quarters of the mechanics and employees who are working on the construction of buildings, roads, etc…. The most interesting part of the camp, however, is further west along the rail road. It is the site of the hangers [*sic*] and aerodromes where the immense mechanical birds are taken care of…. The wonders of an aviation camp attract large numbers of our citizens who visit the camps frequently and marvel at the wonders to be seen.[5]

Once again, the shops and tradesmen of Deseronto were busy, the town thriving and optimistic as the young airmen and mechanics crowded its streets in their well-cut uniforms.

Camp Deseronto became home to more than its share of eccentrics and non-conformists. One of the instructors was Captain Jack Coats, heir to the Coats thread fortune, and former resident of Skelmorlie Castle, the Coats family's imposing mansion in Ayrshire, Scotland. Coats had his large white Marmon automobile shipped to Deseronto by rail. His motor launch was kept in the town's harbour where it was maintained by a Mohawk — who also took care of Castle's two German shepherds. On several occasions Coats's launch was used to rescue downed aviators from the Bay of Quinte. Coats had flown at the front and lost a lung. No longer fit for battle, he was sent to Canada as an instructor. Coats shared Castle's careless attitude towards money, his interest in women, as well as his passion for fast cars. The two men quickly became fast friends.[6]

One of the instructors had a reputation for unusual daring and athletic ability. Lieutenant Ned Ballough was known as "the wing walker" — a sobriquet earned from his trick of leaving the cockpit unattended and climbing out onto the wing where he would walk nonchalantly back and forth as calmly as a stroller on a country lane. A muscular man, he also shone in athletic competitions.[7]

The commander of the camp, Lord George Wellesley, was the great-grandson of the "iron" Duke of Wellington of Waterloo fame. He stood a ramrod six feet tall and looked every inch the former captain of the Grenadier Guards, which he had been before transferring early in the war to the RFC where he saw active service in France and Egypt. An aristocrat who was admired and liked by both his officers and men, he had been ostracized from polite British society. The commander's brother had been killed at the front, leaving behind a talented, beautiful wife and two fine sons. Against Church of England proscription, Lord Wellesley had fallen in love with and married his brother's widow in April 1917. He and his bride, Lady Louise Pamela, hoped to start a new life in Canada.[8]

The Rathbun family rented many of their properties and buildings to the IRFC, including one of their estates, which was occupied by Lord and Lady Wellesley. The Rathbun Company's offices had operated from an elegant three-storey brick building complete with ornate wood panelling and a modern phone and telegraph system. Located on the east side of

*Lieutenant Ned Ballough was known as the wing walker. Courtesy of Deseronto Archives.*

the town's main street, it stood empty for several years. Taken over by the IRFC as Wing Headquarters, it was easily restored to its former utility. The entire first floor was taken up by Wing Commander Wellesley and his staff, including the orderly room and the office of the orderly officer. The second floor was occupied by the supply section.

One of the Canadian instructors was Eardley Wilmot. A native of Belleville who had studied engineering while employed by the Ford Motor Company, Wilmot was born in 1892, the same year as Coats. Wilmot, Castle, and Coats soon became fast friends. Wilmot's place within the triumvirate was cemented when he arranged for Coats and Castle to meet his two beautiful sisters who lived conveniently nearby at their mother's home in Belleville.

There are differing stories as to how the sisters met their brother's two dashing friends. One version has Eardley introducing his sister Audrey to Jack Coats, after which Coats and Castle became frequent visitors at the Wilmot home.

Another version postulates that Coats decided to literally drop in on the lovely sisters in a manner that would make a lasting impression. As the Wilmot back yard was not big enough to land an airplane, Coats had to wait until the sisters were visiting the Burrows family on their large estate before making his fraudulent forced landing.* The estate stretched south for almost a kilometre and was virtually flat and even. The Wilmot sisters rushed out to "rescue" the daring aviator. They helped Coats out of his airplane and invited him in for tea while a servant was sent to fetch gasoline.

The Wilmot sisters were accomplished dancers and excellent horsewomen. Audrey Wilmot had just turned twenty-three, while Gwen was two years younger. They lived, with their mother, in a large rambling home overlooking the Bay of Quinte, about a mile west of Belleville. Since the mysterious death of their father in a Toronto hotel fire, the sisters had survived primarily from the piano and singing lessons given by their mother and the money sent home by their brother, Eardley. Although they lived in genteel poverty, the sisters were high-spirited, strong-willed, and mixed with the cream of local society.

In the spring of 1917, Jack Coats and Audrey Wilmot began dating regularly. Simultaneously, her Titian-haired younger sister, Gwen, fell head over heels for the magnetic Vernon Castle. From all accounts Vernon reciprocated her ardour.

On 30 May, Castle had another brush with death. When shot down over France, he did not suffer either emotionally or physically. But this accident involved the death of a student he was instructing.

The official report states that Cadet Fraser was making a turn at about 200 feet when the nose dropped, frightening the cadet who panicked and pulled the nose up, stalling the wings. With the cadet's hands frozen on the wheel, Castle was unable to force the nose down to avert the stall. The Jenny spun out of control and plunged into the roof of a hangar.

Castle tempted his own death in his efforts to free his student, but was thrown to the ground and knocked unconscious when the gas tank

---

* Known as the Glanmore National Historic Site, the mansion covers over 9,000 square feet and boasts fifteen rooms. It is open to the public as a museum.

exploded. The aircraft burst into flames and burned itself through the roof of the hangar.

Although it was clearly not his fault, Castle felt responsible for the young man's death. He was so shaken he developed shingles and was given leave to rest and recuperate. Before taking his leave, he made a three-hundred-mile rail journey to console the cadet's parents.[9]

Upon his return, Castle made a typically selfless decision. He resolved that he would now sit in the student's seat while his students sat in the safer rear seat. After hours, he plunged himself into patriotic activities, taking the train to Montreal and other centres, where he appeared at recruiting and fundraising balls.

In Belleville, Castle, Jack Coats, and the Wilmot sisters became fixtures on the social scene. Castle and Gwen had fallen passionately in love, as had Coats and Audrey. During the six months that Coats and Castle were stationed at Deseronto, the foursome were frequent visitors to the finest homes in the city, including the stately residence of Judge Arthur Brickenden, the stone manor of Doctor Marshall, and Sidney Cottage, the rural home of Colonel Ponton. They were also guests at the Dundas Street mansion of international industrialist George Graham. More ordinary folk could sometimes see the famous Vernon Castle "dancing divinely" with Gwen Wilmot in the ornate Greco-Roman ballroom of the Quinte Hotel.[10]

*Gwen Wilmot in happier times. Courtesy of Carolyn Heatherington.*

Audrey Wilmot and Jack Coats became engaged and made plans to marry. One of the quartet, possibly Castle, suggested a double wedding. Castle planned to file for divorce, expecting it would take about six months to arrange and another six months for the decree to become final. It was decided the two couples would be married in the fall of 1918. Vernon gave Gwen a large emerald-and-diamond engagement ring. When the war was over he planned to return to dancing with Gwen as his partner.[11]

The entry of the United States into the war led to dramatic changes in the policies and direction of the IRFC. Rather than moving the whole enterprise west to British Columbia for winter training, Hoare negotiated a shrewd deal with the Americans that saw fully two thirds of IRFC cadets move to Texas for winter training. Vernon Castle and Jack Coats were among those officers sent to Texas while the Wilmot sisters waited anxiously for their safe return and for the double marriage planned for the following September.

# CHAPTER THIRTEEN
## HOW TO SUCCEED BY BREAKING THE RULES

The only way to deal with Govt. Departments ... is
to ignore them, they don't care a damn what you do
so long as no-one is asked to take responsibility.[1]
— *Brigadier-General C.G. Hoare*

The severe Ontario winter of 1916–1917 convinced Hoare that the IRFC had
to find a province with less severe winters if flight training was to continue
during the long Ontario deep freeze. In March 1917, he sent two staff
officers to British Columbia to search for possible aerodrome locations. The
officers recommended the selection of two sites, one near Stevetson on Lulu
Island, the other at Ladner on the south arm of the Fraser River. The sites
were separated by a narrow branch of the Fraser River and were located a
few miles south of Vancouver.* After reading his staff officers' report, Hoare
advised the IMB to lease these sites, preferably with an option to buy.

Despite his action, Hoare retained serious reservations as to the
viability of the British Columbia sites. Two months later, he left for B.C.
to examine the sites himself. This meant a three- to- four-day train trip
both ways; an enormous amount of time for a man pressed for decisions
on several fronts. Along the way, he spent a day in Winnipeg where he
quickly concluded prairie winters were too long and severe for winter
flying. Proceeding to Vancouver, he approved the sites already selected
as the best locations available under the circumstances. On his return
to Toronto in late May, he cabled Charlton advising of his decision and
voicing his reservations:

---

* The first airplane flight in B.C. was made by C.K. Hamilton in a Curtiss
Pusher Biplane at Minoru Park Racetrack on Lulu Island on 25 March 1910.[2]

The aerodrome Sites at both Ladner and Lulu are satisfactory provided they do not prove too wet. Macpherson who is putting in the drainage scheme tells me they can be made efficient. B.C. on the whole is bad for flying. The surrounding territory beyond the island and delta is wooded and the opportunities for cross-country flying are somewhat limited.

If it were not for the necessity of having one Wing where climatic conditions are not so severe in the winter, and also the necessity of stimulating interest in Aviation in the West, I should not recommend having a Wing in B.C. at all.

I visited Vancouver Island, it is entirely wooded and hilly. I was able however, to start an interviewing committee for Cadets and get the local people interested. Strubell accompanied me and we left an officer and recruiting staff in Vancouver which appears to be good recruiting area.[3]

While construction did get underway, the aerodromes were never completed, nor did a B.C. Wing come into existence. However, as Hoare predicted, recruiting in the province benefited from the publicity. B.C. proved a fertile recruiting ground for flyers, providing more airmen per capita than any other province.[4]

Yet, even as Hoare was travelling by train to Vancouver, he knew there was a possibility the B.C. aerodromes would not be built. The United States had entered the war on 6 April 1917. A few days later, he was asked by the governor general, the Duke of Devonshire, to travel to Washington and meet with members of the American War Department and some military officers. Hoare cabled the War Office in London for instructions and was told not to commit himself. He ignored these restrictions, observing later that it was the only way to deal with government departments who don't care what you do so long as no one in their department is asked to take the responsibility.

When he arrived in Washington, Hoare lunched with Colonel Hiram Bingham, a Yale University professor and world-famous explorer. Bingham had been placed in charge of ground-school training for the air branch of the U.S. Army Signals department and was anxious to learn about the IRFC training operation. Over lunch at the Raleigh Hotel, the two men discussed their countries' mutual needs. Both were adventurers and got on famously. Hoare made a few notes on the back of an envelope after which he accompanied Bingham to a meeting of the War Production Board. Here, he made a presentation outlining a plan of mutual co-operation in which he disarmed the shrewd Yankee businessmen by telling them frankly that the plan would cost the United States vastly more than it would cost England. The success of his presentation and the warm regard he engendered can be gleaned from letters he received from two conference participants. Bingham wrote:

> You are the only person I know who could give a complete summary without notes immediately after lunch and several cocktails.

Hoare also received a note from Norman Edgar, a successful American businessman in charge of aerodrome selection and construction, who commented:

> I am Scotch and I should like to tell you that I have never met a better negotiator than yourself.[5]

The War Production Board was so impressed with the genial and persuasive Hoare that they made him an honorary member.

Hoare grasped quickly that the Americans were totally unprepared for war and were looking to the IRFC to help kickstart a pilot training program for their fledgling air force. He agreed to bring back three U.S. Army Signals officers and acquaint them with training program operating in Canada. They were shortly followed by a long succession of American military men, all soaking up the methods and experience offered by Hoare's co-operative staff officers. The IRFC provided them with all sorts of training manuals and forms to guide them in setting up their program. A tour of IRFC facilities in

*Commander C.G. Hoare. Courtesy of Alan Sullivan,* Aviation in Canada, 1917–18.

Toronto and Borden impressed the Americans even more. They were particularly pleased to discover that an American, Major Oliver Filley, was the station commander at Borden. The Americans departed realizing they could avoid many mistakes and save a lot of time if they worked co-operatively with the IRFC. In his brief visit to Washington and the treatment he and his staff gave the visiting officers, Hoare laid the basis for trust and friendship with members of the War Production Board, the American military, and, in particular, with Colonel Bingham.

In return for Hoare's assurance that the IRFC would assist the American military with training procedures, he was able to obtain a quid pro quo for one of his most pressing concerns, namely that the supply of airplane engines from Curtiss Manufacturing in Hammondsport, New York, would not be reduced by the Signal Corps' needs for training airplanes.[6] None of this was in writing but, if the two sides were to assist each other, a relationship of trust and co-operation was essential. Hoare offered that and the Americans readily reciprocated.

One example of the IRFC's willingness to assist the United States took place during the summer of 1917. In August, the American military sent a group of some thirty-plus reserve officers to Toronto, headed by Captain C.J. Ryan of New York. Here, they underwent an intensive course on flying equipment, which had been created by Hoare's brother, Lieutenant-Colonel F.R.G. Hoare. All the Americans were college graduates, many having extensive business experience. On the completion of the course, they returned to the United States and were placed in charge of supplies for the flying wing of the American Army.[7]

When it entered the war, the United States was just emerging as the greatest economic power on the planet. Although it had enormous potential, their military power was largely undeveloped. According to Bingham, American air power consisted of two small flying fields, 48 officers, 1,330 men of all ranks, and 225 airplanes, not one of which "was fit to fly over the lines."[8]

Hoare was quick to understand the United States' military situation. He also knew how seriously England had been financially drained by the war. In addition, the Canadian operation was proving more costly than anticipated. As a consequence of the great distances, higher wages, and the initial lack of an air force infrastructure in Canada, the cost of training a pilot in Canada was nearly double the cost of similar training in Great Britain.[9]

General Squire had been away during Hoare's visit to Washington in April. Shortly after his return, Squire, who was in charge of the air branch of the army, accompanied by his staff officer, Major Foulois, travelled to Toronto for further discussions with Hoare. The two Americans lived at the "chummery" during their visit. It was during an informal meeting in the relaxed atmosphere of the chummery that the reciprocal scheme took shape and was later put into writing. Dermott Allen was present during these discussions.

Squire's first question got right to the heart of the U.S. air power problem. He turned to Hoare and asked, "Colonel, we have some 140 millions of population, a vast industrial potential, unlimited money. We want to do something big in aviation. How shall we set about it?"

Hoare cut straight to the nub of the problem. Sitting back, he took up his pipe, which he filled with deliberation, using two matches as he always did to light it properly, and, at length, replied: "Well, General, I would suggest you design an aero engine of not less than 100 H.P. [powerful for the time] produce it in mass and build your various types of aircraft around it. All the rest will fall into place."[10] The result of this encounter was the design and mass production of the Liberty engine, which quickly became a critical component of United States air power.

The meeting of these two men proved one of the most significant of the war. Together they conceived a plan that enabled the United States to train and organize a large air force in record time, thereby materially assisting the Allies in winning the war. The plan saved the IMB at least $1 million by solving the IRFC's problem of winter training at little cost, the burden of building the Texas airfields falling entirely on the United States. Not in the exchange of letters, but understood by both parties, was an understanding that the IRFC could continue recruiting pilot-cadets in the United States. Officially, they would only recruit British citizens residing in the States, but young Americans were recruited on the understanding with Squire that, should the press or hostile politicians catch wind of the practice, it would cease.

The two men agreed on the terms on 9 July 1917. Upon Squire's return to Washington, letters were exchanged setting out the terms of the Reciprocal Agreement. Hoare set out the final terms in his letter to Squire on 12 July 1917. The entire agreement ran to only five pages.

G.A. Morrow, director of the Aviation Section of the IMB, advised Hoare that the arrangements dealing with the supply of aircraft to the U.S. War Department should be governed by a legal document. When the lawyers attempted to put the scheme into a legal document, it was so lengthy, verbose with legalese, and complex, that Hoare's brother, Gurney, after reading it carefully, exclaimed, "Gibberish!"[11] The lawyer's draft was scrapped. The parties agreed the success of the plan depended upon the mutual trust of the parties and a determination to make the scheme work.

From the American point of view, the main purposes of the agreement were (1) to train a nucleus of pilots and ground crew for their Air Service and (2) to learn as much as possible from the IRFC's training methods so they could set up their own schools and get an effective, efficient training scheme operating as quickly as possible.

To achieve the first goal, the IRFC was to train ten squadrons, which would include 300 pilots, 20 equipment officers, and 2,000 ground crew/mechanics. Training was to begin in Canada immediately, but move south before winter arrived.

While the training of American cadets in Canada was underway, the United States was to build and equip three training camps in Texas at sites to be chosen by the IRFC. To this end, Allen left in June for Texas, where he chose three sites near Fort Worth.

The United States was to purchase 200 machines (JN-4 Canucks) from Canadian Aeroplanes Limited and was also to build and supply one flying field comparable to Camp Borden to be used by the IRFC for three winter months in order that the service could continue the training of cadets sent to Texas for the winter. Two more camps were to be built for the training of the American cadets. All running supplies such as petrol, oil, electricity, power, and raw materials were to be supplied by the U.S. government. While they were in Texas, the U.S. government was also to supply the needs of all ranks of the IRFC in the areas of medical attention, supplies, support, personnel, and equipment.

The agreement had an added benefit for the British. The Canadian Aeroplane Company was now producing 200 JN-4s a month, considerably more than was needed in Canada. Hoare's deal whereby the Americans were to buy 200 Canucks was badly needed to keep the plant operating at full capacity. In December of 1917, with the plan in full operation, the Americans ordered a further 250 airplanes, which further assisted the efficient Canadian company. On 26 December, Hoare wrote to the Air Board Office in London setting out the situation at the factory:

> Owing to lack of orders, Canadian Aeroplanes Ltd. have been in a very difficult position.... It would be unfortunate if a Factory employing 2,500 hands, with a value out-put of 200 machines monthly should have to close down. The difficulty for the moment has been overcome by our obtaining a further order for 250 machines from the USA, with Spares which will tide over a couple of months. We shall then have sold them 500 machines, with three months Mob Table of Spares on a generous scale, and in addition supply all the spares we require up to Feb. 15 [the expiry date of the Reciprocal Agreement] at their expense.[12]

Even before Hoare obtained these additional orders, the Air Directory in London had come to the realization that in Hoare they had not only an excellent leader of men, but an officer who combined the invaluable talent of the convivial but shrewd negotiator. He had negotiated an agreement with the United States that pleased this most important ally, that would speed up the American contribution to the war in the air, that would avoid the costly building of camps in British Columbia, and continue the training of Canadian cadets in Texas over the winter. Moreover, all this was accomplished at America's expense. On 1 August 1917, Hoare was promoted, vaulting over the position of full colonel, straight to brigadier-general.

Meanwhile, officers at the Air Directory were taking notice of the way Hoare was getting things done in Canada. On 12 April, Charlton, his immediate superior in London, indicated his confidence in Hoare's ability, making this clear in his cable: "Congratulations on having got on so well with the work. Very shortly, weekly reports can become fortnightly."[13]

After Hoare's deal with the United States, Charlton was even more generous in his compliments, writing to him on 9 August 1917, "I should like to compliment you and all concerned on the extraordinary good show you have put up with the means and time at your disposal."[14]

An officer with the Military Aeronautics Directorate wrote to the newly minted, thirty-five-year-old general, expressing the views of the executive, "The reciprocal scheme of the U.S. is approved and, as you say, is very satisfactory. Parenthetically, you are a wonder!!.... Hearty congratulations on your becoming a Brigadier, no one deserved it more. I think you are a perfect marvel the way you have got things done in Canada."[15]

Nor had Hoare finished negotiating with the Americans. The Reciprocal Agreement called for the IRFC to train ten American squadrons by 15 February 1918, at which time the corps was to return to Canada, where the training of 42 and 43 Wings would resume. It made little sense to move the training operation from Texas to Ontario in the middle of February to resume training. Hoare had prepared a solution. Writing to Charlton in October, he laid out his strategy:

> By the reciprocal agreement the U.S. only agreed to lend aeroplanes and maintain us in Texas for 3 months. We shall be there by November 20th and our time will be up February 20th. From February 20th to the end of March here is almost worse than the period before Christmas, I shall therefore endeavour when our time is up here on February 20th to get them to let us stay on, of course, them paying our own expenses. If I fail we shall have a wretched output from February 20th to April 1st ... if Washington concurs in my plan the 42nd and 43rd Wings will miss the winter altogether.[16] [Washington agreed.]

Hoare had an even more pressing reason for keeping his two Wings in Texas until April. The IMB had run out of money and the Treasury Board in England had not seen fit to grant them additional funds. Consequently, the IMB had not been able to build winter quarters for the cadets passing through basic training. During the warm weather these men had been housed in tents at Long Branch. Had he been forced to bring the two Texas Wings back to Canada in February, he would have been forced to billet the cadets in tents in freezing weather.

The training of the ten American squadrons would take five months, and both parties were anxious to get the plan underway. As a result, American cadets began arriving in Toronto in June with the first contingent consisting of an elite group of 300 U.S. Naval Cadets. In July some 1,400 officers, cadets, and enlisted men from the American Army, Signals Branch, arrived in Toronto and were billeted in tents at Long Branch. A few of these men had military experience, but the great majority were totally raw, untrained, and undisciplined. The arrival of the independent and egalitarian Americans was to prove quite a shock for the British non-coms whose job it was to put these callow youths into first-class physical condition, as well as inculcate respect for military procedures and tradition. The results were often humorous and occasionally disastrous for the non-coms, nor was it a pleasant experience for the Americans, who bristled at British discipline.

# CHAPTER FOURTEEN
## FORGING AN HISTORIC ALLIANCE

We had no battle planes. We had no bombing
planes. We had no high powered engines. We had
no aeroplanes equipped with the numerous devices
war had developed on the other side. We had 135
aeroplanes, useful for training and so on, but of no
other value whatsoever.... We had no standards to
go by; we had no model planes; we had no drawings.
We had nothing.
— *S.G. Blythe,* Saturday Evening Post, *January
1919*

Hoare and General Squire implemented the Reciprocal Agreement. So
quickly, in fact, that large numbers of American cadets and enlisted men
began arriving in Canada on 9 July 1917, three days *before* the letter of
agreement between the parties had actually been signed.

Both Hoare and Allen were appalled at their ally's poor preparations.
The IRFC had provided the Americans with a complete scheme for testing
recruits for trades but the Americans ignored it. Moreover, the Americans
were organized into squadrons strictly by numbers without any regard to
training or trade skills. In addition, they arrived in Canada so lacking in
training of any kind that they could not march from the train to the depot
but, in the words of Allen, "Just ambled along like a baseball crowd."[1]

By July 1917, about 1,400 recruits, cadets, and officer-pilot trainees
had arrived in Canada for training. The recruits were billeted in tents
at the Leaside aerodrome where the IRFC set to work testing them,
instilling some basic military drill and discipline, and assigning them to
the various depots and camps for trades training.

*Recruits Depot, Camp Leaside, summer of 1917. Courtesy of Library and Archives Canada/Department of National Defence PA-022888.*

The Army Signal Corps cadets, including officer-pilot trainees and some two dozen naval cadets totalled nearly 350 men. They were all sent to the University of Toronto to be schooled in the mysteries of flight and, like the recruits at the depots, to learn British military discipline. Inevitably, a conflict arose between the stiff-necked British military tradition and Yankee disrespect for authority. Cadet L.L. Smart described the clash in his book, *The Hawks That Guided the Guns:*

> We disembarked at the University of Toronto — a beautiful campus right in the city which was to be our new home and where we would take our ground school classes. From now on ... [we] were under the direct command of British officers and non-coms. Our quarters were temporary barracks, consisting of a long narrow building with showers and toilets at one end and a separate room at the other end for the sergeant

who was to be our guardian, guard and disciplinarian.

It was here that I was to meet one of the most unforgettable characters I ever knew — a British sergeant-major ... [he] is omnipotent, the supreme being over all enlisted men ... woe betide the sergeant or any others who questioned his command or authority.... One morning ... Sergeant-Major Bissop packed all of us into a small room where the only thing you could do was to stand.

He called the cadets to attention while he stood there — erect, straight as an arrow, heavy set and very formidable-looking. His left arm was half-bent at the elbow and in his left hand he carried his ever-present swagger stick, the other end of it under his armpit. On his face was a deep scowl; his penetrating eyes swept every face in the room. On his upper lip reposed his pride and joy — his waxed mustache twisted fastidiously to perfection. It stuck out like two small antennas. There he stood in all his glory, the personification, the ultimate of the British army. He made the Prussian Guards look like boy scouts.[2]

Sergeant-Major Bissop then proceeded to bawl out the thoroughly intimidated cadets. His bull-like voice thundered through the room, bouncing off the walls, echoing in the cadets' burning ears: "In the words of a common Canadian, I'm an S.O.B. and I live up to my reputation!"[3] He then told the innocents in no uncertain terms what he expected of them and what punishment they could expect for the most minute infraction.

It did not take long for the cadets to bring down the sadistic sergeant-major. Bissop had never visited the United States and, when the cadets invited him on a trip to Buffalo, he readily accepted. In Buffalo, Bissop got roaring drunk and, when the party returned to Toronto, the cadets carried their prostrate superior into his room and wreaked their revenge. Bissop's Achilles heel was an inordinate pride in his waxed mustache. The cadets hit on a brilliant reprisal, shaving off not all his preening glory but merely half of it. In just a few minutes, the spit-and-polish sergeant-major had been transformed into a clownish buffoon. He left the university the next morning and was not seen again by the cadets.

The Americans particularly disliked having to learn the British system of close order drill, which was more complicated than the American system of squads right. Moreover, they could not see the point of learning a drill, which, once they had completed their training and were posted to American units, they would never use again. The British insisted that the Americans were on British soil and therefore had to be instructed in British drill formations. The American officers pointed out they were American cadets and that American drill was therefore mandatory.

A compromise of dubious practicality was reached when it was agreed the cadets and recruits would do American drill in the morning and British drill in the afternoon.[4] This double time for drill, did not make the cadets and recruits particularly happy.

Aside from Bissop, the Americans had a genuine respect for their British and Canadian instructors. The majority of these men were combat veterans whose posting as trainers was a much-needed reprieve from the nerve-shattering combat of Europe. Many of them had been too badly wounded to continue in the front lines but their experience made them invaluable as instructors. As L.L. Smart noted:

> All our instructors were either officers or sergeants who had seen service in France and had been incapacitated in action. They were a fine bunch, especially the commanding officer, Colonel Harcourt, who had lost a leg in combat but could still fly with his wooden leg. We liked them all.[5]

Cadet Smart was commenting upon his training while at Toronto and Borden but Naval Cadet Frederick Ordway who, took his initial flight training at Deseronto, held a similar view:

> The treatment we get here is great. We eat with the officers and have fine, large lounging rooms. The food is

good.... Nothing to do here but work and sleep. Flying is the all-absorbing topic. Nothing else is even mentioned or even thought of.[6]

After Allen had selected the sites for the three flying camps in Texas, Lieutenant H.B. Denton was dispatched to lay out the two camps for the American cadets and the one camp for the IRFC cadets.

The cadets sent to Texas came primarily from Deseronto and Borden; North Toronto cadets remained in Canada. Lieutenant Denton had laid out the various camps in Ontario and was therefore dispatched to Texas by Hoare with instructions to duplicate as, far as was possible, the flying camps in Canada. The press release issued in early August made clear the underlying objective:

> This camp in Texas will mean closer co-operation between the aviation sections of the American and British forces and a further standardization of methods of actual work. The plan is to reproduce in Texas, aviation schools like those at Camp Borden, Camp Mohawk, Camp Rathbun, Camp Leaside and Camp Armour Heights.[7]

By mid-August, the American military and their contractors were rushing to build and equip the three camps near Fort Worth, Texas, which together would be known as Camp Taliaferro.

Shortly before the move to Texas, the flying camps were reorganized into Wings. Borden became No. 42 Wing; Deseronto, No. 43 Wing; and North Toronto, No. 44 Wing. In addition, each wing became a composite flying training school, with three of its squadrons providing elementary instruction while the other two providing advanced training. Each of the advanced squadrons was divided into three flights that individually handled courses in cross-country flying, bombing, wireless telegraphy, and photography. Previous to this reorganization, only Borden had provided advanced training.

In late August, construction finally got underway on the first of the three fields. Known as Hicks' Field or Taliaferro Number 1, it occupied 668 acres and was located about twelve miles northwest of Fort Worth in Tarrant County, Texas.

Construction began on Taliaferro Number 2, also known as Barron or Everman Field, on 8 September. Also in Tarrant County, it was located about five miles south of Fort Worth. At 633 acres, Everman was just slightly smaller than the Hicks airfield.

Taliaferro Number 3, also known as Carruther's Field, was located near the community of Benbrook, about ten miles southwest of Fort Worth. Construction began on 18 September and, when finished, comprised some 640 acres.

In the early hours of 24 September, an IRFC advance party left Toronto by train, arriving at Fort Worth on the twenty-sixth. The advance party was made up of four HQ officers — thirty-four officers constituting a complete wing — plus four American officers, and fifty NCOs and enlisted men. The group was led by Captain Murton Seymour, a young Canadian who later served as the IRFC liaison officer. Seymour claimed the distinction of being the first British officer to command British forces on American soil since the War of 1812.

Allen arrived a few days later and counter-claimed the honour from Seymour, pointing out that he held a court-martial warrant, whereas Seymour did not. The warm Texas hospitality so generously extended to the "invaders" prevented either man from taking the matter seriously.

IRFC headquarters was set up in Fort Worth, as was the purchasing section of the IMB, which worked closely with the IRFC HQ in Texas. The School of Aerial Gunnery, under the command of Major Ballard, was moved from Borden to Hicks' Field, the first of the three camps to be completed and fully occupied by the military.

In the absence of Hoare, Allen commanded the IRFC operation in Texas. Allen noted with wry humour that the new HQ offices allocated to the IRFC by the U.S. brass had formerly been the site of Fort Worth's most infamous brothel. The officer commanding in Texas dryly observed that, "My room had been the bedroom of the leading lady and still had some blood stains on it." Whether this facility's previous use was known to the American authorities in command is unknown but it is clear from Allen's reminiscences that some American officers were not only aware but found the situation highly amusing.[8]

The condition of Camp Taliaferro Number 1, however, was distinctly unamusing. A depressing sight greeted the IRFC inspectors as they toured the fields where IRFC and American cadets were to begin training in just a few short weeks. The construction crews had fallen far behind schedule: hangars and barracks were not finished and, at some fields, construction had barely started; water mains, sewage disposal facilities, and power lines were incomplete, and at Benbrook, even the basic infrastructure had not begun.

Before their departure for Texas, the American cadets had smiled inwardly as their Canadian counterparts chattered eagerly of going south to warm and sunny Texas for winter training. Many speculated that the weather in Texas was comparable to Florida, others to Bermuda or the Bahamas. Naval Cadet Halstead knew better. He and his American counterparts made every effort to complete and pass their training while in Canada. Halstead noted in his report to his superiors that "We were all much amused at the enthusiastic anticipation displayed by the Canadian personnel who all believed hopefully that part of Texas would be like Florida as to which we all carefully refrained from disillusioning them."[9]

Most of the officers at headquarters in Toronto knew Texas was no tropical paradise. Allen had made a reconnaissance trip to the Lone Star State in June when he approved the aerodrome sites to be constructed. While there he heard about the Texas "northers" and read the climatological reports published by the American government. Wisely, he decided to keep that knowledge from the cadets, but did make arrangements with the Americans at Fort Worth as to the procedures to be followed when notice was received that a "norther" was expected. One of the earliest orders published by Advanced Headquarters at Fort Worth, required that a "norther" warning was to be followed by the cessation of all flying, aircraft were to be safely stored in hangars, and all ranks were to change into their warm blue serge uniforms.[10]

In early October, Hoare decided to form a provisional gunnery school at Fort Worth. This would minimize any loss of training time when the cadets arrived in Texas. They were scheduled to begin their course on 3 November, the same day this training ended in Toronto.

He took the same approach to all aspects of training. For example, in order that Borden could keep flying up to the last moment before leaving for Texas, he ordered the formation of a ground crew squadron, which he named Z Squadron. Three days before Borden's personnel moved south, Z Squadron would begin the task of repairing and overhauling the equipment and airplanes so there would be no delays at Borden when flying recommenced in the spring.[11]

The transfer of the cadets, instructors, and other staff was accomplished with considerable secrecy. Rumours flew as to just when the men would be leaving, but train routes were classified information. Moving two complete Wings — Borden (42) and Deseronto (43) — by train was a complex logistical task, but was carried out smoothly. One airman, Cadet Jim Powers was killed when he fell from a train outside Chicago. As the cadet's wife lived in Chicago, it is probable he was trying to jump so as to spend time with her.[12] Aside from this mishap, the 1,600-mile movement of the men was uneventful. They arrived at Camp Taliaferro Number 1 on 17 November, just three days after leaving Ontario. The cadets were flying the same day.

Much to the dismay of the naive Canadian cadets, the day after their arrival at Camp Taliaferro, a "norther" hit, carpeting the three aerodromes with an unusually heavy snowfall. All flying ceased and was further delayed when the fields turned into a thick, sticky mud as the landing fields had no proper sub-drainage. As a consequence, the melting snow lay in puddles, draining away slowly. This resulted in many nose-over landings and broken props. In one morning's flying, the thick mud resulted in some forty propellers being broken.[13]

Fortunately, Allen's earlier visit led to measures to minimize the cadets' discomfort. Colonel Roscoe and Hoare agreed that the Americans should obtain from the IRFC or American suppliers, certain facilities and equipment prior to the cadets arrival in Texas. The camps were to be outfitted with extra blankets and the tents were to be equipped with wooden floors and walls, electrically lighted, and supplied with heating stoves.[14]

*Camp Benbrook, Texas, welcomed Canadians with a snowstorm. Courtesy of Alan Sullivan,* Aviation in Canada, 1917–18.

The cadets quickly discovered that even without the northers the weather was unreliable and subject to wide swings and sudden storms. Unfortunately, the winter of 1917–1918 was unusually wet, with much rain and the occasional snowstorm; calm air was the exception.

A greater problem arose from the lack of completed barracks, sewers, and water facilities. Some units had to sleep in tents that had been rushed to Texas from Canada and proved fairly comfortable. Posted to Camp Hicks, Cadet Herbert Andrews of Regina complained, "This camp is a big place but dusty as hell and the mess is rotten ... It sure is a dreary looking country. We are sleeping in Hangers [*sic*] and there is not a drop of water in the place."[15] Disillusion had set in early.

In spite of these inconveniences, Allen was able to keep the men flying. In one instance, an American squadron arrived at Camp Hicks and was posted to new but unfinished barracks without camp equipment, water, or sewage. Moreover, the squadron's hangars were packed with aircraft still in their crates, without the tools to assemble them. In spite of these obstacles, the Americans displayed typical Yankee ingenuity, and had the airplanes assembled within eight days.

Despite the initial shock created by the norther, it soon became evident that the weather was usually favourable for flying and the cadets were soon racking up a great many hours in the air.

Once back on American soil, the Yankee cadets' irrepressible natures bubbled over. Floyd Lewis recalled that, after spending some time quartered in a hangar, the cadets were rounded up to march the length of the field to put up some tents to be used as quarters. An officer headed up the detail, but as they marched past each of the many buildings en route, a few cadets would disappear until, when the destination was finally reached, only a handful remained. The officer postponed the project until the following day and managed to keep the detail intact by having the men march in front of him.

Cadet Tom Abernethy stated that discipline was non-existent, observing that, "They started a calisthenics formation for us at six in the morning but about the third day the Lieutenant-instructor said, 'If you fellows won't come out for this formation there is no use having it.' And that was the end of that."[16] The cadets became so unmanageable that a marine major had to be assigned to discipline them.

Nor were these hijinks confined to the ground. Once in the air, the cadets — American, British, and Canadian — indulged in all manner of stunts, which, while dangerous, did serve to improve their flying skills.

Cadet Abernethy noted two especially daring cadets who soon mastered the loops, stalls, and standard aerial acrobatics before devising one of their own; an unusually perilous contest. The two cadets would meet in the air and each would then put his plane into a spin and aim for the ground; the one who could spin closest to the ground and beat the other in the coming-out process would be the winner. The contest ended when, "The winner spun right into the ground and a brave, likable boy ended his days after only a few hours of exciting life. His name is well-known today as an air field is named after him [March Field]."[17]

Fortunately, only a few cadets took such extreme risks, although regular flying was too tame for many. These daredevils scorned the regular approach to a landing, preferring instead to spin or side-slip above the airfield, levelling off at the last minute as they went in on their final approach.

Being able to master a forced landing was a prerequisite to obtaining one's wings. Practice in this manoeuvre was sometimes achieved in unorthodox fashion. While landing at school grounds was expressly prohibited, the regulation did not prevent two cadets from landing in a cotton field next to a girl's seminary where they spent the afternoon fraternizing with two of the more lovely inmates. Back at base, the colonel noted their undercarriage, and observed wryly how surprised he was, "That cotton was being grown up in the clouds."[18]

There was no dearth of female companionship for the dashing airmen. The ladies of Fort Worth competed for the attention of the cadets and officers. In 1992, Mrs. C.F.A. McCluer, then ninety-one, recalled the halcyon days when the British and Canadian flyers arrived in Texas:

> We were all excited when we heard that the British and Canadian cadets were coming to Fort Worth. We soon discovered that they would be off-duty on Friday afternoons and many of the girls I knew couldn't wait to get in their cars to drive to town and would ride up and down the streets to see if they could pick up some of the RFC cadets and officers. A lot of the Fort Worth boys were jealous of the British and Canadians as they looked so grand in their uniforms. A lady called Mrs. Galbraith held a list of a group of girls that (she) could call on when the officers were going to hold a dance. We would then go to the officers' club, down on West 7th St., but were always chaperoned. Once the officers had met the girls they would telephone them to invite them to hanger [sic] parties. I used to go to the hanger [sic] parties and always had a good time. There were also a lot of parties at the Riverside Country Club, where it was so lovely to walk from dance floor out onto the veranda, and to sit in the moonlight. Vernon Castle would always be at these parties. He wouldn't dance

but would go up and join the orchestra where he used to play the drums, and I surely do remember his pet monkey, Jeff, beating the drums.[19]

A short time after the dashing cadets arrived in their midst, the welcoming Texas belles unexpectedly turned frosty. The British and Canadian cadets were both puzzled and dismayed at this change in reception. What had happened? Had they breached some obscure rule of Texas etiquette? For over a week, the once sought-after cadets found themselves utterly devoid of female companionship. Finally, the cause of the calamity was uncovered.

Not surprisingly, elements of the American military were not pleased when the arrival of the fly-boys led to an abrupt decline in female attention. They had formerly been the recipients of that same attention now so generously lavished on the airmen. The uniforms of the invaders were part of the problem as they were more attractive and better tailored than those of their American competitors.

A distinctive item of attire separating the IRFC's cadets from the American soldiers was a white band worn on the caps of cadets. Once a cadet had received his wings, the band was removed. An inspired American soldier came up with a solution to their problem. He started a rumour that the white band was issued only to those cadets suffering from venereal disease. Fuelled by jealous American rivals, the rumour spread as rapidly as the bubonic plague in medieval Europe. In the view of the suddenly lonely and libidinous IRFC cadets, the fall-out from the white band rumour was nearly as disastrous.[20]

It did not take long however for the Texan ladies to learn the true reason for the white band and to return to their previous warmth. Inevitably, a few marriages resulted. A Canadian named Vandervoort returned after the war to settle in Texas and marry his sweetheart. He subsequently founded a large dairy in Fort Worth. The Vandervoort dairy continued to operate in Texas for several decades.

Despite the alpha-male rivalry, much good will developed between the British and Canadian airmen and their American hosts. Fort Worth society went all out in making the visitors feel welcome. The officers were invited into exclusive private clubs; various facilities were created by the city for both cadets and enlisted men, and many of Fort Worth's citizens opened their homes to the visitors. A particularly warm relationship developed between the Texans and the Canadians, many of whom shared the western culture of horses, ranching, and the outdoors.

During the Christmas of 1917, petitions poured into division headquarters for permission to entertain some of the IRFC men on Christmas Day. As a result, "Canadians from the Royal Flying Corps headquarters staff were entertained on Christmas day in many of the most prominent homes in Fort Worth while scores of others spent the day with friends they had made since coming to Texas. Half the airmen and HQ staff were granted four day furloughs for the Christmas holidays, while the remaining fifty percent were granted furloughs over the New Year."[21] Many a lonely airman was welcomed into a Texas home for a bountiful Christmas dinner, complete with generous helpings of hospitality.

Shortly after the first anniversary of the IRFC in Canada, the British brass threw a large dinner to celebrate the occasion. *The Toronto Star*'s account captures something of the atmosphere prevailing between the three allies:

> One hundred officers of the Royal Flying Corps and a large number of guests of the American air service drank the health of the King of England and the President of the United States at a dinner Saturday night.... The dinner was to have been given on the anniversary date, January 25, but was postponed in the hope that Brig.-Gen. Hoare might return from Toronto by Saturday. Neither Gen. Hoare nor Lieut.-Col. Roscoe, commander of the fields, was present. Col. Roscoe is in Washington.
>
> The dinner was given at the Fort Worth Club with Major Ballard, commandant of the School of Aerial Gunnery, and the staff [were] ... hosts. Major Ballard ... toasted Brig.-Gen. Hoare. He told of the many difficulties which the general met in the organization of the corps and the wonderful success with which he had met.

In the absence of the general, his brother, Lieut.-Col. G. Hoare, responded.

Lt.-Col. Wanklyn proposed a toast to the American Aviation Service.* He paid high tribute to the American as a flyer. He made it clear that the Canadians were not exactly pleased with the weather conditions. He said they had come here expecting to find a sunny south land, but had been disappointed. He said they had found only a sunny hospitality.... After dinner all went to the River Crest Club for a dance program.[22]

Of all the British and Canadian airmen, Vernon Castle received the warmest reception. Not only had he lived in the United States since 1907, he was a star of Broadway married to an American socialite. While the gallant captain was teaching American cadets how to fly, Irene Castle was starring in silent movies and appearing on the stage. Her husband was always generous with his time and talents both as an airman and as an entertainer. Moreover, his lifestyle was widely approved by Texans. His servant, Walter Ash, had himself joined the IRFC in order to remain close to his captain who, in turn, treated him with consideration and kindness.

In February, Castle was informed that he was being appointed CO of the new camp being built near Beamsville, a small town in the Niagara Peninsula. The Beamsville camp would provide advanced training in combat flying and gunnery. It was a prestigious appointment, but Captain Castle's winning streak was nearing its end.

Ever since his student, A.W. Fraser, had been killed at Mohawk, Castle had insisted his students sit in the safer rear seat while he took the more dangerous front seat. It was this gesture, perhaps more than any other, that endeared the instructor to his students. It typified his courage, unselfish nature, and genuine concern for his students' welfare.

---

* Fred Wanklyn was a debonair, well-travelled graduate of Royal Military College. A native of Montreal and a career soldier, he was awarded the Military Cross in 1915 and was the last commanding officer at 43 Wing in Deseronto. He spent most of his later years in Bermuda.

Above: *Vernon Castle was killed in this crash. Courtesy of Deseronto Archives.* Below: *Vernon Castle's funeral, Fort Worth, Texas. Courtesy of Hastings County Historical Society.*

*Vernon Castle's caisson, Fort Worth, Texas. Courtesy of Hastings County Historical Society.*

On 15 February 1918, Castle was instructing Cadet R. Peters from the American Signal Corps. They were coming in for a landing when a plane took off in front of them. Castle took evasive action, attempting an Immelmann turn in the hope of missing the aircraft and righting his plane in time to land. At a height of only forty-five feet, he must have known it was an impossible manoeuvre. The other aircraft hurtled past, grazing Castle's airplane, which dove straight into the runway with a sickening crash. Cadet Peters, sitting in the rear seat, suffered only shock and a black eye. Castle was lifted, crushed and bleeding, from the aircraft and rushed to the hospital where he died twenty minutes later without regaining consciousness.[23]

He was given a hero's funeral. All other traffic came to a halt as the citizens of Fort Worth turned out en masse to watch the caisson carrying his casket. It was draped in the Union Jack, and drawn by a team of six U.S. Army horses, which proceeded slowly through the city to the train station. A U.S. military band played a dirge while tearful women heaped flowers on the casket and caisson. When the train arrived in New York, hundreds of Castle's friends from the IRFC and Fifth Avenue were waiting. Political dignitaries from both England and the United States, as well as the military and entertainment world, filled the church while hundreds were forced to wait outside. Irene Castle was there, dry-eyed and pale.

The three nations were unanimous in their admiration and affection for Castle. But there were matters on which the allies did not agree. Given that an imperial power was commanding the troops of a former colony on that sovereign nation's soil, it is hardly surprising that friction and tensions developed. How these were resolved would be crucial to the success of the training plan.

# CHAPTER FIFTEEN
## FRICTION BETWEEN THE ALLIES

> The British Empire and the United States will have
> to be somewhat mixed up together in some of their
> affairs for the mutual and general advantage. For my
> own part, looking out upon the future, I do not view
> the process with any misgivings.
> — *Winston Spencer Churchill, British House of*
> *Commons, 20 August 1940*

Despite generally good relations between the British and Americans, the IRFC was in a delicate situation. Americans would find it galling to be taking orders on their own soil from their former colonial masters. Conflict of some sort was bound to arise. The situation was further complicated by the deal made by Hoare, which called for the Americans to provide most of the supplies, including hospital services.

When a "norther" struck, the U.S. military was totally unprepared, having no serge uniforms and only one or two blankets per man. American preparations compared unfavourably to those of the IRFC, which issued four blankets per man and had additional reserve blankets for those struck down by the flu and children's diseases. Not surprisingly, the American troops were swept with disease and flu, overwhelming their medical services, which were unprepared to handle illness on such a scale.

Under the Reciprocal Agreement, IRFC manpower needing medical services were to be treated in American military hospitals by American medical staff. But these units were totally overwhelmed; they were unable to treat even their own men with reasonable promptness. Consequently, some IRFC crash victims did not receive beds and instead were left on stretchers on ward floors.

When he heard of the situation, Allen immediately telephoned his senior medical officer, Major Brefney O'Reilly, who took the first train out of Toronto for Texas, arriving within forty-eight hours. The decisive SMO went directly to the military hospital where he found some of the IRFC's crash cases lying on the floor. He immediately arranged for their transfer to the newly constructed civic hospital in Fort Worth, which had a surplus of beds. He also arranged a lien on some twenty to thirty beds at that hospital for the IRFC's more serious cases. As an emergency measure, Allen arranged that the extra cost be paid by the IMB. The expenditure was eventually refunded by the American War Department.

Overlapping jurisdictions and bureaucratic obtuseness caused some friction. An American MO (medical officer) at one of the aerodromes refused to follow O'Reilly's directive and continued to ship IRFC cases to the overflowing and understaffed military hospital. When confronted by Allen, he advised the major that he took orders only from his U.S. medical chief in Washington and no one else. The resourceful Allen turned to Lieutenant-Colonel Lord Wellesley, IRFC commanding officer at the camp and told him, "Lord Wellesley, you will ensure that all IRFC crash cases go to the Civic Hospital. Put an armed guard on the ambulance if necessary."[1]

The camp MO exploded at this affront to American sovereignty, whereupon Allen replied that he took full responsibility, and, turning to Lord Wellesley, he asked if that was quite clear. Wellesley, realizing the Wing Commander was bluffing, played his role with aplomb. Blessed with height and a commanding presence, the one-time Grenadier Guardsman clicked his heels loudly and barked, "Quite, sir," then, offering Allen his smartest salute, turned sharply on his heel and marched out, boots rapping on the floor. The bluff worked; no armed guards were needed, and IRFC casualties went directly to Civic Hospital. When the crisis subsided, IRFC casualties were transferred back to the military hospital and relations between the two medical services eased somewhat.

In the view of Allen, disputes with the American Medical Corps arose primarily because the U.S. medical and quartermaster services were independent of the U.S. commanding officer and very much a law unto themselves. Any variation of the original scheme agreed to by the U.S. commander was not necessarily accepted by either the medical or the quartermaster service. This often resulted in heated discussions and, occasionally, in serious disputes.

Such a dispute occurred when Allen infringed on the jurisdiction of the U.S. Quartermaster corps major. Under the Reciprocal Agreement, the U.S. Army was to supply forty light trucks; these were essential to keep the JN-4s flying. Three days before the squadrons were due to arrive from Canada no trucks had been received. A railway freight agent offered to let the IRFC have forty similar trucks consigned to U.S. squadrons at Waco, Texas, where the aerodrome was still under construction and the trucks not yet needed. The agent required that Allen provide only a signed receipt for the trucks. Allen knew that waiting for approval from Washington or Hoare would delay the start of training. With some trepidation, he signed for the trucks and awaited the storm; it was not long in coming.

Immediately after requisitioning the trucks, Allen informed the U.S. commanding officer, Colonel Rosco, who took the matter surprisingly well. Despite this, the major in charge of Quartermaster services exploded with rage, charging that the IRFC had hijacked U.S. Army equipment and had done so in U.S. territory. Allen pleaded military urgency and the failure of the U.S. to supply the trucks as agreed. His explanation failed to assuage the irate major. Eventually, the matter was smoothed over by a U.S. captain who had served with Allen's brother in India.[2]

There were also minor incidents arising from profound differences in the attitudes of the two allies towards the First World War or, as it was then called, "The Great War." To most Americans, the "war," meant the "Civil War," — they regarded the Great War as merely a war in Europe.[3] Old Europe was seen as corrupt, imperialistic, and remote from America's ideals of democracy, liberty, individual rights, and the personal realization of success through effort and ability. Europe was seen by Americans as the antithesis of American values.

Consequently, while the Canadians and British saw the war as a life-and-death struggle between freedom and tyranny, requiring all-out effort and sacrifice, the Texas attitude was more a "let's enjoy ourselves" approach to the whole business of training and flying. There was very little urgency in the Texas approach to military matters in general.

Although disputes did arise, generally, the two forces co-operated effectively. For example, although the camps were ravaged that winter by flu and children's diseases, they continued operations throughout an unseasonably wet winter. The medical staff managed to limit death from disease to a mere seven, a considerable achievement for a medically understaffed, hastily constructed military camp without the modern-day advantage of penicillin and sulfa drugs. By the winter of 1917–1918, the population of each camp, not counting HQ staff, numbered approximately 2,000 for a total of more than 6,000 personnel. Seven fatalities due to illness out of 6,000 personnel was considered an admirable achievement.

The original agreement called for the IRFC to train ten squadrons, involving some 300 pilots, plus ground crew, mechanics, and administrative staff in a three-month period ending on 20 February 1918. This timetable was delayed by the contractor's inability to keep to schedule. On 25 March, the last of the ten squadrons left for Europe, but in January 1918, at the request of the American Army, Hoare signed a supplementary agreement which he had deftly manoeuvred to obtain. Under this agreement, which extended the time from 15 February to 15 April, the IRFC would train a further eight American squadrons and approximately 100 additional pilots.

From Hoare's standpoint the deal was critical, enabling him to continue training British and Canadian cadets in relatively mild Texas weather while Ontario remained locked in the grip of an unusually harsh winter. Moreover, during the winter of 1917–1918, the IRFC had lacked sufficient barracks to accommodate all its cadets in the Ontario camps. This situation arose from the IMB's lack of funds. The British Treasury Board refused or was unable to supply the funds needed for constructing the extra barracks. As a consequence, had Hoare not made the supplementary Texas agreement, many cadets would have spent the latter part of the winter in frigid Ontario, sleeping in tents. Tents had been the primary accommodation at Long Branch but had never been utilized during an Ontario winter. The Texas agreement allowed Hoare to move most of his cadets to winter accommodation provided by the Americans. In the meantime, he had to find accommodation for the influx of new cadets coming in for ground training in Canada. This problem he solved in his flexible make-do fashion.

Hoare outlined the problem and his solution in a letter to Charlton dated 22 October 1917:

> The weather is getting bad (we have already had snow at Borden) and there is no doubt we should only get very poor results after November 15th ....
>
> I have large numbers of men under canvass, 500 at the Long Branch Cadet Wing alone. I must house them as soon as possible. Practically all possible existing accommodation has been taken up. To build barracks would be very expensive and besides is impossible as there are no funds. The only solution is to occupy the barracks the 42nd and 43rd Wings are vacating.[4]

Had there not been a supplementary agreement, the cadets sent back to Ontario in mid-February would have spent the remainder of the winter in heated tents.

The supplementary agreement set dates for the arrival of the various squadrons to be trained, which the U.S. Army Signal Corps, unfortunately, was unable to meet. The men did not arrive until just five to six weeks prior to the departure of the IRFC. Despite these problems, the IRFC was able to fully train 408 American pilots, and partially train an additional forty-eight.[5]

Although the Americans, Canadians, and British were intermingled and their relationship, particularly concerning command, was complicated, the plan was a huge success. When the IRFC departed in April 1918, the ten American squadrons as stipulated under the Reciprocal Agreement had been trained and, by the end of March, all ten squadrons had been posted to Europe where, in a short time, they proved themselves excellent pilots. Relations had been so good that many of the Americans were attached in flights to RFC squadrons in Europe.*

---

* The bulk of the American cadets trained by the IRFC had graduated from the nation's most prestigious universities. They were the cream of American youth and learned quickly; they made superb pilots.

During the five months the IRFC was training in Texas, a total of 67,000 flying hours were racked up and 1,960 pilots, including IRFC, Army Signal Corps, and U.S. Naval cadets, were fully or partially trained. In addition, another 4,150 men and 69 officers were trained in various ground trades and skills. Moreover, in spite of the dangerous stunting, flying fatalities made up just 1.88 percent of pilots trained, considered excellent for the times. The Medical Corps was especially effective. Winter weather and inadequate clothing supplies led to an outbreak of flu and children's diseases such as measles, yet only 3 percent of cadets were incapacitated from all medical causes.[6]

The major participants in the plan were fully satisfied with the results. Roscoe, commander of the American operation in Texas, reported to his superiors after the British had departed, making these observations in his official report to General Squire:

> There has of necessity been a great deal of dual control and without the closest cooperation between officers and men of the two services, the situation would have been intolerable. In making the military systems — so different in most respects — to dove-tail and harmonize there may have been a great many unforseen problems, difficulties and petty annoyance which, but for the determination of all concerned to make a success of the reciprocal agreement, must have surely resulted in a great deal of friction.
>
> In obviating this, I desire to express my sincere appreciation of the soldierly qualities and broad vision displayed at all times by the General Officer Commanding Royal Flying Corps.
>
> A smoker and entertainment was given by our officers for the officers of the Royal Flying Corps in the Chamber of Commerce Building in Fort Worth on the eve of their departure. The good fellowship displayed on that occasion was an eloquent attestation of the comradery which existed between the two forces and of the earnestness which actuated all in the tasks before them.

The condition in which the Royal Flying Corps left all buildings, hangars, etc., is worthy of remark. There was simply no fault to be found.[7]

Hoare did not fully reciprocate Roscoe's admiration. Writing to Allen, some years later, he assessed the U.S. officer tartly, "Roscoe was ... incompetent and quarrelsome. I hadn't much to do with him but we ended quite good friends. He was too small and petty a man to bother about. However, no necessity to emphasize this. Better to be friends than enemies. I got him made a C.B.E. after the war."[8] As Hoare made these observations forty-four years after the war, his recollections could be faulty.

Allen served as Hoare's chief administrative officer and was responsible for the implementation of the plan worked out by Hoare and the Americans. Moreover, Allen was the CO in Texas longer than Hoare and took an entirely different view of Roscoe, writing that:

There had been frictions between Canadians and Americans at all levels, and this might have become serious had we not been fortunate in having such a courteous, good tempered, and understanding senior U.S. Officer in Col. Roscoe. Brigadier General Hoare as a fellow cavalry officer always got on well with him as I did when I was in command of the RFC units at Fort Worth from Oct. 1917 to Jan. 1918 [9]

Hoare has received most of the credit for the success of the Texas experiment, but it is clear that other officers were also critical to the plan's success. Hoare acknowledged Allen's contribution when, upon his arrival in Texas, he wrote HQ in London, stating:

I am sending Allen back to Toronto, now that I am here. He has had the brunt of the work during this move and his initiative and common sense in getting this place started and co-operating with the U.S. officers, has been of the greatest value and assistance to me. The move has been a successful one and he deserves the credit.[10]

The importance of the training provided by the IRFC has been noted by many Americans, but perhaps the most perceptive was penned by an elite naval airman who trained at both Toronto and Texas. J. Sterling Halstead, a naval aviator, wrote an assessment of the training program for the U.S. Naval Institute. He concluded his report with these comments:

> As to the contribution made by the detachment sent to the Royal Flying Corps, as a whole, history should record that it collected and absorbed and brought back to the Navy and the legions of Naval Aviators who have been trained and served in both wars, a system of training in a new and fabulous weapons system, incorporating the lessons learned in three years of war by one of the great powers ... a weapons system which has revolutionized the waging of war probably as much as the introduction of the cross-bow, the invention of gun powder or the building of steel ships.[11]

As to the impact of the plan on the air division of the American Army Signal Corps and on the outcome of the war in Europe, forty-four years after the event, Allen observed that:

> It can fairly be reflected that the merits and far reaching effects of this Scheme have never fully been appreciated. Through the scheme the Americans quickly acquired an enormous amount of "know how." Ten Squadrons of the U.S. Army Air Force were within 9 months trained from scratch to readiness to take the field after their pilots had had a few hours flying instruction in combat types of aircraft. They were in fact among the first U.S. Squadrons to engage the enemy.[12]

The last word on Canadian and American cadets goes to Hoare. More pithy and more aware of the frictions between the two military forces than Halstead, Hoare simply told Allen when he reported that the last units had just arrived home (to Canada) from Texas, "Well, we have just got away with it."[13]

The experiment in close co-operation between two great powers had worked well, but could easily have gone awry. Moreover, the IRFC brass now knew that should the war continue past 1918, training pilots during the Canadian winter was eminently practical. While the Texas plan had been underway, another experiment had been taking place in Canada where 44 Wing (North Toronto) was learning to fly in open-cockpit Canucks during one of the worst Canadian winters on record. The results of these winter-flying experiments would have a major impact on the development of aviation in post-war Canada.

While there was some friction between Canadian and American airmen, overall relations were good. The British and Canadian airmen seem to have made a favourable impression on the Texans. Before the United States entered the Second World War, more than 600 Texans travelled to Canada to join Canada's air force. In the spring of 1949, a seventy-man contingent from the RCAF, headed by an air vice-marshal, flew to Austin, Texas, to present a totem pole in memory of the Texan boys who served with the RCAF during the Second World War; a war which the Western world now regards as crucial to the survival of democracy and freedom.[14]

# Chapter Sixteen
## Frostbite Flying: Beating the Canadian Winter

> When the RAF [first] established training squadrons in Canada it was considered so difficult if not impossible to continue flying under the ordinary conditions of winter, that for the winter of 1917–1918 the bulk of the training camps were transferred to the South, only a small number remaining, more as an experiment than anything else.
> — M.R. Riddell, chief engineer, Canadian Aeroplanes Limited, 1919[1]

Hoare made quick decisions and relied on his principal officers to carry out his policies with little or no supervision. This was particularly evident in his decision to continue flight training in Canada during the winter of 1917–1918. As in Texas, he relied heavily on two men to carry out the experiment: Major J. Stanley Scott of Robervale, Quebec, CO of the North Toronto Wing, and F.G. Ericson, chief engineer at Canadian Aeroplanes Limited. (M.R. Riddell replaced Ericson as chief engineer some months after winter flying had been perfected.)

Hoare's decision to keep an entire Wing in Canada to solve the problems of winter flying was based on limited experience. The CO did not arrive in Canada until late January of 1917 and so had never experienced an entire Canadian winter. He appears to have made his decision on the basis of the recommendation of F.G. Ericson plus a single day in the air. He had been flying in late February 1917 and observed, "The conclusion I came to when flying the other day is that there will be many winter days that will be ideal for flying and the snow will only hamper us to a limited extent. When it is below zero [-18°C], I think the cold will be a problem."[2]

Hoare's enthusiasm for Ontario winter flying flagged considerably when the winter of 1916–1917 continued remorselessly into spring. Even in April, winter weather continued to torture Ontario. It was April's chilly, windy weather of snow, sleet, and drizzle that convinced Hoare to abandon training in an Ontario winter and proceed with leases at Ladner and Lulu Island in British Columbia. Once the IMB had signed the B.C. leases, they began laying sewer and water lines — a preliminary step to building another wing.

Despite its mild weather, Hoare had reservations about British Columbia. The area around Vancouver and southern B.C. was heavily forested. This would make the inevitable forced landings and crashes highly dangerous. Moreover, damaged airplanes would be extremely difficult, if not impossible, to recover. Another problem resulted from the greatly extended lines of communications and supply with HQ and Canadian Aeroplanes. Shipping airplanes, parts, and materials would be time-consuming and costly. As telephone communication between B.C. and Ontario was in its infancy, communication between HQ and the staff in British Columbia would be slower and less efficient.

Three months later, Hoare put the B.C. plan on hold in favour of training in Texas while, at the same time, experimenting with winter flying in Ontario. Pilot training would continue on a trial basis at North Toronto, chosen because its winters were milder than those at Borden or Deseronto.

Scott was kept behind to superintend the winter flying experiment at North Toronto while the majority of the Deseronto and Borden Wings decamped for Texas. Winter came early in 1918 when a large snowfall was dumped on Borden in the third week of October. Toronto received its first heavy snowfall in early November. Shortly thereafter, Captain H.V. Ackland took off from Leaside in a JN-4 equipped with wheels and successfully landed in eighteen inches of snow.[3] This sealed Hoare's decision to keep 44 Wing in Canada.

Subsequent experience revealed Hoare's optimism was premature. Scott quickly discovered it was not practical to make wheeled landings in more than six inches of snow. There were too many nose-downs resulting in broken props, smashed tail skids, and collapsed undercarriages. But the decision to fly in winter had been made, leaving Ericson, his

*Experimental winter flying had many problems. Courtesy of Hastings County Historical Society.*

engineers, Scott, and the Repair Park to find solutions in a winter which the meteorological office described as the worst in five years.[4]

Neither Scott nor Allen appear to have shared General Hoare's optimism for winter flying. Allen worried, "We had nothing to go on. The prospect of the 44th Wing sitting on their backsides for months producing no pilots had us scared stiff."[5]

The winter of 1917–1918 can be summed up in one word — brutal. Not only was it bitterly cold, it dumped unusually large amounts of snow on the province, sometimes bringing all traffic to a halt for days on end. With the exception of Toronto, Hamilton, and a few of the larger cities, trucks and automobiles did not operate in Ontario during the winter. The movement of people and goods between cities and towns was by train or, in rural areas, by horse and sleigh. The winter of 1917–1918 was so severe that it frequently brought even those reliable means of travel to a complete standstill.

On Saturday, 12 January, high winds and heavy snow forced most railways to cancel service. From Friday night until the following Wednesday. Only a few main lines managed to keep open.

A CPR train left Toronto for Buffalo on Saturday but got only as far as Islington (now the west end of the city) before returning to Union Station. Travel to Islington normally took about a half an hour, but the train and passengers did not return for a chilly twenty-six hours. At Brantford, a Grand Trunk train was stuck in a huge snowdrift; the crew who battled to clear snow from the track suffered frostbite for their efforts. Travellers were stuck for days, waiting for the lines to clear so that service could resume. By Wednesday, 16 January, all main lines were running, although hours behind schedule. On average, most trains operated from one to three hours late.[6]

Despite its impact on normally reliable modes of transport, the onslaught of snow did not keep the North Toronto flyers grounded. During the previous winter, Ericson had suggested the adoption of skids or skis to Hoare. Hoare requested the engineer have several experimental pairs constructed. The engineers appear to have adopted the general design principles found on Canadian horse-drawn sleds. A number of experimental constructions for the undercarriage were tried before one proved successful. It had to be lightweight but strong enough to withstand the frequent heavy-impact landings made by student pilots.

It was also known to the British that the Russians had used skis as landing gear on the eastern front. However, the Canadian Ericson was more familiar with the Native use of snow shoes, toboggans, and skids to move articles in winter. The early terminology of the IRFC reflects these traditions. The IRFC consistently referred to them as skids or sleds, never as skis.[7]

The pilot making the majority of test flights was Lieutenant Younghusband, who made flights on various types of terrain, including grass, bare ground, sand, and even gravel — all with excellent results. Other pilots were involved in the winter flying program but few proved as skilled as Younghusband. Cadet William Ptolemy was fairly typical, smashing a propeller on 22 December 1917. He did not make a successful landing on skis until 29 January 1918.[8]

By the end of January, Allen was able to report to the Military Directorate in London:

*An early example of skis used for winter flying. Courtesy of Hastings County Historical Society.*

> Skis have really been a great success. Wheels cut up the Aerodrome a lot — resulting in rough surface and many broken Propellers and Tail Skids. Skis tend to flatten out inequalities and to improve the surface. Far fewer Propellers and Tail Skids have been broken since the Wing changed over to skis. There has also been less breakage in undercarriage struts and Fittings. Instructors have been landing outside the Aerodrome without any difficulty.[9]

The efforts of Ericson, his engineers, the Repair Park, and Scott succeeded admirably in overcoming the problems of taking off and landing in heavy snow. But the problem of protecting pilots from frostbite in severe winter temperatures in open-air cockpits remained unsolved. During January, temperatures at 44 Wing dipped to -30°C, but the lows at which the pilots flew their aircraft were well beneath the lowest temperature recorded by the available thermometers (-40°C).

These figures take into account the wind-chill factor, a concept only vaguely comprehended at the time. We now know that an aircraft passing through still air at the Jenny's cruising speed of 100 km per hour when the outside temperature was - 23°C would have a wind-chill temperature of - 44°C.[10]

It is not surprising that the initial attempts to fly Jennies in January resulted in severe frost bite for the pilots. The weather in which the Toronto pilots flew was described in *The Daily Intelligencer* of Thursday, 3 January 1918:

> Lieuts. Armstrong and Stevens went up [at Leaside] on Saturday, the one in the morning and the other about noon. Both had, as a preliminary, coated their face and hands with antifreeze and wore specially thick protective garments. The morning experiment lasted four minutes. Armstrong's nose and hands were frozen and he received immediate attention from the medical officer. In the second case, a flight of 3 minutes was accomplished, the aviator's nose being frozen. The medical officer refused to permit further flights. The thermometer in each case dropped to the lowest limit of record[-40°F, or -40°C].

This experience taught the IRFC that flights could not safely be attempted when ground temperatures fell below a certain point. As Allen observed, "There was no hang-up in training unless the air temperature went lower than -10°F [-23°C.]. Below this temperature there were too many cases of frost-bite to make it worth while."[11]

During January, the pilots of 44 Wing tried various substances and materials to protect themselves from the extreme cold. Vaseline and antifreeze were both tried and found to be ineffective. Used by Arctic sailors and explorers, whale oil proved more effective in preventing frost bite. Unfortunately, the evil-smelling substance had unpleasant effects on the pilot's stomachs, especially when performing spins, dives, and rolls. The risks attendant on a queasy stomach were particularly unpleasant if the pilot was recovering from a night of revelry. There was general relief amongst the flyers when whale oil was replaced with the more effective and less nauseous chamois masks, which covered the entire face except for holes for the eyes and mouth. Long heavy gloves and thigh-length boots completed their protection.[12]

Ironically, while these developments were taking place, pilots at the front were wearing electrically heated suits invented by Lieutenant J. Werden Edwards, a Kingstonian with the RFC in Europe.

According to reports, "By using this invention, the birdmen are able to stay aloft for hours in the bitterest weather."[13] The invention never reached the IRFC (Canada).

Only one obstacle remained to ensure safe winter flying. With proper clothing the men could withstand the bitter temperatures, but what of the aircraft? In the Yukon, men were found to recover more quickly than the sturdiest of horses, would the JN-4 prove as tough and durable as the men who flew them?

Modifications were made to make the aircraft easier to start in the morning and less likely to develop problems during flight. These included: covering the bottom three-quarters of the radiator with felt-covered beaver board, adding anti-freeze to the radiators, and wrapping exposed water hoses with felt and cloth. Some squadrons drained the engines of both radiator fluid and oil every night, heating them up before returning the fluids to the engine in the morning. This made early-morning starting easier, but otherwise made no appreciable difference to the performance of the engine. One mechanical alteration was made and incorporated into new machines. The oil gauge was moved from the rear to the front seat, thereby shortening the connecting pipe between the engine cylinders and the gauge.

The fears that the compression or shortening of the wires caused by the extreme cold might damage the areas where rigging connected with wings or fuselage led to more careful inspection by the ground crew after each flight but no damage was detected. Consequently, the IRFC was able to ascertain that no accidents were attributable to mechanical or structural failures arising from cold-weather flying.[14]

The minor structural changes made to the JN-4 combined with modifications to the flyers' clothing and the precautions of grounding the cadets when the temperature dropped below -23°C overcame what had previously been considered the insuperable problems of flying in a Canadian winter. For example, during one of the coldest Januarys in Ontario's history, Major Scott and the men of 44 Wing could take credit for having got their flyers airborne on twenty-six days of the month. The weather office later reported that the average temperature in January was a full nine degrees below the mean for that month.[15]

In February, the weather was less frigid, but more variable. Despite this, 44 Wing managed to get cadets and instructors into the air on no fewer than twenty-one of the month's twenty-eight days.[16]

During the winter flying experiment, the IRFC's casualty rate appeared to climb even higher. This was dramatically underlined by the death in Texas of Vernon Castle. The press, which had barely tolerated the IRFC's secrecy and aloofness, finally unleashed their pens. The IRFC discovered it could no longer ignore the press and Canadian pubic opinion. Legally, the Imperial Royal Flying Corps answered to the governor general, and no one else in Canada. *The Toronto Daily Star* was having none of this. It took an increasingly critical interest in the legal status of the IRFC and in the welfare of young Canadians serving with that service in Canada.

Hoare and his officers knew they needed the co-operation of the Canadian Militia, particularly in matters of recruitment. This was put at risk if they lost the support of public opinion, and recruiting could decline. Without a continuous supply of cadets, the whole scheme would be an expensive failure.

# CHAPTER SEVENTEEN
## SURVIVING TRAINING

So numerous are the accidents to aviators that
people begin to ask if there are not as many of them
killed when training as in actual combat.
— Mail and Empire, *20 February 1918*

Although training fatalities were high from the very beginnings of the
IRFC's operation in Canada, it was not until the death of Captain Vernon
Castle that the press turned its full attention to the problem. Once alerted,
a few papers proceeded to pummel the IRFC for what many editors and
reporters believed was an unacceptable loss of young men training to be
pilots. *The Toronto Star* was particularly caustic, calling for the Canadian
government to intervene and halt what it regarded as unnecessarily
wasting the lives of the finest young men in the Dominion.

The extent of the problem became clear a few days after Castle's
death when the *Mail and Empire* weighed in with an editorial criticizing
the high number of training fatalities in the IRFC. A loyal supporter of
Prime Minister Borden and his policies, the *Mail and Empire*'s criticism
of the IRFC's training methods was a wake-up call to both the prime
minister and the flying service. Only the most obtuse failed to realize
that the IRFC needed to re-examine its training methods.

Until the death of Castle, English-speaking newspapers in Canada
generally supported the prime minister's policy of letting the British pay
for and run the air training plan in Canada. A prime example of this bias
was *The Intelligencer*, a mid-sized newspaper in the eastern Ontario City
of Belleville. In an editorial following the death of Captain Castle, the
paper was unwilling to accept that there was anything wrong with the
IRFC training plan or that fatalities were too high. The paper quoted the

arguments of Lieutenant-Colonel Charles E. Lee, a spokesperson for the IRFC. Lee argued that an aviator must be taught dangerous stunts. Lee argued persuasively that:

> That they are attended by considerable risk is not to be denied, but it is better to run the risk when the aviator is training than, not knowing how to perform them, to become the certain victim of the first enemy aviator the young flier encounters at the front.... Unless a pilot can turn his machine any way and every way, at any time, in order to manoeuvre for position, all the straight flying in the world will not help when he has to fight. In an encounter between enemy aviators it is the man who can out-manoeuvre the other who wins. The flier who is not used to side-slipping, nose-diving, and other tricks, will be at a serious disadvantage if, when he desires to employ one of them for the first time, he is under enemy fire. The more he has practised these stunts in training the more automatically will he perform them when his life depends upon their execution. Aerial acrobatics are a necessary part of the training of an aviator. It is unfortunate that they demand such a toll in human life but the casualties among our flying men would be ten times as great if they were not instructed in what may look to the ordinary spectator as mere useless showing off."[1]

Privately, some of the IRFC's top officers were seriously concerned at the high number of training accidents and casualties. Both the chief justice and the governor general frequently raised the issue in private conversations with both Hoare and Allen.

The high number of training fatalities can be attributed to several factors. A major cause was the pressing need for pilots at the front. The emphasis was necessarily on numbers trained rather than on safety in training. Another cause was the training process; preparing pilots for dogfights with enemy pilots was an evolving process. Training pilots on ordinary flying manoeuvres had been going on for just a few years, but training in the complicated and dangerous manoeuvres of dogfighting was wholly new. It did not begin until mid-1915 and was still evolving at war's end. A third factor was the youth of the men at the top of the IRFC. Hoare was only thirty-four and his staff officer, Allen, was just twenty-seven. As Thornton Wilder wrote after the war, "There were no grey-haired officers above them." It is probable that older, more cautious officers would have placed greater emphasis on safety and reducing the risks of training the eager youths in their charge. But there were few older officers who knew anything about flying and certainly none with experience in dogfights. Moreover, the veterans returning from the front to instruct the cadets were mere youths themselves. Almost all these veterans had seen the wastage of fighter pilots, but their own survival confirmed their sense of indestructibility and, like their charges, they often lacked both fear and caution.

Hoare and his staff accepted the basic principle of training used in England, which was to get the pilot flying on his own as soon as possible and with a minimum of dual instruction. This principle was seriously flawed and not accepted by the United States naval air arm, which required that all cadets receive a minimum of ten hours' dual instruction before allowing them to fly solo. In the IRFC, no minimum amount of dual instruction was stipulated; it was the job of the instructors to decide when a cadet was ready to go up on his own. According to J.S. Halstead, an American naval officer who trained in Canada, cadets went solo on a maximum of six hours and, in one instance, as little as forty-five minutes.[2]

There is no question that this practice contributed to the high accident rate in Canada. Several cadets crashed on their first solo and at least nine died on these flights. Cadet Vivian Voss learned basic flying at Camp Mohawk. He wrote a book about his experiences in which he captured both the thrill and the terror of that memorable first flight made with no instructor sitting behind to guide the student and, when necessary, to save his skin. Voss's account captures the terror of that first solo:

> At last one morning Lt. Stuart got out of the machine in
> the middle of the aerodrome and said to me, "Vee, you

had better take her up now. I wouldn't send you up if I had not every confidence in you. (The usual formula! I thought.) Hold her straight while you are taking off, and then climb slowly till you reach a safe height. Then bring her round very slowly to the back of the hangars. You need only make one circuit. Well off you go!"

While he was talking, my heart was gradually sinking. By the time he had finished, it was in my boots. I hoped he did not notice how my teeth were chattering as I climbed over into the pilot's seat. Things looked strange from the back seat and the nose of the machine seemed so far away — then I opened the throttle. I managed to take off pretty well. I had a horrible feeling that this big thing was running away with me. She swayed a bit as we got into the air, and I kept her straight as we climbed slowly for several minutes. I was thrilled with a sense of great adventure on this first solo flight. After a while, when I thought I had reached a safe height, I made a very gradual turn. It was all very well banking steeply when there was an instructor in the back seat, but not quite so well when one was absolutely alone up in the air. It seemed safer now to make a gradual turn with less bank. I flew round to the back of the hangars and then made another gradual turn. When I got her near the hangars, I shut off my engine. She seemed to be sinking so rapidly that I was afraid of hitting the hangars and so "gave her the gun" [opened the throttle], till she was over the hangars.

Now I shut off again and began gliding down, but although the aerodrome was large, I was too high now to land on it, and realising that I was going to overshoot it, gave her the gun once more and made another circuit. The same thing happened the second time. The third time I shut off some distance from the hangars, and this time, got into the aerodrome. But my fear of stalling the machine made me land it too fast and she ran for a long distance on her wheels, finally running into a bush.

This worried me very little. I was delighted to have the first solo safely behind me. It had never occurred to me how comfortably solid and secure the earth could feel under one's feet.[3]

Voss was in the prime of his youth and had benefited from several hours of dual instruction. His recounting of that first solo flight vividly illustrates the dangers in getting cadets airborne too quickly.

While academically gifted, Voss was not a natural pilot. But even gifted pilots were critical of the IRFC policy of getting cadets flying on their own so quickly. Alan McLeod, a natural-born flyer, was fearless in the air, he nevertheless complained in writing about the lack of dual instruction.[4]

Writing of his training experience in Canada some years after the war, U.S. naval officer J.S. Halstead believed the major reason for the large number of crashes was the lack of dual instruction, stating:

> The principal reason for the large number of crashes was insufficient dual instruction. Whether this insufficiency was due to lack of instructors or a studied policy based on the theory that it was more economical ... was hard to determine.... In any event the time was too short.[5]

Another cause was the unreliability of the OX-5 engine, which had a soft camshaft and tended to quit or lose power unexpectedly, forcing the cadet to crash-land. Fortunately, the aircraft tended to fold around the pilot, often allowing the flyer to emerge with only minor injuries. However, anyone sitting in the front seat was at greater risk. If the plane fell into the ground or buildings, the man in the front seat was usually killed or seriously injured.* The IRFC had a strict maintenance policy but it could not eliminate the basic weakness of the OX-5 engine.

---

* See Chapter 6 for a detailed examination of the strengths and weaknesses of the OX-5 engine.

Unaware there might be a better system of instruction, Hoare and his staff concentrated on making the training program more thorough. In the fall of 1917, the commander made plans to open a new camp to house the School of Aerial Gunnery in order that graduating cadets would be better prepared offensively when they faced the enemy in battle. Initially, the Gunnery School consisted of three squadrons and operated out of Camp Borden. In November 1917, the school moved with the rest of Borden to Texas. Hoare planned to resume gunnery training in the spring at a new camp where cadets could get practice using the most advanced methods then in use in England. He selected a site near the town of Beamsville, located approximately forty kilometres south of Hamilton. The three-hundred-acre site was close to Lake Ontario; a distinct advantage as the corps had learned that firing over water made it easier to see where the bullets were actually striking.

Hoare's decision to locate at Beamsville was influenced by the need to find the warmest location possible. He was already looking ahead to the winter of 1918–1919, optimistically convinced that the North Toronto Wing would prove the feasibility of winter flying. On 22 October, Hoare wrote to Charlton in London advising the Air Directorate of his financial problems and his arrangements to expand the number of training squadrons:

> To cope with next year, I have got an excellent site in the warmest part of Canada, short of going west, where I will get a more complete [gunnery] school going in the spring. It is at Beamsville near Hamilton in the peach growing district. I shall require at least 50 machines there.[6]

Construction of the Beamsville camp got underway in the fall of 1917. In early November, some 300 carpenters arrived to erect nine hangars and various buildings, including: quartermaster's stores, blacksmith shop, ice house, gunnery office, guard house, latrines, storage depots, office and administrative buildings, and buildings for coal and wood storage, as well as one for photography. As the IMB was short of money, no barracks were built and ads were placed in the local newspaper for rental accommodations for the officers. Cadets and mechanics were to be housed in tents until the fall. The camp officially opened on 1 April 1918, when the gunnery school returned from Texas. Beamsville's first CO was Major F.M. Ballard, a British officer sent specifically to set up the new school.

Beamsville differed from the camps at Borden and Deseronto in terms of its proximity and convenience to both Toronto and Hamilton. At Beamsville, members of the RAF could take advantage of the street railway system to travel to Toronto or Niagara Falls. It took some time to travel to Hamilton, but from there the journey to Toronto was cheap and took only an hour. If an officer or cadet at Beamsville had a weekend pass, he could take the radial tram to Toronto, just an hour or two by tram but light years distant in its diversions and entertainment.

A decision was made in March to open an armament school in Hamilton. Its purpose was to thoroughly train cadets in air weaponry. This would take pressure off the No. 4 School of Military Aeronautics. When word got out that the IRFC was looking for premises, the Canadian Westinghouse Company patriotically offered the use of a large factory (8,808 square feet), together with the surrounding grounds; all at no cost. The Hamilton Golf Club then offered the school the use of its nine-hole golf course, which conveniently adjoined the factory. Captain J.C.C. Afleck, OC of the new school, was quick to accept.[7]

With the site for the school determined, the IMB and Royal Engineers moved to convert the factory for the use of the cadets and instructors. Gunnery ranges were built and equipped and alterations were made to the interior of the factory, providing for lecture rooms, workshops, and an armoury. A section of the building was modified into a small hospital. Renovations began in May and were complete by mid-June. On 20 June, the Armament School was able to move into its new quarters. By the summer of 1918, the officers and staff at the school totalled eighty-two, of which fourteen were women. During its operation the school turned out an average of 400 students a month.[8]

The course was four weeks in duration and dealt thoroughly with both the practical and theoretical aspects of the Vickers and Lewis machine guns, as well as with aerial bomb sights, bombing, and the mathematical principles involved when synchronizing gears with propellers. The most important of the theoretical training involved the mathematics of calculating how to aim a gun from a moving aircraft at another moving object such as trains, boats, balloons, and other aircraft.

The Armament School operated in close co operation with the Gunnery School at Beamsville. Their proximity to each other expedited the transfer of both theoretical and practical information. Theory could be put into practice at Beamsville where the applied results could be immediately transferred to the staff and officers at Hamilton. The principles of deflection sights were taught in Hamilton, but their practical application took place at Beamsville. This implementation took many forms: shooting at banners towed by other aircraft, firing at fast-moving armoured boats racing across Lake Ontario, and firing at full-sized aeroplane silhouettes mounted on rafts. Camera shooting was also employed.

Despite these advantages, the Beamsville camp had its problems. Hoare found a surprising lack of discipline, writing to the air ministry that, "Beamsville does not seem to be all that is to be desired … it was reported to me that the Fire Gong has been destroyed by being used as a target for revolver practice."[9]

Hoare, who inspired leadership and an esprit de corps, did not tolerate sloppiness in either discipline or performance. Major Ballard was the camp CO and therefore the shoddy behaviour was his responsibility. Within three months, Ballard had been returned to the front, replaced as CO by Lieutenant-Colonel B.S. Huskisson, DSC (Distinguished Service Cross). The new CO had a brilliant record, serving first with the RNAS and then with RAF for a total of three and a half years, much of it at the front.[10]

The summer of 1918 also saw major improvements to camp facilities. In anticipation that the war would continue into 1919, the IMB obtained financial approval to build sufficient barracks to replace the tent accommodations at Long Branch and Deseronto. Construction of barracks and new hospital buildings began at Deseronto and Long Branch in mid-summer and were completed that fall.[11] The YMCA also opened a comfort station on the outskirts of the Long Branch camp.

In addition, further changes were made to the training facilities. Besides the Gunnery School at Beamsville and the Armament School in Hamilton, the Leaside camp was converted to a new and advanced Artillery Co-operation School.

In an attempt to build public support for the IRFC and to offset the criticism resulting from the numerous fatalities, Captain Seymour kept the press informed of training improvements, sending out press releases to any newspapers of consequence. Even small newspapers received detailed press releases similar to the following:

> The Artillery Co-operation School at Leaside just completed is one of the finest anywhere. There are three groups of seven batteries of miniature artillery, and seven targets to each group. All the targets are connected by telephone with the squadrons. The batteries fire at the targets, the pilot flies over and observes the shot, and directs the artillery fire. In addition, there are two big sand tables with 13,000 feet of electric wire like a net work [with 1,360 electric light bulbs, each of which simulated a shell burst]. The tables are 40 X 20 feet, and are miniatures of the battle front. To the wires are attached electric bulbs. Above the tables on an elevated platform 20 cadets can work simultaneously, each with a wireless apparatus. The operator at the switches flashes the electric bulbs, which correspond to shell fire [there were 80 enemy batteries], and the cadet sends his wireless message to the artillery and directs the fire.[12]

Although these improvements added to a cadet's skills, they had little impact on the number of training fatalities, which remained disturbingly high.

Hoare did not normally grant press interviews but privately both he and his staff officer were concerned at the high casualty rate. They had already implemented a few safety measures, such as requiring flyers to wear safety belts to prevent them falling from their airplanes. In the summer of 1917, as casualties grew, they introduced the first systematic flying regulations in Canada.

These required that flyers not take off until a signaller with a flag gave the go-ahead. When an aircraft was coming in for a landing, no other machine was allowed to take off until the other machine had landed safely. Aviators in the air had to keep at least one hundred yards away from each other or at least 200 to 300 feet above one another. Windsocks were made mandatory at all aerodromes so that any pilot could easily determine the direction of the wind. Henceforth, he could take off and land only if he was going into the wind. Moreover, a thorough inspection of each airplane was mandatory before it could be taken up. Every aircraft had a mechanic specifically responsible for each airplane's air-worthiness and only he could give the plane clearance to be flown.[13]

Despite these precautions, fatalities continued at an unacceptable rate. Late in 1917, Hoare and Allen decided to send one of their most capable officers to England to study the latest training methods. The officer selected was Lieutenant-Colonel Arthur Kellum Tylee, regarded by Hoare as the most indispensable member of his staff.

Tylee was born in Lennoxville, Quebec, but lived for a decade in Boston, graduating from the Massachusetts Institute of Technology in 1907. He later returned to Quebec as a heavy machinery agent for an American company but, shortly after the outbreak of the war, enlisted in the Canadian Militia as a second lieutenant, later transferring to the RFC. In February 1917, Captain Tylee was posted to Canada, serving initially as squadron leader of No. 81 CTS at Borden, being promoted in September to wing commander of the Borden station. Except for a few hundred mechanics and maintenance crew, the cadets and staff of the Borden Wing were moved to Texas in mid-November 1917. Tylee could thus be spared from his administrative duties and was sent to England to study their training methods.

While there, he learned of a radically new method of training. Developed by Major R.R. Smith-Barry, this system caused a transformation in RFC training methods. Prior to Smith-Barry, flying instruction depended on the whims and temperament of the instructor. There was no systematic step-by-step procedure, no comprehensive theory of flight, nor any agreed-upon explanation of how controls worked, merely one or two accepted principles; the most noteworthy being to get the aspiring pilot flying on his own as speedily as possible where he would learn by doing. The mysteries of flying were not then fully understood.

In July of 1916, Smith-Barry was posted to France with No. 60 Squadron, then one of the few fighting squadrons in the RFC. When he returned to England in December with experience in the development of air fighting on the Western Front, he was given command of the training squadron at Gosport. It was here that he developed his system of training, a step-by-step process whereby the pupil learned the hitherto mysterious principles of flight and how to apply them. It quickly came to be known as the Gosport System. A School of Special Flying to teach the system to instructors commenced at Gosport in August 1917, under the command of Major Smith-Barry. Pamphlets explaining the system were printed by the War Office to assist both instructors and students.

The gospel that Smith-Barry preached was, in the words of one of his instructors, that:

> The aeroplane was a nice-tempered, reasonable machine, that obeys a simple honest code of rules at all times and in any weather. And by shedding a flood of light on the mysteries of its control [the instructor] drove away the fear and the real danger that existed for those who were flying aeroplanes in the blackest ignorance even of first principles.[14]

Gosport revolutionized the training of combat pilots. Not only did it turn out much better pilots, it dramatically lowered training fatalities. Incredibly, although the Gosport School was established in August 1917, no mention of it was sent to the organization in Canada. Considering that by that time the Canadian organization was sending approximately 100 pilots a month to England for final training and that these pilots had to be retrained in the Gosport System, this oversight was incredibly inefficient. Particularly in view of the achievement of Hoare and his staff who, by December 1917, had doubled Canada's output of pilots to 200 per month for overseas service. Despite this achievement, the Military Command in London failed to advise Hoare of the new system. It was a costly mistake, as was demonstrated by the success attendant on RAF (Canada) immediately following its implementation of the Gosport System in the spring of 1918.

An example of the time lost in training can be seen in the training of Cadet Malcolm Plaw MacLeod. MacLeod had completed two years of engineering at the University of Toronto when he joined the IRFC in late May 1917. After completing the standard curriculum, he spent August through October instructing beginning pilots. By November he was as well-trained as many of those being sent to the front. He continued flying in Canada until February 1918, at which time he was sent overseas for final instruction.

When he arrived at No. 1 Training School in England, MacLeod had already amassed over ninety-two solo hours and completed 141 landings. Rather than spending two or three weeks learning to fly high-powered scout airplanes, he was put through the entire Gosport System. In effect, much of his training in Canada was not necessary as he was taught to fly using the new system. His training in England lasted from February until mid-August; a total of six months, during which time he flew Camels, Avros, a Sopwith Pup, and various SE 5s. He was commissioned a full Lieutenant on 13 August 1918.

Although he had lost an additional six months in retraining, MacLeod undoubtedly improved his skills. Sent to France to join No. 41 Squadron where he flew SE 5s, he quickly proved his value, qualifying as an ace by shooting down five aircraft and two balloons in just three months. For his achievements, he was awarded the DFC and the Belgian Croix de Guerre.[15] Yet the fact remains that if MacLeod had initially been trained under the Gosport System, he could have been fighting in France five to six months earlier. Equally important, had Gosport been implemented as soon as it was proven in England, Canadian deaths from training accidents would have declined and the lives of many excellent pilots would not have been lost. The failure of the directorate of Air Organization to communicate with Hoare resulted in the unnecessary loss of fine young men both at the front and at the training schools of Canada.

When Tylee returned from England in March 1918, he brought copies of the booklet printed by the War Office entitled *General Principles of Teaching Scout Pilots*. When Hoare returned from Texas two weeks later and read the pamphlet, he immediately grasped its import and wasted no time implementing the "Gospel according to Gosport." The new system was to be taught immediately to the instructors at Armour Heights and extended as quickly as possible to all wings engaged in flight training. The school opened in late April and was named the School of Special Flying. By July, the school had a staff of twelve fully trained Gosport instructors and was turning out graduates to teach the revolutionary principles to cadets graduating from the standard program.

With the implementation of the Gosport System, casualties declined dramatically, dropping in a few months from 5 percent of pilots under training to just 3 percent. Once it became clear how effectively the new system was reducing fatalities, Hoare wrote to the secretary of the Air Ministry in London, offering a solution to the communication problems of the RAF: "I think that in the past there has not been sufficient information sent out regarding training methods, alterations in graduating tests, etc. If some officer of the Training Staff could be made responsible for keeping us fully informed monthly, it would lead to greater efficiency."[16]

The statistics show that by comparing the number of hours flown with the number of fatalities, the rate of Canadian fatalities was roughly equal to that of the United Kingdom. The statistics and Seymour's cogent argument were effective. Many English-language newspapers in Canada printed Seymour's press release. *The Vancouver Daily Sun* headed its coverage with the reassuring message, "Few Casualties to Flying Cadets." In Barrie, *The Northern Advance* ran a similarly reassuring message. The heading claimed, "Canadian Flying Casualties Light."

The press release did not include statistics from the earlier period when fatalities had been disturbingly high nor did it mention that the lord chief justice of Ontario, the governor general, and the chief of the Canadian general staff, had all been concerned by the high fatality rates. That period was now over and Seymour wisely chose his statistics from the recent past when the numbers had greatly improved.

Seymour had an advertiser's knack for dramatizing statistics in a manner that would impress the general public as the following excerpt demonstrates:

> It will also be noted that the above flights in Canada cover approximately … thirty-four times around the

globe; thus we have one fatality for 116,280 miles or five times around the globe. The conclusions to be drawn from the above figures are so evident that no further explanation is required.[17]

Hoare and Allen quickly realized they had chosen a man who could not only work with the press but knew how to put a positive spin on a difficult subject. Seymour knew how to persuade.

*The Toronto Star* did not print Seymour's press release, but it did back off the casualty issue. A more important political issue now absorbed its attention. The peoples' paper was now aiming its typewriters at eliminating the British-run Imperial Royal Air Force altogether, arguing the need for a Canadian-run air force, a cause which it believed an increasing number of Canadians supported, a cause Joe Atkinson sincerely believed in and felt he could win.

It was true that, during all of 1917 and well into 1918, fatalities had been disturbingly high both in total numbers and in relation to the number of hours flown. However, during August through to the end of October, the impact of the Gosport System of training began showing up in the statistics; the average number of fatalities fell to just 5.3 deaths per month from the rate of 12.14 that had prevailed during the first seven months of 1918. Under the Gosport/Armour Heights System, training deaths had fallen by more than 50 percent. A more accurate measurement of the improvement in training safety was the number of hours flown per fatal accident. Prior to the full impact of the new training methods, the average number of hours flown per fatal accident ran in a range of 1,500 to 2,000 hours for each fatality. By October of 1918, the Gosport System had lowered fatalities dramatically; to just one fatality for every 5,300 hours flown.[18] Had the war continued, fatality rates would have almost certainly continued their decline.

# CHAPTER EIGHTEEN
## PUMMELLED BY TYPEWRITERS

> I strongly advise you not to fight the press, but to
> conciliate and make use of it; otherwise you will be
> set upon by masked men with poisoned weapons,
> and they will do you to death.
> — *Chief Press Censor Chambers to Allen, 28
> February 1918*[1]

Given the autonomy of the Imperial Royal Flying Corps within Canada
and its obsession with secrecy, a conflict with the Canadian press was
inevitable. Both the British cabinet and the generals at the Imperial Air
Board were fully aware that this situation was rife with potential difficulties
for the British government and particularly for the IRFC in Canada.

A delicate problem arose from the fact that the IRFC was training
the cream of Canadian youth in a highly dangerous activity, one leading
to numerous accidents and often death. It was inevitable that some
elements of the Canadian press would be offended by the IRFC's many
infringements on Canadian sovereignty. Unfortunately for the IRFC,
the champion of those picking up the cudgels of Canadian sovereignty
was Joseph Atkinson, publisher of *The Toronto Daily Star*. Once the
IRFC's immunity from Canadian law came to Atkinson's attention, he
proceeded to use his newspaper's massive circulation to challenge the
force's autonomy within Canada. By the summer of 1918, Atkinson
and *The Star* were challenging the very existence of the British Force in
Canada, arguing for a separate and distinctive Canadian air force and an
end to a British-controlled flying corps in Canada.

As *The Star*'s campaign got underway, an already-sensitive situation
was exacerbated by the attitude of British officers who treated all

TRFC matters as subjects of the greatest secrecy and were not used to accommodating the press. This unwillingness to divulge information, combined with barely concealed contempt for the press, alienated many reporters and influenced their coverage of fatalities; some of which were legitimate targets of criticism.

Initially, the British military command had been reluctant to participate in an operation contrary to the direction in which relations with the Dominions had been evolving for over four decades. They had only proceeded with the training plan when Prime Minister Borden gave his blanket assurance that the Canadian government would fully cooperate and that his government had no reservations as to the operation of the British force on Canadian soil. The military situation on the Western Front had finally forced the hands of the British Air Board and they were forced to go ahead because Borden had no intention of Canada operating and sharing in what Borden perceived as the prohibitive cost of an air-training scheme.

A minor conflict between the officers of the RAF in Canada and the Dominion's judicial system revealed RAF (Canada)'s unwillingness to comply with Canadian civil authority. It arose over the theft of a Model T Ford by a member of the Deseronto camps from the nearby town of Napanee.

Apparently some cadets, lacking a convenient means of transport back to camp, decided to "borrow" a new Model T Ford from Centre Street in Napanee. This occurred in the early evening of 25 April 1918. Some days later the automobile was found parked on the outskirts of Camp Mohawk. To Napanee Chief Constable F.W. Barrett, it was clear that the automobile had been used several times, probably with the complicity of the camp's military police.

Barrett was determined to find and arrest the culprits and enlisted the aid of U.M. Wilson, crown attorney for Lennox and Addington County. Wilson put pressure on the camp's officers to turn the miscreants over to the civil authority. The crown attorney wrote to Camp Mohawk's adjutant, Captain Barnsdale, as follows:

> There is unmistakable evidence on the ground where
> the car was found that the car had been used several

times subsequently to Thursday night last and surely not without knowledge of your military police. We do not wish to have any clash with the military authorities here while it can possibly be avoided but conditions are such that the civil authorities must assert the supremacy of the law even among members of your Corps.[2]

As events unfolded, it became clear the OC of the camp was not about to co-operate with the Canadian civil authority. The chief constable had located the stolen car on the south side of Camp Mohawk near the train tracks. A lap rug, bearing the name of R.L. Wright, had been stolen and there was evidence that the gasoline tank had been filled at least once. The few garages in and around Deseronto and Napanee were checked and all claimed not to have sold gas for the new Ford since it had been stolen.* Barrett and Wilson could only conclude that the gasoline had been obtained at the RAF camp, logically concluding the military police were aware the vehicle had been on camp property and knew who had been driving it.

Captain Barnsdale stonewalled the civil authority, claiming that a thorough investigation had been conducted and that he had been "unable to obtain any information that would lead me to suspect any one of this Unit to have been complicated [implicated] in the stealing of the Ford car in question."[4]

W.M. Alkenbrack, a long-time MP for the riding, claimed that both Wilson and Barnsdale knew very well who had stolen the car, but "The prospects of the RAF handing some culprit over to a boondocks Crown Attorney were dim indeed."[5]

The incident demonstrated where the power lay in any dispute between the RAF and Canadian civil authority. Moreover, it demonstrated that RAF officers were not disposed to co-operate with that authority. It is unlikely the culprits involved went unpunished. The RAF did not welcome clashes with the civil authority and it can be assumed that those responsible suffered some form of punishment. As far as the RAF was concerned, the stolen car

---

* In 1917 there were less than 200,000 vehicles in all of Canada or one car or truck for every forty persons.[3]

fiasco was an unfortunate incident best managed by minimizing conflict with the Canadian civil authority. The less said by the RAF the better. The press did not get wind of the incident and, had the civilian authorities not retained the correspondence, the incident would never have surfaced.

Barnsdale typified the attitude of the British military, which emphasized secrecy and felt itself under no obligation to appease the press. When Cadet Vernon Stoddard of New Glasgow, Nova Scotia, was accidentally shot by another cadet, Barnsdale refused the press any particulars. The newspapers only become aware of the shooting when Stoddard was taken to the Belleville General Hospital. Stoddard died a few hours later, which led to an autopsy. As the autopsy was open to the public, local newspapers were able to get a few details. Barnsdale refused all comment; an approach that led to local speculation as to the truth of the accident and further soured relations with the press.[6]

Reflecting back on the conflict that developed between the RAF and Toronto newspapers, Allen explained why they had handled the press so inadequately. He quoted the Canadian press censor, Colonel Chambers, who wrote, "The average newspaper man on this side of the Atlantic is accorded very much more freedom and is in the habit of asserting privileges etc., an attitude which tended to require the RFC to give an account of its policies and actions."[7]

This attitude was one which Allen admitted the RAF could not subscribe to for reasons of military secrecy. However, he countered, the RAF was willing to allow the Dominion and provincial governments to fully investigate every aspect of their operation.

There had been little criticism of the IRFC/RAF in Canada until the winter of 1917–1918. But the death of Vernon Castle in the middle of February focused the attention of the press on the high number of training fatalities. There was a spate of criticism in several Toronto newspapers, including the *Mail and Empire, The Globe,* and a particularly searing editorial by *The Toronto Daily Star*, which quoted various sources damning the IRFC for poor maintenance of its aircraft. What made the criticism particularly devastating was the statement of a returning RFC officer who told *The Star* that aircraft maintenance in France was far more thorough than that performed in Canada.[8]

As a result of this criticism, Colonel J. Earnest Chambers, chief press censor for Canada, called a conference with the press to discuss the IRFC. Following the conference, Chambers wrote to Allen outlining the grievances of the press. One reporter complained of the Imperial Royal Flying Corps:

> They appear to think that as they are Imperial Officers administering a branch of the Imperial Services in Canada that their actions are entirely beyond criticism and beyond the reach of Canadian laws and Canadian institutions. This not withstanding that the lives of young Canadians are in their charge. When these gentlemen are asked for news they seem to take pleasure in refusing it.[9]

The attitude was common among many British officers who, unlike Hoare and Allen, held both the press and Canadians in low regard. Lieutenant-Colonel Burke was not untypical when he wrote of Canadians, "There are a number of men who would make good pilots but only a small proportion … would make officers."[10] Burke thought Canadians lacked the character and breeding to make "gentlemen" and recommended the Canadian flyers be made sergeant-pilots.

This assumption of superiority grated on the democratic attitudes prevalent among both Canadian and American cadets. No one in Canada was more egalitarian than North American newspaper reporters, particularly those working for the liberal *Toronto Star*, a paper that reflected Atkinson's view that you earned your position by hard work and achievement.

Chambers wrote to Allen on 28 February setting out the position of the Canadian government in dealing with the press. He also explained why the IRFC was held in such poor esteem by elements of the Toronto press:

> I think I gave you some idea of the somewhat delicate relationship which exists between the press censorship authorities and the Toronto press. There is a certain legal authority to take drastic action, behind the press

censorship system, but the policy of the Government of this service is to abstain as far as possible from invoking the law, and to all effects and purposes the press censorship as administered depends entirely upon the cordial and loyal co operation of the press.[11]*

A few days later, the chief press censor sent a copy of his letter to Gwatkin with the comment that, "Unless an improvement takes place in the feelings of the Toronto press towards the RFC that an injury will be done to the service and to the Country."[12] In his earlier letter, Chambers gave Allen the best advice he would receive on solving the problem, suggesting, "I really think that if you could appoint some discreet young officer of your Corps to act as a medium of communication between your staff and the press useful results would be obtained."[13] Fortunately, Allen and Hoare took Chambers's advice and appointed Captain Murton Seymour as the IRFC's first press officer.

As a Canadian, Seymour understood local sentiment and had the added advantage of being well spoken and persuasive; he proved an excellent choice for what proved a difficult job. Seymour kept the contagion from spreading beyond *The Toronto Star.*

The Royal Air Force came into official existence on 1 April 1918. Unfortunately, the new force contained certain provisions that went against Canadian values. In the new force, graduating pilots would not necessarily become officers. The RAF created a new class of cadets, men who did not have the education or aptitude to qualify as officers, implying they did not meet the standards of a British gentlemen, and therefore would be classed as B cadets and receive pay of two dollars daily. Those who qualified as A cadets would receive $1.18 a day plus a $0.95 flying allowance. The B class received no flying allowance during training. When they had qualified for their wings, they became sergeant-pilots and received significantly less pay than a second lieutenant.

---

* *The Toronto Star* reported that the government of Newfoundland had invoked the Emergency Measures Act to shut down *The Daily Star* in St. John's for printing articles that hampered the operation of the Conscription Act in that country.[14]

*The Toronto Star* seized on these distinctions weighing in with an editorial which caustically observed, "It is understood that the distinction [between A and B classes] is one which does not at all appeal to Canadian sentiment."[15]

In 1917, the Russian Army had ordered a large quantity of blue serge cloth from the British to be used in manufacturing uniforms for its military officers. The collapse of Russia in the fall of that year left the British cloth industry encumbered with an estimated million square yards of unsold material. The pragmatic Brits lost no time in deciding this material would be ideal for the uniforms of the new air service. In Canada, those members of the IRFC who had purchased or already ordered the green uniforms could continue to wear them but any new uniforms would be made from blue serge. Thus was born the tradition that RAF uniforms would be blue.

*The Toronto Star* continued its role as the watchdog and protector of young Canadians serving in the IRFC. Any perceived abuse of these rights brought a swift response from the ever-vigilant editors and reporters at *The Star.*

The first of these incidents arose when three cadets stationed at Deseronto interpreted the contract transferring them from the IRFC to the RAF, to mean that they were signing up for four more years and not just for the duration of the war. Unfortunately, the wording of the contract was ambiguous and easily misinterpreted. *The Star* devoted much ink to this latest transgression of Canadian rights, under the heading, "'Signing Up' in the Royal Air Force":

> The young American cadets training in the Royal Air Force at Deseronto interpret the new contract they, and all the others, are now required to sign as meaning that they tie themselves up for a straight four year period in a permanent service.... It is said that they are sending a protest to Washington asking President Wilson to interest themselves in the matter.
>
> Thousands of young Canadians are in the air force.... They are in the service because a war is on;

many of them are boys half through their schooling and meaning to complete their education if they survive their adventure. It never entered into their calculations that if they volunteered in this war service they would be conscripted into a permanent Imperial Air Force. The Government should look into this.[16]

Seymour moved decisively to staunch the flow of critical ink, granting *The Star* an interview, which it published the next day. The young press officer stated unequivocally that the contract did not mean another four years but merely to the end of the war. Seymour's frankness and charm defused the incident. While *The Star* accepted his explanation and printed the full content of the interview, it still managed to jab its sharp pencil in the eye of RAF (Canada), suggesting the Canadian government should be involved in RAF matters when Canadians were involved.

Seymour had more difficulty defusing a controversy that arose when a senior RAF officer made a judgment which reinforced the view of British officers as insensitive and/or indifferent to Canadian public opinion. A seventeen-year-old Canadian cadet had failed to make the cut as a pilot and was recommended for discharge by Lieutenant-Colonel Tylee, OC of Training. Unfortunately, an administrative officer at HQ reversed that decision and ordered the underage cadet to report for service as an air force mechanic. This action caught the attention of *The Star*'s editorial staff who launched a series of broadsides against the IRFC.

In the meantime, the officer who had ordered the demotion of the young cadet offered a defence that managed to offend as many Canadians as possible, blithely explaining that, "We are trustees for the Imperial Government, which is spending the money in Canada and we must have something to show for the money which we spend here.... In the course of his instruction as a pilot the cadet was fully taught the mechanism of the aeroplane and he is a fully trained mechanic now. I think it would surprise you to know that the cost of the training which pilots receive runs to $10,000 or more."[17]

Shortly thereafter, the RAF beat a strategic retreat on the issue of the underage cadet. On 1 June, Seymour released a short statement to the effect that, as Cadet Argot was underage, he would not be forced to serve as a mechanic but would be released from military service.

Atkinson had sensed a growing support in his readership for the idea of a Canadian air force. He was always quick to spot trends in public opinion and, when they coincided with his values, to take the lead in championing that opinion in the pages of his newspaper. Canadian military accomplishments at the Somme, Ypres, and especially the victory at Vimy Ridge had led to an increasingly confident nation; a nation finding a separate identity attached to, but not subsumed by, the British Empire. Atkinson would lead only when he believed his readership would support his cause.[18] He correctly sensed that Canadians were increasingly finding their identity within Canada and, while some rival papers disagreed with his criticism of the RAF, few newspaper editors attacked his call for a truly Canadian air force.

Atkinson's assessment of the public mood was reinforced when, five days after *The Star*'s editorial, *The Globe* came out strongly in support of a Canadian air force. *The Globe* began its argument by first acknowledging that the British War Office had spent vast sums of money on the aviation camps, factories, and training programs. Having outlined the case for a continuance of the present program it turned to the arguments for an independent service, pointing out that, "The young manhood of Canada has rewarded it [the RFC] with a special enthusiasm for the air service." According to *The Globe*, so much so that "At least forty percent of the members of the Royal Flying Corps in England and France come from the Dominion, and Canadians are among the most brilliant airmen developed by the war." The paper concluded its case by noting:

> The time is ripe for rounding out the Canadian military establishment by a Canadian air corps, officered and controlled by Canadians. We have outgrown the present arrangement which involves some methods at variance with a self-reliant Canadianism.
>
> The newspaper pointed out that Regulation 12 of the Military Service Act provided that, if a cadet fails his pilot's certificate, he could be transferred to another branch

of the Imperial Service at "the discretion of the Officer Commanding the Royal Flying Corps" or the cadet could be retained as a mechanic in the RAF, or he could be discharged from the Royal Air Force and immediately re-enlisted into the Canadian Expeditionary Force.

In other words, whether the Canadian cadet succeeds or fails as a pilot, when he enlists with the RAF in Canada, he passes out of the control of Canadian authority and into that of Imperial authorities; he can then be forced against his will to serve in any Imperial unit. *The Globe* argued this state of affairs was not consistent with "Canadian pride and freedom" and was one of the arguments for placing the aviation branch under Canadian control.[19]

Whether or not Canada would have its own air force was a delicate political issue and not one on which a military organization could safely comment. Seymour and the RAF had no choice but to watch without comment while *The Globe* and *The Star* carried on their campaign for an independent Canadian air force.

On 25 May, *The Star* employed arguments provided by Sir Sam Hughes who, as minister of militia, had insisted on a Canadian army. The newspaper pointed out the same arguments should now apply to the air service. In early June, it got another opportunity when *The Ottawa Journal-Press* criticized *The Toronto Star* for its attacks on the RAF (Canada), arguing that it was none of Canada's business because English money was paying for it. *The Star* gleefully demolished that argument and returned to its hobby horse, ending a long editorial with its strongest denunciation of Borden's air force policy to date:

We should have our own Air Force in Canada, in England, and at the front. Particularly we should have no war service recruiting and operating here independent of the supervision and control of the Government of Canada. To have such a service operating here is two

generations behind the times, and it isn't working and
it won't work.[20]

Ten days later, on 13 June, when a cable from the British War Office put the
number of Canadians in the RAF at one third of the total force, *The Star*
seized on those statistics and made a fresh argument — namely that post-
war commercial opportunities for air travel required that Canada have
an air force as well as aerodromes such as already existed at Deseronto,
Borden, North Toronto, and Beamsville. *The Star* pointed out that the
RAF could not be expected to maintain those stations after the war.

Despite Hoare's Canadianization of RAF (Canada), *The Toronto Star*
remained virulently hostile. Unlike *The Star*, most Canadian newspapers
were either neutral or supportive. A few — *The Orillia Packet* was
particularly active — frequently rebutted the criticisms levelled by *The
Star*. In one exchange, *The Packet* accused *The Star* of trying to stir up
trouble in the air service whereupon *The Star* replied that it was trying
to prevent and end trouble in the air service without waiting for it to run
its full course. *The Packet* dryly observed that, "*The Star* is taking a queer
method of preventing trouble."[22]

Ironically, *The Star's* attack on RAF (Canada) reached its peak during
the summer of 1918 just as the force was attaining its highest degree of
perfection in its facilities, training syllabus, and methodology. This was
supported by the decline in accidents and training fatalities.

*The Toronto Star* would continue its attacks until the Royal Air Force
withdrew from Canada completely. Even the creation of two Canadian
air forces did not end their vituperative editorials. How Canada came to
have two Canadian air forces, in addition to RAF (Canada) operating on
its soil, reveals much about the state of the Dominion's growing sense of
nationalism that emerged from the radically changed world following
the First World War.

# CHAPTER NINETEEN
## TOWARDS A CANADIAN AIR FORCE

Canada is the only country in the war that has not got a Flying Service — Australia, New Zealand, South Africa, all have their Flying Corps, while Canada, having probably more flying officers on active service than probably all the other colonies put together, has so far failed to give recognition to this vitally important branch.
— The Toronto Star, *13 June 1917*

*The Star's* campaign against RAF (Canada) had been waged, at least in part, with the goal of convincing the prime minister that the government should create a Canadian air force. Ironically, Borden had been converted to that need for some months before the newspaper's campaign had even begun. But he had kept his views confidential. Behind the scenes, he had directed two of the government's senior members to look into the feasibility of creating a Canadian-run air force. The prime minister had determined on this direction as early as May 1917, when he became convinced that Canadian flyers in the RFC did not share equally in the promotions or recognition with their British counterparts. This knowledge, although not wholly accurate, infuriated the normally patient and phlegmatic leader.

In November 1916, Borden removed the refractory Sir Sam Hughes as minister of militia, replacing him with Sir Arthur Kemp. He then reorganized the ministry, hiving off the command in London by establishing a HQ for the Overseas Military Forces of Canada. This was done to curb the independence and power of the minister of militia. Borden placed this newly created office under the command of the British High Commissioner, Sir George Perley. It was to Perley that

Borden revealed his change of mind concerning a Canadian air force. On 22 May, he sent a cable to Perley in which he angrily complained of the treatment of Canadians by the RFC in England:

> There seems to have been a disposition from the first to assign them [Canadians] to subordinate positions and to sink their identity. They were forbidden to wear any distinguishing badge to indicate that they were Canadians. They have been discriminated against in promotion ... I am afraid this is only another indication of a certain tendency which I took pains to correct ... during my recent visit to England. The question of a Canadian Flying Corps demands immediate and attentive consideration. I am determined that Canadians shall not continue in any such position of unmerited subordination. Please give that subject immediate and attentive consideration and make such thorough enquiries through the best independent means available to verify the truth of what has been represented to me. I am inclined to believe that the time for organizing an independent Canadian Air Service has come and that we must ask the Imperial authorities to release all Canadians now in the British Flying Service.[1]

Fortunately for the RFC, the RNAS, and the prosecution of the war, Borden did not pull the Canadians from the British flying services but ordered a careful study of the situation by both his minister of militia and his high commissioner to London. A while later, Perley reported back that there was no basis in fact to the rumours that Canadians were not being promoted as readily as their British counterparts.

Nevertheless, the matter continued to be studied and the British were made aware of the Canadian government's sensitivity to the lack of identity accorded Canadian airmen serving in the British air service. They were also made aware that Canada's government might move to create a distinctive air force unless Canadian airmen received more recognition and a fair proportion of the senior positions in these services. The prospect of Canada pulling its flyers from the British forces was a serious concern to the British High Command and one they worked to prevent.

As the war progressed, Borden and the majority of his generals became convinced that while it would not be practical to form a completely separate Canadian air force, it would be feasible to designate three or four squadrons as a Canadian air force, without disrupting the Allied effort to maintain control of the air. One hurdle was to obtain a guarantee from the British that these squadrons would be supplied the latest, most up-to-date fighter airplanes. This could not be guaranteed should the Canadians pull all their pilots from the British service and create a fully independent Canadian service.

But other more pressing matters intruded, forcing the prime minister to defer action on air force matters which continued to be studied but did not receive top priority. Borden at this point was fully occupied with the problem of conscription; a policy he believed he had to impose in order for Canada's front-line troops to receive adequate support but which would almost certainly divide the nation along ethnic and regional lines. Quebec was fiercely opposed to conscription, the prairies resentful, and labour demanding that wealth be conscripted before working men were made to serve overseas. Any illusion that war was glamorous had been annihilated — along with a million men — in the mud of the Somme.

Ignorant of Borden's conversion, *The Toronto Star* carried on its campaign for a Canadian air force. The newspaper's campaign, by highlighting concerns shared by many Canadian generals and politicians, may have helped to persuade the British War Office to offer concessions to Canadian officials.

One of those championing the idea of separate Canadian units in the RAF was Brigadier-General Hoare. By the summer of 1918, Hoare was recommending the establishment of an "all-through training wing" in England, staffed primarily by Canadian flyers and commanded by a Canadian. He recommended Tylee, his inspector of training, for the job. This wing would complete the training of those pilots who had graduated from RAF (Canada) and were sent to England to complete their training on advanced fighter planes.

Hoare proposed this idea to Sefton Brancker, the master-general of personnel, who referred Hoare's letter to the director of training, Brigadier-General Hearson. Hearson's reply to Hoare in late September suggests he held a low opinion of the Canadian training program:

> I am not quite clear as to exactly what you mean with regard to Canadian cadets being hung up for months in England. These semi-trained officers and Flight Cadets go through exactly the same training as our own pupils, and do get through more quickly than our own people owing to their having done a considerable amount of flying before. I do not think they would get through any quicker if your proposition was adopted. Your scheme that a Wing Commander of your proposed Wing should have authority to communicate direct with Canada is most undesirable The whole object of the organization of the Royal Air Force is to prevent short-circuiting, and I am afraid your proposition would absolutely nullify this organization.[3]

Hoare had made a success of the Canadian training and recruiting scheme precisely in the manner Hearson was criticizing, by short-circuiting the organization, bypassing regular channels, and bending rules and regulations to reach his targets. His success in recruiting Americans had been the result of just such tactics. His promotion to brigadier-general was at least partially a reward for the deal he had made with the Americans when he disregarded instructions not to commit England and went ahead and did just that.

As in any organization, the RAF Command contained officers with varying opinions on the Canadian training scheme. Not all were as critical as Hearson. General Brancker provided a very different reason for turning down Hoare's idea for a Canadian all-through training wing. Brancker believed that separating the Canadian cadets from the Brits would have a negative impact on the latter, noting that the Canadians were of a better quality than the recruits the RAF was receiving in England.

Although the Air Board turned down Hoare's request for a Canadian Wing in England, they did make some minor concessions, agreeing to provide at least one Canadian flight commander at each of several British training stations.[4]

Even as the British military was moving ponderously towards an accommodation with Canadian nationalist sentiment, the politicians were bypassing them. A conference was convened in London on 28 May 1918 with members of the British Ministry of Air to discuss the matter of a Canadian air force. The Canadian view was represented by the minister of militia, Sir Arthur Kemp, accompanied by Lieutenant-General R.E.W. Turner, commander of the Overseas Ministry Office in London and, like Kemp, a strong believer in a Canadian air force. The British were represented by newly appointed secretary of state for Air, Sir William Weir, along with several of his officials and staff.

It was at this conference that Weir stated he had no objection to forming two or more squadrons manned and commanded by Canadians. Weir also agreed that Canadians could wear Canada badges as an identifying mark. He also promised the RAF would keep Canadian authorities informed of those Canadians being listed in *The London Gazette* so that Canadians back home could be kept informed of their countrymen's achievements. A follow up conference took place on 5 June at which some hard bargaining took place but, as Weir had earlier agreed to the formation of the two-squadron air force, that agreement could not be retracted and the Canadians emerged with this concession intact. The Canadian Air Force would remain within the RAF and would consist of two squadrons, numbered Squadron 1 and Squadron 2. This arrangement would mean a minimum of disruption to the operations of the RAF in the field.

On paper, the Canadian Air Force came into existence with the passing of an order-in-council by the Canadian cabinet. The order authorized the formation of the Canadian Air Force for the purpose of the war and confirmed the agreement reached by Kemp and Turner with the British authorities. However, it would be some time before the CAF came into operational existence, primarily because the RAF hierarchy was not enthused, viewing its creation as a distraction from winning the air war that was at a critical stage in the summer of 1918.

Hoare's main concern was to keep RAF (Canada) running smoothly. He had no wish to have his organization involved in the training of the CAF. While the CAF posed no danger to Hoare's recruiting goals, the emerging need to protect Canadian shores posed an unexpected threat. While the Brits and Canadians had been quibbling over the details of creating the CAF, the Imperial Royal Navy had been exerting pressure on the Canadian government to form a Royal Canadian Naval Air Service. They were aided in this campaign by the U.S. Navy and State Department. The Dominion, which had no air service for the first four years of the war, now found itself moving, very reluctantly, towards the creation of two air forces.

The Royal Canadian Naval Air Service originated in the American and British need to have America's Atlantic coast protected from Germany's long-range submarines. These new weapons could range the Atlantic for three or more months at a time. They had already invaded the St. Lawrence, where their presence terrified the villagers. They had also sunk shipping both in the St. Lawrence and off the east coast of Canada. This led to the development of the convoy system with Sidney and Halifax becoming assembly points for eastward bound convoys. It was decided by the British and Americans that the best air-protection could be provided by building seaplane bases at Halifax and the north shore of Cape Breton. From these locations they could provide much-needed protection to the convoys; neither the British nor Canadian navies could adequately provide this protection.

The Americans stepped into the breach. They were to supply the personnel, seaplanes, airships, and kite balloons for a new Royal Canadian Naval Air Service. Canadian Aeroplanes Ltd. was to start gearing up to provide the seaplanes. While the Americans would initially supply the personnel, it was expected that Canadians would eventually man the stations.

On 5 September 1918, Canada's cabinet passed order-in-council # PC 5154, officially creating a Royal Canadian Naval Air Service for the duration of the war. The order-in-council further provided for eighty aircraft cadets, twelve airship (balloon) cadets, and up to 1,000 ratings. The recruits would be dressed as airmen and had their own distinctive uniforms.

Officers in the new service wore a naval cap and a dark-blue serge uniform with a brown leather Sam Browne belt. RAF rank badges and pilot wings were used, but the wings were modified to include a green maple leaf with RCNAS in the centre.[5]

On the day PC 5154 passed, the minister of naval service, C.G. Ballantyne, issued a press release to the media that put the best possible spin on the new force. Its birth, after all, had been forced on Canada by its larger allies. Ballantyne somehow made it sound as if the pregnancy was Canada's idea. The headline did not mention that all the men in service and all the equipment in use was supplied by the U.S. nor that they were on loan to the newly minted RCNAS. This arrangement conveniently bypassed the delicate problem of Canadian sovereignty as the two stations would be on Canadian soil. The press release of Minister Ballantyne maintained the fiction that the new force was Canada's idea, as illustrated in the following excerpts:

NEW AIR FORCE PATROLLING COAST
*Royal Canadian Naval Air Service Already in Operation*

The establishment of an air service in Canada, intended primarily for the defence of the Canadian coasts during the war, has been under consideration for some time, but various difficulties, chiefly concerning the supply of the necessary material, have prevented this being formed before. Early in 1918, however, the Government considered that the formation of an air service for coastal defence was of vital and immediate importance to Canada. As it was felt that this service should be of a naval character and should work in conjunction with the R.C.N., the matter was brought strongly before the notice of the British Admiralty [*sic*, by the Americans, not the Canadians] ...

Admiralty and Air Ministry [*sic*, American] consented to send out further officers.... These officers arrived in the country on Dominion Day, and have, up to date, been settling details of the preliminary organization in conjunction with the Director of Naval Services, Admiral Kingsmill.

> Machines are flying on the Atlantic Coast ready to bomb hostile submarines and to escort convoys, and perform other efficient services. This has been accomplished with the splendid aid and assistance of our ally the United States [a gross understatement].[6]

Despite some criticism from *The Toronto Star*, as well as *The Globe*, the response from ordinary Canadians was enthusiastic; the Canadian Naval Department was flooded with applications. To reduce the paperwork, A.K. Masterson, acting minister of the department, released a statement to the press asking candidates not to send hasteners with their applications and promising that within a few days a reply would be sent to everyone. He also placed greater restrictions on those who could apply.[7]

By mid-September, sixty-four cadets had been accepted and sent off to the Massachusetts Institute of Technology for ground school. Twelve airship cadets had also been sent to England for training. One of those accepted for service in the administration was Ernest Lloyd Janney, formerly the captain of the short-lived Canadian Aviation Corps. The resourceful Janney, despite dubious qualifications, was now Sub-Lieutenant Janney of the RCNAS.

During its brief existence, the RCNAS flew regular submarine patrols and carried out searches beginning in late August from Baker Point and commencing from North Sydney a month later. Three German submarines were cruising off the Atlantic Coast between Newfoundland and Cape Hatteras, but only once was one reported in Canadian waters. None of these submarines were spotted by the crews of seaplanes in the RCNAS. When the war ended in November, PC 2154 came into effect and the service was quickly disbanded.

While these developments were taking place, Hoare continued to perfect the operation of RAF (Canada). Among his many improvements was the continued Canadianization of the service. This had been going on from the beginning when the Air Board asked him to find instructional staff among the recruits the cadre of British officers were training. Hoare gradually extended the principle until it applied to the top levels of administrators and wing commanders.

The only Canadian in the group of officers who had accompanied Hoare on his initial trip to Canada had been Second Lieutenant Brian Peck, the first OC of the School of Military Aeronautics. By the summer of 1918, the Canadianization of the force had advanced to the top levels of administration; Canadians were in charge of two of the three wings. Major J. Stanley Scott of Roberval, Quebec, commanded Borden (42 Wing), Lieutenant-Colonel Wanklyn of Montreal commanded Deseronto, and Major Jack Leach, the one-legged flyer, was OC of the School of Special Flying at Armour Heights. At HQ the OC of training was Arthur K. Tylee of Quebec.

In June, Seymour released statistics showing the numbers of Canadians in top positions. Of the staff officers at HQ, four of the twelve were Canadians, while four out of the ten squadron commanders were Canadians. However, out of thirty flight commanders, fully seventeen were Canadians. This pattern applied down the line so that 80 percent of all officers were Canadians, although a majority of the first and second tier officers were primarily British and the third tier primarily Canadian. As Canadians gained experience, Hoare and General Brancker steadily moved them into the top levels of responsibility. In addition, the ground crew, which initially had been more than ninety percent British, by war's end, was almost entirely Canadian.[8]

At the School of Aerial Gunnery in Beamsville, the OC was Lieutenant-Colonel Huskisson, a British officer. In late September, Huskisson was replaced by Major Earl Godfrey of Vancouver. At this point all but one flying Wing and Long Branch camp was under Canadian command. In addition, the Medical Corps was staffed entirely by Canadians commanded by Major Brefney O'Reilly, a Toronto physician.

Thanks to Hoare's confidence in the ability of his Canadian officers, by the fall of 1918, most of the top positions in RAF (Canada) were in the hands of Canadians. Almost all of these officers had worked their way up during the war whereas the majority of the British officers posted to Canada had been career soldiers with years of experience. Nevertheless, the service was not totally run by Canadians; almost all the section heads were British, including those in charge of wireless, photography, aerial gunnery, and bombing.

# CHAPTER TWENTY
## PERFECTING THE TRAINING PLAN

> An interesting Booklet, "Air Heroes in the Making" describes fully the R.F.C. course of training. A copy will be sent post-paid to anyone who contemplates entering military life. Apply to one of the following addresses.
> — The Winnipeg Free Press, *30 January 1918*

At the end of January 1918, large ads began appearing in newspapers across the Dominion, inviting young men between the ages of 18 and 30 to join the Imperial Royal Flying Corps, not as pilots but as aerial observers. They were the first such ads to appear in Canada and were placed in response to a request to the IRFC from the Air Board in London to recruit and train cadets for this specific role. The ads specified that the applicant had to physically qualify for Class 1 under the Military Service Act, be "fairly well educated, clear headed, and keen for achievement." The successful applicant was promised that the work was of "supreme importance" and offered "scope for individual achievement." The observer-cadet's starting pay was the same as that of a pilot-cadet, $1.10 a day, and, on successful completion of the training, he obtained a commission as a flight officer.[1]

Cadets training to be observers did not learn to fly. Nevertheless, in the early stages, their training parallelled that of a pilot-cadet. Like the pilot-trainee, the cadet spent the first two weeks at the recruits depot in the Jesse Ketchum School where he learned the basics of military life. From there he transferred to the Cadet Wing at Long Branch where he followed the same syllabus as the pilot-cadet, learning the basics of military law, signalling, aerial navigation, map reading, and further honing his skills at telegraphy. After eight weeks, the cadet was transferred to the intellectually challenging environment of the No. 4 School of Military Aeronautics at the University of Toronto.

At this point his training diverged from that of the pilot-trainee. The observer-cadet's syllabus was ninety hours versus 143 for the pilot-cadet.[2] The former spent less time on aero engines, airframes, and the theory and principles of flight. Both groups deepened their knowledge and skills in the fields of telegraphy, signalling, artillery co-operation, bombing, reconnaissance, navigation, instruments, and photography. These skills were much needed by the observer, one of whose functions was to report back to HQ on what he and his pilot had discovered concerning enemy troops, their movements, artillery placements and size. While carrying out these assignments, he might also be required to photograph certain of the enemy's installations, often under enemy fire.

Upon graduation from the No. 4 School, both groups proceeded to the Armament School at Hamilton where the observer-cadets took a special three-week course designed to meet the specific needs of observers. The pilot-cadet course took five weeks to complete. The observer-cadet course put great emphasis on handling, stripping, and loading the Lewis machine gun, which, with its Scarfe mounting, was the principal weapon of the observer. The Scarfe mounting allowed the observer to rotate the Lewis machine gun in a circle, enabling him to aim the gun at a target coming at him from a variety of angles, whereas the pilot's weapon, the forward-mounted fixed Vickers machine gun, did not rotate.

After successful completion of the armament course, the observer was sent to the Artillery Co-operation School at Leaside where he honed his skills at spotting artillery bursts and reporting their location back to HQ via telegraphy. From Leaside he transferred to the School of Aerial Gunnery at Beamsville where he obtained invaluable combat experience with the Lewis gun, including practice at deflection shooting. He also got practice at aiming bombs at both stationary and moving targets

The last two schools closely approximated the training of pilot-cadets. After successfully completing his training at the School of Aerial Gunnery, the pilot cadet obtained his wings and the observer obtained his single wing. At this point they went on leave before being posted overseas. A few would be held back and sent to Armour Heights for training as instructors.

*Machine-gun deflection practice using Rocker Nacelle, Camp Mohawk, 1918. Courtesy of Library and Archives Canada/Department of National Defence PA-022773.*

The entire observer course took about six months, two to three months shorter than the training of a pilot-cadet. The first observers graduated in mid-July of 1918 and, by the armistice, a total of 137 observers had successfully completed the course. Of these some eighty-five had proceeded overseas. The output of observers continued to increase monthly until the war's sudden end. Hoare anticipated that, by late fall, they would be graduating 100 observers per month.[3]

In the summer of 1918, there was little expectation the war would end in November or even that year. Hoare had advised his superiors at the Air Board that he would not be able to repeat the previous year's Texas arrangement. The United States was now fully involved in the war and needed all its aerodromes and planes for training American pilots and ground personnel. In order to continue training during the winter, RAF (Canada) desperately needed winter barracks at certain camps.

The continued supply of pilots trained in Canada was essential to maintaining Allied air superiority in Europe. As a consequence, the British Treasury found the money for the expanding needs of RAF (Canada). By the summer of 1918, the IMB had authorization from the Treasury Board to build the long-delayed barracks.

In early August, it was announced that workers were now enlarging the facilities at Camps Rathbun and Mohawk, including some new hangars, but more importantly, the contractors were erecting barracks to house the cadets and enlisted men for the winter ahead. In addition, a new military hospital was being built to replace the cramped quarters of the leased Rathbun family home. The hospital was commanded by Major Ken Mundell and staffed by five nursing sisters, six medical officers, (some of whom were dentists), a senior NCO, two junior NCOs, and thirteen other ranks. Even serious crash cases could be handled at the new hospital.[4]

By June 1918, RAF (Canada) was sending more than 200 pilots monthly to England, and the number was steadily increasing. In addition, the pilots were better trained than ever before; a consequence of having adopted the Gosport System and the improvements instituted at Leaside,

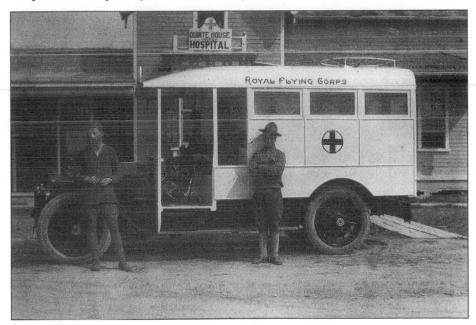

*A house converted into a hospital supplied the medical needs of 1,500 men at Camp Rathbun. Courtesy of Hastings County Historical Society.*

the School of Military Aeronautics, the opening of the Armament School at Hamilton and, in particular, the new School of Aerial Fighting at Beamsville. All these additions and advances vastly improved the effectiveness of RAF (Canada)'s training program. Consequently, other components had to be expanded and streamlined.

The Mechanical Transport Section had been steadily enlarged and improved since it came into existence in March 1917. Initially, its staff was made up of just one officer and fifteen non-commissioned officers and airmen. They oversaw a complement of fifteen vehicles that had been shipped over from England and distributed throughout the various sections of the brigade. The staff and vehicles increased steadily and in August 1917, now cramped for space, the section moved to newly built premises on Dupont Street. The building covered 27,000 square feet and was sub-divided into bays where each vehicle was checked and repaired for a different component. For example, steering repairs would be handled in one bay, tires in another, and so forth until all aspects of the vehicle had been checked and repaired as necessary. The building also provided administration offices and storage for new and rebuilt parts. The rebuilding of worn parts began with the opening of this new facility, and resulted in a considerable saving.

The section grew rapidly until, by the fall, the Toronto section alone was logging an average of 1,200 miles every day. This included miles logged by the Packard ambulances, the trucks hauling a multitude of supplies for the various flying stations at North Toronto, as well as for the depots within Toronto. Supplies for wings outside Toronto were hauled to the nearest train station.* The section also provided fire trucks, motorcycles for carrying mail between units, as well as the movement of personnel. In addition to a large male staff, some fifty women were employed as drivers and clerical staff. They proved particularly well suited for the job of truck-driving, silencing the critics who accused RAF (Canada) for allowing women to do work traditionally reserved for men.[5]

---

* Highways were unpaved and had terrible signage, while most rural roads were impassable in winter and spring. As rail transport was far more reliable, deliveries outside the city were handled by rail. The highway corridor between Toronto and Hamilton was the only exception.

In October, the section moved into new premises on Avenue Road, keeping the former building for repair work only, thereby enlarging and speeding up the section's capacity to repair vehicles and affecting economies of scale. The Mechanical Transport Section was now handling a wide variety of vehicles, including Packard ambulances, motorcycles, chemical trucks used in firefighting, repair lorries, and general delivery trucks of various tonnage.

To meet the increase in the number of pilots training, all sections were expanded. At the School of Military Aeronautics the staff had increased from forty-seven instructors on 1 July 1917 to 256 the following April, an increase of 500 percent in just nine months. Shortly thereafter another flight was added to accommodate the training of observer-cadets. In May the school graduated 360 pupils. Graduates peaked in July 1918 when 680 cadets successfully completed the course.[6]

In 1918, RAF (Canada)'s largest expense was the construction of the Beamsville camp, which began in late fall of 1917 and continued throughout the winter and into the spring of 1918. Due to budget restraints, the IMB had to lease the land. Nevertheless, as an article in the St. Catharines Post of 11 April 1918 makes clear, the camp was an enormous expense. This description of the camp also reveals something of the attitude of the townspeople towards this intrusion into their bucolic existence:

LARGEST AERIAL GUNNERY CAMP IN THE WORLD IS NOW LOCATED JUST 12 MILES EAST OF ST. CATHARINES ON THE Q. AND G. ROAD

Over eight hundred mechanics, cadets, and aviators and instructors arrived at Beamsville Camp on Monday morning from Texas. There were two special trains. More are expected shortly.

Beamsville has now the largest Aerial [gunnery] Camp in the world. The main body of the camp which parallels the Q. and A. Stone Road runs eastward for over two miles and has a depth of about three-quarters of a mile to the next concession road. The block of land which contains close to a hundred acres has all been cleared of fruit trees, bushes, and fences, although all the farm buildings have been left standing and will be utilized. The land has a nice gradual slope northward toward the lake and this made it easy for draining although thousands of feet of tile drain have been placed in the ground.

All the side roads are being torn up and new solidly built stone roads are being laid. New stone roads of good width are also being laid all through the camp. At present there are on the ground at different points nine hangars for the housing of aeroplanes. Each one of these hangars accommodates six machines, making a total housing capacity of fifty-four machines which is, in all probability, all the machines that will be necessary at the camp this summer.

Machine shops have been built and are being equipped with all the latest and most modern machinery. Big garages with room enough for fifteen and more automobiles are up and in use. Office buildings have been built and some are still under construction. Buildings for the holding of lectures and other uses are built and still there are more to be built. Cook-shanties and dining rooms for the men have been erected and they are massive big buildings having accommodation for thousands of men. Bunk houses are up and are being occupied by the mechanics that are already on the grounds.

There is a saw mill and planing mill on the grounds and it is working every day. Big storage houses for the storing of parts and materials have also been erected. Up on the hill on the south side of the Q. and G. will be found the hospital and it is most modern in every way. There are several big white ambulances connected with this hospital which will be fully staffed with doctors and nurses.

All the buildings are of frame construction and covered with heavy tar paper, all the joints and cracks being cemented. The number of carloads of lumber, timber, shingles and paper used run into the hundreds, while the window frames and lights run into the thousands.

Down at the lake a second big piece of land has been secured and rifle ranges and targets are being built here. A large breakwater will be built out into the lake of about three-quarters of a mile and will extend east and west for a distance of about 3,000 yards. This will be used for bomb dropping and aerial target work from the "planes." It is rumoured that a real submarine will be playing around in the lake for the cadets to shoot at. [The rumour was true.]

Water mains have been laid from the village and placed all over the camp. Special springs were secured by the Beamsville Council from land owners along the mountain to feed the reservoir in order to supply the camp with water ...

A switch has been run in from the G.T.R. [Grand Trunk Railway] and runs all through the camp for the bringing in of supplies and equipment. Automobiles of every kind, size and description are now at the camp and are used for all different kinds of work. There is still much work to be done ... and we doubt it will be done this year. It is estimated that there will be at least a thousand men at the camp by the end of the month and close to four thousand there by the end of May.

The erection of the camp in Beamsville has given the village a great boost in every way. Houses to rent are at a premium and during the past winter every householder who could accommodate men at all were jammed full. Several restaurants and pool rooms have been opened in the village and no doubt there will be many businesses of other kinds opening in the near future. The Y.M.C.A. has secured quarters close to the grounds and will look after the boys in their usual splendid manner.[7]

During construction, which lasted through the summer, the cadets, NCOs, and enlisted men slept in tents. Officers found accommodation in private homes or nearby hotels. Finally, on 5 October, the contractors completed the construction of the barracks. The men of RAF (Canada) moved eagerly into their new and much-awaited quarters. Although there were ninety-one female employees at Beamsville, no quarters were built for them. They were expected to find their own accommodation off camp.

The IMB construction team was highly competent; although constructed in wretched winter weather, the team was unfazed and undeterred. The crews worked seven days a week, with twelve-hour shifts day and night; construction even continuing on Sunday. The churches were not amused at these breaches of the Lord's Day Alliance Act but were powerless to enforce that law on the RAF.

Although smaller than both Borden and Deseronto, Beamsville was a considerable achievement. It covered 347 acres of land and included nine hangars — later increased to twelve — as well as a sewer and water system, well-built stone roads, both enlisted men's and cadets' barracks, officers' quarters, HQ's offices, garages, blacksmith shops, oil storage depot, guard house, quartermaster's stores, ice house, and separate buildings for photography, coal and wood storage, and ordinance storage, plus a hospital and medical building, as well as indoor and outdoor machine-gun ranges.

Despite its short period of operation, Beamsville was highly successful as the final stage of cadet training. During the six full months that the School of Aerial Fighting functioned, it graduated no fewer than 1,744 pilots and observers. The peak number of graduates was reached in October when 281 cadets successfully completed their training.[8]

Hoare was proud of his team and their accomplishments. Shortly after Beamsville came on stream, he received a cable from the secretary of the Air Ministry, which set out what a cadet must accomplish to achieve his graduation and hence his commission. Among other things, the rules specified that graduation required the cadet to have flown a service machine, something RAF (Canada) lacked. Hoare's response was to point out that pilots trained in Canada were "further ahead in their training than Graduation A Pilots in England." He explained that in Canada they received extra training at the School of Artillery Co-operation at Leaside and at the School of Aerial Gunnery at Beamsville.[9] The Air Ministry wisely decided not to enforce in Canada the requirement that the cadet operate a service machine before graduation.

The lack of an advanced trainer was about to be remedied. The Air Ministry decided it was time to provide a more suitable training airplane for the cadets in Canada and an order for 500 of the Avro 504K was awarded to Canadian Aeroplanes Limited. The company was already busy filling an order for fifty of the F-5 type flying boats for the U.S. Navy but quickly assigned some of its top engineering staff to the new project. Delays resulted from design changes that needed to be made, as some materials were difficult to obtain in Canada. Design changes were also required to comply with the decision to make certain parts interchangeable with the JN-4. Production was just getting nicely underway when the war ended. Nevertheless, two airplanes were completed and saw some service at Beamsville and Rathbun from June until war's end.[10] The Avro 504K remained the prime pilot trainer for the CAF and RCAF until the early 1930s.

By the fall of 1918, both RAF (Canada) and Canadian Aeroplanes Limited had reached new peaks of production and efficiency. Beamsville had come on stream as an advanced aerial gunnery and fighting facility, the Armament School at Hamilton had come into operation, further improving the cadet's training and, most importantly, the Gosport principles of training were now fully in use. The new system, known in Canada as the Armour Heights System, now formed the foundation for the training of instructors who could impart these principles to their pupils.

The consequence of this special program at Armour Heights meant instructors were now able to teach the principles of flight to cadets during their dual instruction. Perhaps most importantly they knew the whys governing the use of the controls and the theories governing how they operated on the airplane.

Had the Avro 504K trainer replaced the JN-4, the RAF training plan in Canada would have been as good or better than the training in England. That this did not happen by war's end was due to hesitation by the Air Board in London.

# Chapter Twenty-One
## A Pandemic Engulfs Canada

> Mr. Editor, in conclusion let me state my firm belief
> that the reason there are so many more fatal cases in
> this epidemic than in the former or previous attacks
> is due entirely to the fact that good liquor being
> out of reach of the masses [due to Prohibition] they
> have nothing to help the system to give the disease a
> knockout blow on the start, and it therefore gets the
> upper hand and knocks out the victim in the end.
> — *Letter from D.H. Ackrill, VS*[1]

The Spanish flu pandemic was the worst epidemic to strike Canada in the twentieth century. The crisis was heightened by a totally inadequate public health system that was overwhelmed by the disease. When the epidemic struck a community, doctors and morticians were forced to work around the clock, struggling vainly to tend to the sick and bury the dead. Coffin-makers were unable to keep up with the demand, but the greatest burden fell on the nurses who had to care for the victims on a continuing basis until their patients either recovered or died. As they came in daily contact with the infection, a high percentage of nurses contracted the disease and many died. Public facilities were so overwhelmed that records fell behind or were ignored entirely; undertakers could neither keep up with the demand for their services, nor with the accurate recording of deaths.

When the epidemic finally wound to a close, the number of lives lost in Canada was estimated at somewhere between 30,000 and 50,000. Modern researchers believe the death toll was much higher.

Like most pandemics, the Spanish influenza moved from east to west; its velocity increased by the transfer home of sick and wounded troops, lodged in close quarters on troop ships. These ships discharged their weakened and infected humanity at ports along the Atlantic seaboard; one of these was Halifax, another Quebec City. Those soldiers were then put on equally packed trains and carried to their destinations, primarily to the west. Again, they were in close quarters with other soldiers, many of whom had already contracted the disease. No special precautions were taken to isolate the sick from the healthy.

Usually the most susceptible victims to the flu virus are the very young and very elderly, but the Spanish flu favoured young adults. The records of the vital statistics branch of the Ontario Board of Health reveal that 65 percent of the total fatalities in the province took place among adults between the ages of twenty and thirty.[2] This was the same age group that suffered the greatest casualties during the Great War.

One casualty was Alan "Bus" McLeod, teenaged holder of the Victoria Cross. When he returned with his doctor father to Stonewall in Manitoba, he received a much-deserved hero's welcome. The town declared a civic holiday in his honour. From the speaker's podium, the nineteen-year-old shyly stammered, "I am no speaker. I want to thank you very, very much. I only hope I deserve it."[3]

While he was recovering from his wounds, Bus hoped to return to the front and was notified that he was to be promoted to captain. But, in late October, the young hero contracted Spanish influenza. He was too weakened to fight it off and developed pneumonia. On the evening of 6 November, he died in his sleep at the Winnipeg General Hospital.

Initially, neither the public, press, nor pundits were alarmed by the rumours that Spanish influenza had appeared in Canada. Quebec was the first province to be hit hard but the situation was minimized by the Civic Health Bureau. Consequently, word of the epidemic did not reach Toronto until it too was struggling to contain the virus. Many municipal and provincial authorities tried to play down the seriousness of the epidemic, believing that panicking the public would only worsen the situation.

There were many examples of this head-in-the-sand approach. In Ontario, the Board of Health under Doctor McCullough, the provincial officer, reported from Toronto on 24 September that the influenza outbreak was not alarming, nor was it as serious as the measles. His statement was reinforced by Doctor Schutt, in charge of contagious diseases, who stated there were no indications of any cases of influenza in the city.[4]

A few days earlier, Doctor McCullough had reported that the outbreak of Spanish influenza at the Polish infantry camp at Niagara was now under control and he felt the department had this new but aggravating complaint well in hand. This complacency gradually gave way to a sense of impending doom. On the last day of September 1918, *The Toronto Star* reported hopefully that hundreds of cases had developed in Ontario over the past three or four weeks but all were of a mild form and that there had been no deaths locally. *The Star* also reported that the largest number of cases were in the RAF (Canada) where about 150 were already in the military base hospital and that fifty airmen had been taken to the hospital the previous day. *The Star* and medical authorities remained ignorant of the true nature of the disease. It was most lethal in its final phase after pneumonia had set in.

A few days later, news of the deteriorating situation at the Polish military camp reached the press. Deaths at the Polish camp due to influenza had now grown to fourteen. Despite this, officials continued to regard the situation with blinkered optimism, releasing an announcement on 3 October that, "The fight against Spanish influenza in the Polish Camp is progressing favourably and today the number of cases is down to 146, the lowest in a couple of weeks." This sanguine spin on a situation growing rapidly out of control was proving difficult to maintain.

Even as officials were minimizing the situation at Niagara, *The Star* reported that the town of Renfrew was overwhelmed with five hundred cases and ten deaths from the sudden onslaught of the disease. There was an immediate reaction from the provincial government, where the member for Renfrew was Thomas McGarry, a prominent member of cabinet who held the post of provincial treasurer. McGarry held a conference with the previously obtuse provincial officer of health, Lieutenant-Colonel McCullough, who was made to realize there was a serious problem. Telegrams were sent to numerous surrounding cities and towns asking their hospitals and provincial institutions to reply at once, stating how many doctors and nurses were available to go to Renfrew. Arrangements were made by the government for the immediate and free transportation of these health professionals to the little town where, coincidentally, McGarry was town solicitor.[5]

Two days later, the Provincial Board of Health, now suddenly alert to the gravity of the situation, placed a large ad in newspapers across the province headed, "Ontario Emergency Volunteer Health Auxiliary" and below, in large black type, "Wanted: Volunteers!" The ad explained that volunteers were needed for a short training course so they could supply nursing help wherever needed to combat the influenza outbreak. Training had already started at the Parliament buildings in Toronto and a syllabus of learning was being sent to all medical officers across the province. Those taking the course would be issued an official badge bearing the initials SOS, standing for Sisters of Service and could expect to be called at anytime to serve anywhere in the province.

By early October, the situation in Toronto had reached crisis proportions; officials were forced to take over several buildings as emergency hospitals. These included Burwash Hall at the University of Toronto and the women's building on the Exhibition grounds. The various hospitals of RAF (Canada) were soon overcrowded, with the surplus at North Toronto, HQ, and the Repair Park sending patients to the base hospital, which had beds for 400 but which, by 4 October, had 714 patients. Two days later, the number of patients began to decline until, by 26 October, the number was down to 387.[6]

Across the province, the overwhelming number of patients was beyond the capacity of most hospital staffs to deal with adequately. The situation was further aggravated by the spread of the virus amongst the hospital staff themselves. Consequently, many cadets had to be temporarily deployed from their training to assist at the hospitals. A future governor general of Canada was one of those cadets. In his memoirs, Roland Michener recounted his experiences:

> In the fall of 1918 I was in Toronto with three friends from the University of Alberta, beginning our training in the Royal Air Force as pilots.... It was cold in Toronto, especially in the RAF recruits' depot, which was then housed in the Jesse Ketchum school on Davenport

263

Road…. In the meantime the epidemic became a very personal experience. Almost daily we were sent with other recruits to the base military hospital, a wooden building on Church or Gerrard Street. It was built and furnished to accommodate 300 patients but by then was overcrowded with 900 or more. We worked as orderlies, taking out used blankets for fumigation, stretcher-bearing the sick, and carrying out the dead. This is no exaggeration; the toll in one day in October was as many as twelve.

Michener's friends soon contracted the virus and became patients at the base hospital themselves. A few days later Michener joined his buddies at the base hospital. He had this to say of his ordeal:

Of the next two or three days I have almost no recollection. I must have slept continuously until the fever subsided. I was soon sufficiently over the crises to be sent for convalescence to the East House, one of the residences of University College. For ten peaceful days I enjoyed a life of ease, until I was well enough to go on happily with my routine training at Long Branch.[7]

What Michener failed to mention was the danger posed by the hospital to both staff and patients. At the inquest held into the death of Cadet Davidson, one of the fatalities at the base hospital, Toronto Fire Chief Smith testified he never thought the building was suitable as a hospital and, although the military had done everything possible to make it safe, its wooden construction made it too dangerous. Fortunately, no fire occurred and the death rate remained relatively low. Of 1,811 admissions to the base hospital, the military suffered seventy-one deaths for a 3.9 percent death rate. Of those patients who contracted pneumonia, following the flu, the death rates were unsatisfactory. Of the 218 patients who came down with pneumonia, seventy-one died for a fatality rate of 33 percent.[8]

O'Reilly also stressed the highly contagious nature of this strain of influenza. He surprised both the jury and the chief coroner when he testified that the infection rate among cadets kept in heated tents at Long Branch was almost non-existent whereas the infection rate among cadets in barracks was quite high. His message was apparently lost on the Toronto School Board, which continued to keep the schools open on the grounds that children were less likely to catch the virus in the classroom than when playing outdoors.

Aside from Toronto, RAF (Canada) was generally adequately supplied with hospital space. At Camp Rathbun, where the chief medical officer was Captain Sam Cronk, a new hospital had been built over the summer. Opened in August, it handled all RAF cases for the area other than convalescent patients. The situation for the RAF in Deseronto was true for Military District #3 generally. At the end of October the adjutant for the district released the numbers for the military hospitals in District #3, noting that the figures spoke for themselves, making the observation that hospital accommodations were ample and the mortality very low. The maximum number of patients in the district military hospitals was reached on 18 October when 642 were under treatment. Up to 28 October, there had been a total of twenty-five deaths from influenza and pneumonia. After that the number of patients declined steadily until, by the end of October, there were just 452 patients in the various military hospitals within the district.[9]

A critical factor lowering the infection rate was the Medical Corps policy of housing cadets in heated tents rather than in crowded barracks. Camp Borden had been equipped with a new hospital from the beginning and hence survived the epidemic without serious difficulty.

Initially, it had been intended to have one base hospital for serious crash cases, but it was soon realized that convalescent hospitals were needed. For example, at Long Branch a hospital with a capacity for 150 patients was built to house those cadets and other ranks suffering from venereal disease. Another hospital, housing twenty-five patients, was constructed at Long Branch in the summer of 1918 for general cases. The Leaside hospital could accommodate another forty and the hospital at Armour Heights only ten. These facilities — while adequate for normal times — were overwhelmed by the Spanish flu, an epidemic of tsunami proportions.

An additional convalescent hospital was acquired through the generosity of Mr. and Mrs. Charles Beattie, who loaned their country home to the force for the duration of the war. Known as Longwood House, it was situated eight kilometres north of Toronto on a beautiful ten-acre estate. It had an initial capacity for twenty-four patients, but was later expanded. After the war, it continued to serve as a convalescent hospital for injured flyers until early 1920.

In Ontario, the peak of the epidemic was reached in late October after which the disease began to subside. In Toronto, statistics at the end of the month revealed that 1,802 people had died out of a population of 489,687 or one out of every 272 persons. Over 65 percent of the fatalities were between the ages of twenty and thirty.[10]

The disease would rage across the province well into 1919, spreading out from Toronto into the nearby rural areas. In December, more than a month after peaking in the capital city, the Barrie *Northern Advance* reported that influenza was spreading with alarming rapidity into the surrounding townships.[11] The RAF at Camp Borden had discharged most of its cadets by the time the full impact of the epidemic struck and suffered few casualties.

Despite the epidemic, RAF (Canada) continued to turn out observers and pilots with barely a pause. The number graduated in October was 250, only slightly below the peak of 270 reached in August and better than September's 210 graduates.[12]

Decades later, Allen was fulsome in his praise of Major O'Neill and his medical team, observing that, "Medical officers all from the Canadian Army and their staffs coped magnificently and had the situation well under control by the time of the Armistice."[13]

The people of Ontario performed equally well, displaying considerable grace despite personal loss and suffering. A scrim of humour trickles through the heartbreak and pathos. Writing in *The Daily Intelligencer*, the editor ruminated wryly that, "The only oasis from the influenza epidemic seems to be the Kingston Penitentiary, where it is said there are no cases of the disease. As a health resort the 'pen' seems to be the real thing, but a good many more people are more anxious to keep out of that health resort than to escape the flu."[14]

# CHAPTER TWENTY-TWO
## CANADA'S FIRST AIRMAIL

AERIAL MAIL TO COLLINGWOOD
The first mail to come to Collingwood by air route
came on Tuesday week, when Capt. R.E. Carroll
from Camp Hoare dropped a packet on Hurontario
Street near the corner of Third Street. The packet was
addressed to the Postmaster and was delivered to
Mr. Darroch by a young lad who picked it up on the
street about half past 5 o'clock.
— The Northern Advance, *12 September 1918*

The first official airmail delivery in Canada took place eight weeks
before Captain Carroll's ersatz mail delivery to Collingwood — which
was not simply a gratuitous flying stunt. Carroll was carrying out his
role in a promotional effort, advertising an upcoming athletic event at
Camp Borden. Inside the "air-mail parcel" were a number of posters that
the postmaster obligingly arranged to have plastered on a number of
prominent locations around Collingwood.

The first recognized airmail delivery took place in June 1918, when
the dashing Captain Peck carried out a successful delivery of airmail,
endorsed and partially sponsored by the Royal Mail of Canada. The
mail was carried from Toronto to Montreal while the return trip, from
Montreal to Leaside, featured an equally valuable case of Prohibition
whisky going the other way. To understand the difficulties and risks
involved, we need to examine a few less challenging cross-country flights
attempted before Peck made his famous journey.

In September 1917, Cadet T. Talbot took off from Deseronto airfield
in a brand-new JN-4 and flew to Camp Barriefield, thirty-five miles east of

Deseronto. After a successful landing on the Barriefield parade grounds and hearty congratulations from the camp commander, Brigadier-General T.D.R. Henning, Talbot prepared for takeoff. The parade ground was not quite long enough for the JN-4 and, when he attempted to get airborne, the cadet just managed to clear a fence on the parade boundary before crashing. Fortunately, Talbot was unhurt but the Jenny's engine was wrecked beyond repair.[1]

A lack of proper airfields was just one of the many hurdles facing a pilot attempting to travel any distance by airplane. Additional risks were added by the Jenny's temperamental engine and its almost complete lack of navigational aids. RAF accident files are full of crashes due to engines stalling or lost pilots. A typical example of both phenomena was the trip attempted by Cadet Jensen who was making a relatively routine flight from Camp Borden to Toronto, forty-five miles to the south and normally an easy flight to navigate by following the rail lines.

On the way to Toronto, Jensen got lost in the clouds; a common occurrence as the only navigational instrument in the JN-4 was a constantly swinging magnetic compass. Unlike pilots of small planes today, he had no instruments to assist him in flying straight and level, nor a radio, let alone a directional system. Jensen decided to drop below the clouds but failed to recognize the countryside, nor was he able to pick out any landmarks. Unwittingly, he had gone nearly 60 kilometres (37 miles) off course, and was just a few miles outside of Kitchener. With no idea where he was, Jensen decided to land in a nearby field and make inquiries.

The cadet's descent towards a smooth-looking field went well until the crosswind leg when the engine unexpectedly quit; abruptly, the airplane descended steeply towards the farmhouse. Fearing he might kill himself as well as others in the house, Jensen banked into a turn, a dangerous manoeuvre, as turning without power causes the airplane to lose height more rapidly. The aircraft struck the ground nose-first a mere twenty feet from the house. Miraculously, Jensen was not seriously injured and the plane proved repairable.[2]

This one accident demonstrates several of the risks involved in cross-country flying. First, the dangers posed by inadequate navigational aids and second, the unreliability of the JN-4 engine. Add to this a limited capacity gas tank and a dearth of proper landing fields and you have a recipe for disaster on a long flight.

As the pilot training program became more sophisticated, fewer accidents occurred until, by the summer of 1918, cross-country flights were somewhat less dangerous. Round trips from Deseronto to Montreal were not quite routine, but a few had been made without serious incident. One of the earliest of these flights took place on 5 June 1918 when Major F.V. Woodman and Captain E.M. Smith made the trip to Montreal in just two hours. While the newspaper described them as "fresh as a daisy" when they landed," the reporter was exaggerating more than a little. Interviewed in Montreal, Captain Smith stated, "The trip was very agreeable. High in the air we had some rain, also had for two miles to struggle against a strong north-west wind, but these added zest to our journey, enabling us to test our pilotage thoroughly."[*]

By mid-summer of 1918, the round trip from Deseronto to Montreal was becoming almost commonplace. Still, mishaps did occur, generally due to the problems of navigation. Lieutenants Burwash and Henry set out for Montreal on a sunny Sunday morning where, after a short visit, they headed back to Deseronto. Although they followed the St. Lawrence they managed to become lost and, in the early hours of the evening with their fuel running low, were forced to land in a farmer's field. It turned out they had landed in a field belonging to a Frank Lajoie, near the separate school in Tweed. Despite the ease of following the St. Lawrence River and later the coast line of Lake Ontario, the two experienced pilots had managed to wander about thirty miles north and west of their intended destination. Overcast clouds probably were responsible for their wandering off course.

As a consequence of their unexpected landing in the rural community of Hungerford-Tweed, telephone party lines hummed with the news, resulting in the formation of a large, gawking crowd gathered to view the "huge bird." On Monday morning, hazy weather conditions prevented Henry and Burwash from making an early-morning departure.

---

* Ordinary citizens can be forgiven for thinking these elements didn't add zest so much as discomfort and fear. An open-cockpit airplane is hardly a comfortable refuge in a storm.

Consequently, an even larger crowd gathered from the surrounding countryside to watch the "great event."

The impact of this unscheduled landing on the rustic residents of Tweed-Hungerford, most of whom had never seen an airplane, can be gleaned from this description of the Jenny's takeoff which appeared in the *Tweed News:*

> It was just twelve o'clock noon when they started the great buzzing, whirling thing on its course down the field between the rows of sheaves lined up on either side. The machine just went a few rods when it began to rise as gracefully as a great bird. Over the fences, over the wires, over the trees, over the lake and the distant hills, it went and soon was lost to view of the wondering, gaping throng.[4]

Forced landings caused by bad weather, lost pilots, or failed engines were commonplace among both cadets and seasoned flyers; the newspapers were full of such happenings. Hence the first airmail flight in Canada, even when made by a seasoned combat pilot, was an endeavour fraught with risk. The circumstances of the first officially recognized airmail flight in Canada were particularly hazardous.

A few days after Lieutenants Burwash and Henry's unscheduled landing near Tweed, Captain Brian Peck and his mechanic, Corporal C.W. Mathers, set out to make Canadian history.

It did not start out that way. After some months at the front in France, Peck was repatriated to Canada to assist with the RAF training program. He was posted to Camp Leaside to train cadets in advanced artillery co-operation, a function which he had carried out with distinction on the European front. But Peck found instructing tedious and looked forward to visiting Montreal, where he could visit with his family, renew friendships, and enjoy some lively nightlife. Toronto was not only in the grim grip of war, it was firmly in the control of Ontario's righteously dry prohibitionists; potable alcoholic beverages were nowhere to be found.

Peck convinced his superior officer that a low-level display of acrobatics over downtown Montreal would improve flagging recruitment in Canada's largest city.* It was no coincidence that the quartermaster at Leaside was getting married and his fellow officers needed someone to pick up a case of Old Mull whisky in Montreal. The Old Mull was intended to enliven a party planned for the officers' mess in celebration of the quartermaster's impending marriage. No doubt Peck's superior officer took the party into account when giving his approval for the "Recruitment Trip."

By fortuitous coincidence, the Aerial League of the British Empire, a civilian organization dedicated to the general advancement of aviation, was planning to demonstrate the feasibility of improving mail delivery by using airplanes. The major problem with the scheme was the lack of both an airplane and a competent pilot. Peck's arrival was superbly timed for this purpose.

George Lighthall and Edmund Greenwood, respectively president and treasurer of the Montreal branch of the Aerial League, had conceived the idea of carrying mail on the return flight to Toronto. They obtained permission from R.F. Coulter, deputy postmaster at Ottawa, who authorized a special rubber cancellation stamp for the envelopes. Greenwood was appointed acting aerial postmaster and authorized to stamp and thereby cancel the envelopes in Peck's aircraft as Canada's first airmail.[5] The letters were chosen at random from the general mail at Montreal.

Peck's flight to Montreal was made with little difficulty on Friday 20 June 1918. Although JN-4 #C203 had been equipped with a special long-distance fuel tank, Peck still needed to land in Deseronto to refuel. Another difficulty was the lack of an airfield at Montreal. These were minor challenges and the capable Peck handled them without difficulty. The Bois Franc polo grounds at Montreal were converted into a makeshift landing field and Peck managed a smooth landing on the short field.

Unfortunately, the aerobatic display planned for Saturday had to be cancelled due to a persistent and heavy downpour. On Sunday, under

* Peck's superior was Lieutenant-Colonel Fred Wanklyn, then in command of 44 Wing, which included Leaside. Both men were urbane and sophisticated, familiar with the upper echelons of Montreal society.

*Lieutenant Brian Peck shortly after completing his historic airmail flight. Courtesy of Crossman Collection.*

ominous, leaden, low-lying clouds, Peck and the stoic Mathers prepared for takeoff. Peck gunned the Jenny into the wind, skidding across the sodden turf in their heavily overloaded machine, finally rising slowly into the air. Even before the well-wishers were gone, the two men were back. Visibility was too poor to chance going more than a few miles from the polo grounds.

Early Monday morning, the weather still threatening, Peck and Mathers made ready for a second attempt. Peck cut a dashing figure in his leather helmet and goggles, high-flared gloves, fur-lined leather windbreaker, knee-high leather boots, and swagger stick. Mathers sat in the rear seat, uncomfortably perched on a case of Old Mull, his arms clutching the precious sack of official letters. Mathers was acutely aware of his responsibility. There was no room to stow the letters in the tiny cockpit so he had to be constantly vigilant lest the sack be blown from his hands by high winds or sudden turbulence.

After two days of rain, the Jenny's fabric was sodden with water, making turning difficult and slowing her responses to the controls. Handling was further slowed by the extra weight. In addition, the runway looked dangerously short of what Peck would need to get the JN-4 airborne. Nevertheless, he had to try. As a fighter pilot, he was used to risks, basing his decisions not on mathematical formulas, but experience in tight situations.

Again the Jenny charged through the grass. Peck couldn't seem to gain flying speed. Dead ahead lay the perimeter of the grounds; railway tracks skirted the perimeter. Along the tracks ran telegraph lines. Suddenly, the aircraft lurched uncertainly into the air, passing well below the telegraph lines. Peck pulled into a tight jiggery turn and began following the railway right of way, thereby avoiding the trees, fences, and wires, he was unable to fly over. It took five more miles before the Jenny managed to stagger a mere forty feet into the air.

As the pair struggled westward they encountered more or less continuous headwinds and heavy rain squalls. With their fuel supplies perilously low, the flyers put in at Camp Barriefield, east of Kingston. There was no aviation fuel at the camp or in Kingston, forcing the flyers to rely on lower-octane automobile fuel. This got them to the RAF camp at Deseronto where the ground crew drained out the auto gas, replacing it with proper airplane fuel. At 4:55 p.m., after nearly six hours in the air, Peck landed at Camp Leaside.

He immediately requisitioned a car and personally delivered the mail to Postmaster W.E. Lennon at Toronto's general post office. Lennon gave the mailbag to Peck as a memento. In the meantime, Mathers ensured his own popularity, if not renown, by slipping away from the crowd and delivering the Old Mull to the grateful officers. Today, the airmail bag is on display at the Canadian War Museum. Unfortunately, no one thought to save the whisky case or even a few of the empties. They would have made an interesting addition to the exhibit.

Aside from the War Museum, the only reminder of Peck and Mather's historic flight is a small blue-and-gold sign at the corner of Eglinton Avenue and Brentcliffe Road in Toronto. Erected by the Ontario Archaeological and Historic Sites Board, which draws attention to the old Leaside Aerodrome, the field where Canada's first official airmail plane landed in 1918.[6]

# CHAPTER TWENTY-THREE
## WINDING UP THE RAF IN CANADA

> One of the wonders of the war in Canada was the celerity with which the Royal Air Force was put into working order ... the commanding officer, Brigadier-General Hoare has come in for many favourable comments on account of the fine work. Now he is proving to be no less efficient in time of peace, for the demobilization of the RAF in Canada is being facilitated without delay.
> — Toronto World, *14 December 1918*

The Great War, the war to end all wars, the war for freedom and democracy, had become the war that would never end, the war that almost wiped out an entire generation of young men.

Previous wars had been limited geographically to a continent. This war had spread from Europe to the Middle East, most of Asia, much of Africa, brought in North America, and finally spread to a few countries in South America. After the First World War, commentators throughout Europe agreed the world would never be the same. They were right in more ways than they imagined.

In Canada, celebrations broke out spontaneously across the nation. As was to be expected of young, exuberant, but well-bred sky pilots, the personnel of RAF (Canada) were energetic and noisy, but not violent. Parties, parades, dances, and dinners took place at the various camps and depots. The officers were feted with balls and dinners in an interminable round of parties sponsored by the upper echelon of Canadian society. These celebrations carried on throughout November, December, and well into the new year.

At Deseronto, the personnel of both camps Rathbun and Mohawk paraded through town, whooping and singing. It was not enough for the exuberant young cadets; there were limitations to the diversions the tiny town could provide. Moreover, Prohibition held sway, and the available supply of bootleg alcohol was quickly exhausted. Another problem was the lack of young women. The population of the mostly male camps was nearly equal to that of the entire town of Deseronto. The ratio of young men to young women was roughly ten to one. Over time, the majority of the cadets and mechanics had used the convenient rail connections to travel to the larger centres of Napanee, Kingston, and Belleville. The informal celebration committee at Deseronto decided their chosen centre for a "real" celebration would be Belleville, the closest of the larger centres to the camps. The day after the signing of the armistice, several hundred cadets and other ranks travelled to Belleville on the Great Northern Railway, disembarking at the train station (since torn down) near the corner of Dundas and South Front streets. *The Daily Intelligencer* of 13 November captured the flavour of the celebration:

> Those from Mohawk and Rathbun camps had a celebration all their own last evening. They formed a parade at the Victoria Park and marched up Front Street, Bridge Street, Victoria Avenue and many other main streets, in a zig zag fashion, paying a visit to the Palace Theatre, pool rooms, cafes, Hotel Quinte, Armoury grounds, and many other places which happened to be open. The Palace Theatre was soon evacuated by the movie fans. [Many of them joined the festivities.] The music consisted of tin cans, pie plates, baking dishes, and pieces of tin, clashed together and pounded by sticks and pieces of steel. Flags were also carried and various signs, the leading one being from *The Intelligencer Peace Extras*, published Monday morning, with large headings such as, "The war is over, Bring on your wild, wild women," "Where do we go from here? Home," "We fly tomorrow, MAYBE," "A fly in the air is worth 2 in the soup." "Injuns

from Mohawk," and many others. They proceeded to the back of the various business places and carried off large numbers of boxes, barrels, paper and cardboard, saturated them with oil and placed a number of fire crackers in the boxes, and had an enormous bon fire on the corner of Front and Bridge Streets. The birdmen are to be congratulated on their orderly conduct.

Whoever dreamed up the sign "We fly tomorrow, MAYBE" had been on the mark. Three days after the armistice, RAF headquarters in Toronto issued orders that there was to be no more flying by the RAF in Canada and that all aerial instruction was to cease in order to avoid any possibility of casualties. The RAF had good reason to be cautious. *The Toronto Star* had never been sympathetic to the British aviation presence in Canada, and would be quick to pounce on any action that might lead to the death or injury of any Canadian cadets or officers.

Almost immediately, the RAF began to have second thoughts about their decision. What were they to do with the nearly 12,000 men and women on the payroll during the months it would take to demobilize them? The thought of all these keen, energetic young men just sitting around with nothing to do was disquieting in the extreme. Youthful energy and enthusiasm would inevitably boil over into other activities, not all of which would be positive or desirable.

In addition, protests against the "no flying, no instruction" rule were sure to be made by those cadets just a few training-hours short of graduation. Some had already ordered uniforms in expectation of the proud day when they would receive their commissions and graduate as fully trained pilots. The staff at HQ reconsidered, and, on Friday, a day after the announcement, they reversed the no-fly order. By Monday, flying had resumed at all camps. A few days later the announcement was clarified, HQ announced that flying and instruction would commence until further notice.[1]

During October, two cadets and one lieutenant had been killed in flying accidents. It was the lowest fatality rate for any month since November 1917, when two pilots and a corporal had been killed. But

November was kept artificially low by the move to Texas and the delays in flying brought about by the unprepared camps when they arrived. The number of hours flown in November had been substantially below those flown in October of 1918. It was clear that the October fatality rate had been substantially lowered by the new training methods. But there was always the possibility of a fatality should large numbers of cadets and officers be permitted to continue flying.

Late in the afternoon of 21 November, a full ten days after the armistice, the inevitable happened. Second Lieutenant E.S. Sexton was struck by the propeller of an airplane as it was warming up for takeoff. The young flyer, whose parents lived in Strathroy, died that evening in Camp Borden hospital before his parents could reach the base.[2]

The day after Sexton's fatal accident, another flyer was killed, this time at the Beamsville camp. Lieutenant Thomas Logan, an experienced flyer from New Glasgow, Nova Scotia, crashed and died while practising aerial combat. As he had already received his commission and would not be posted overseas, it appeared his death was the result of recreational flying. RAF (Canada) could hardly justify this death to the press.

Only the day before Sexton's death, the RAF had wisely issued a demobilization order, making it clear that cadets who flew were doing so solely because they wished to continue their training in the air. They were required to put these intentions in writing or cease flying. The order was clear yet did not prevent press criticism. Here is the text of that order:

> No Canadian cadet should leave for the air this morning until he has personally put in writing a statement that he wished, on his own responsibility, to continue his flying training for air service. This order will apply to all Canadian aviation camps in the RAF in Canada.

The demobilization order went on to state, "All officers and cadets are freed from the dangers and difficulties of air work since the war has ended unless they, of their own free will, volunteer to continue their training. Such officers and cadets as wish to carry on their training in the air will be permitted to carry on, while the lesser ranks may go on with their regular work."[3]

In the meantime, various celebrations were being planned or were underway. On the evening of 20 November, Hoare and Colonel Tylee were feted by the Mount Royal Club of Montreal with a lavish dinner and many complimentary speeches.*

Hoare had received orders from the Air Board in England to commence the demobilization process with all possible speed. HQ staff in Toronto regarded this as a monumental task, especially as all airmen would have to be medically boarded (examined) before discharge. In Canada, the RAF had only thirty doctors for the nearly 12,000 men and women making up the brigade. To speed up the demobilization process, the RAF asked the Canadian military to supply a further thirty doctors. But the CEF had the equally daunting task of demobilizing a military district already short of medical men. All soldiers in District No. 2 (Toronto), except those needed for the demobilization process, such as pay officers, were to be disbanded before the RAF (Canada) could demobilize. Three weeks were allotted for this task. To assist them, the CEF found the needed doctors for the RAF in other military districts where the pressure of demobilization was less acute.

In the meantime, the RAF proceeded to demobilize some 2,000 cadets at their training camps. This included: the cadets at Jesse Ketchum School, the camp at Long Branch, the School of Military Aeronautics at the University of Toronto, and the Armament School in Hamilton. These cadets were placed on a six-month reserve list, meaning they could be called back into service at any time within that period. In practice, the process was the equivalent of being discharged, as the cadets could immediately return to civilian life. It was expected that virtually all members of the force would be discharged by the end of January 1919.[4] The RAF wasted no time, moving quickly to close the School of Military Aeronautics; on 4 December, the University of Toronto announced that university residences had been vacated by the RAF and would soon be open to students.[5]

Meanwhile the flying camps were demobilizing swiftly. At Deseronto, Sergeant Sharpe put his organizing skills into play. To help maintain

---

* Hoare tried to avoid social activities, regarding them as a waste of time. But he knew they were sometimes necessary and reluctantly did his duty.

morale during demobilization, he organized weekly dances beginning early in December and continuing every Tuesday night at the Camp Mohawk mess hall. Music was provided by local musicians and the hall was decorated by a committee headed up by Lieutenant Phillips. Beginning on 6 December, the dances continued until late in the month when almost all of 43 Wing had been demobilized.[6]

By 28 November, several dances had been held at Beamsville. A farewell dance was held by the village for the cadets and mechanics. The officers were treated to a special farewell dance at the Gibson estate. Just eight months earlier, this magnificent home had been the temporary head quarters of the officers of the Beamsville camp. The dance was the final social event held at the School of Aerial Combat to honour the Royal Air Force in Canada.

By Christmas the camp was almost deserted and private guards had to be hired to protect what remained of Air Force property. The camp's water and sewage facilities were offered to the municipality by the IMB for $5,000. The village councillors thought the price preposterous but did agree to purchase a fire siren, some sheds, and a few feet of hose. The dismantling of many of the buildings, including the barracks, got underway. In February, the last of the RAF staff moved out of their offices on the Gibson estate, leaving only a few buildings and some JN-4s stored in a hangar. Later that month, the aircraft were flown to the RAF camp at Leaside.

On 28 February, Dr. E. Ryan, director of the Department of Soldiers' Civil Re-establishment announced that the Beamsville hospital would be taken over as a sanatarium for tuberculosis patients.[7] In March, the Provincial Highway Commission purchased some of the remaining buildings. Aside from one hangar, the few buildings still standing were later purchased by private individuals and rented out as living quarters.[8] The runway at the west end of the camp, while not officially recognized as an airstrip, was used by local aviators until the 1960s when the pavement that the town had applied in the 1920s was finally torn up.

Demobilization in the Toronto area was proceeding at a rate averaging approximately 100 men daily. On 28 November, Lieutenant-Colonel Tylee announced that the training of flying cadets had virtually ceased in Canada; the camps at Leaside and Beamsville had been closed; the forty cadets at Borden had finished their work. Only four cadets elected to proceed to Deseronto for the final stage of their flight training and the rest dropped out. By 20 December, the four cadets had finished their training at Mohawk. It was closed that day and all staff were immediately demobilized or transferred to HQ. Except for a few hangars, the remaining buildings were torn down. A few hangars were used by the Anglin Company of Kingston to store wood from the initial dismantling of buildings. The last remaining hangar at Mohawk was torn down on 29 December 1921 by the Anglin Company to make use of the wood. Only two empty hangars remained at the Rathbun Camp.[9] One of these was purchased privately and made into a private dwelling.* The other was moved to Deseronto where it is still in use by the town's works department.

Prior to the activity at these camps, a party of Toronto newspapermen accompanied Captain Seymour on a tour of Camp Borden. The camp had cost the British government more than a million dollars to construct, and the IMB was anxious to publicize its facilities in the hopes of attracting buyers. *The Toronto Star* described Borden as the finest and largest aerodrome in the world with sixty-eight modern buildings, a water system, heating plant, sewage system, and miles of macadam roads. The buildings included barracks for officers, cadets, and men, as well as eighteen hangars. Thirty-two of the buildings could be converted into hospital accommodation and barracks for troops, the hospital provided five thousand beds with thirty-six other buildings to be used as needed. All buildings were electrically wired, contained hot-water radiation, modern toilets, shower baths, mess rooms, and sleeping quarters. A few were equipped with modern, well-equipped kitchens.[11]**

---

* The hangar has been shortened but the house is visible on the east side of Boundary Road, about a kilometre north of Deseronto. The town also purchased the pipes and fittings; the rest of the plumbing was torn out and sold.[10]

** Of the eighteen hangars, eight are still standing and a few are in use for storage. These hangars were declared heritage buildings in 1989. Retired Lieutenant-General Chester Hull presided over the ceremony. Built in 1917, the hangars were intended to be temporary structures, lasting for the duration of the war.

The IMB, in co-operation with the British War Office, may have arranged the tour to bring the camp forcefully to the attention of the Canadian government, which was well known for its equivocation when large expenditures were involved. This tactic put the government under pressure to make a decision. Had the tactic not worked, the IMB would have been forced to dispose of the camp piecemeal. Fortunately, the strategy worked and, early in December, it was announced that the Department of Militia and Defence had taken over Camp Borden. The price was not revealed. *The Toronto Star* stated there were rumours in air force circles that Borden would now be used as a permanent HQ for a new Canadian air force.[12]

On 28 November, the editor of *The Toronto Star* sprang once again to the defence of Canadian cadets, arguing forcefully that the forty young men who had completed their training, and were due to receive their commissions as well as 180 dollars in uniform allowance had been required to sign their discharge papers.

*The Star* argued that the young men had survived the accidents and risks involved in flight and had successfully completed their training and, following the custom of past graduates, had ordered their uniforms expecting to graduate as pilots. But the war had ended and they were no longer needed. The RAF explained that they had received instructions from England to send no more men; as a result no more commissions could be granted.

Hoare's powers allowed him to grant temporary, but not permanent, commissions. However, he believed that granting the men their commissions was the fair and right thing to do and he cabled the Air Ministry for permission.

In an announcement on 9 December, the RAF informed the public that, with the exception of about 300 who had been disabled while on duty, all the cadets in the RAF, numbering 5,000, had been discharged; only 7,000 mechanics and some officers remained. The process of discharging the mechanics began that day.

As they were not members of the service, but civilian employees, the discharge of the women proceeded more swiftly. The first 200 were discharged on 30 November but many clerical employees remained on staff as large numbers were needed to handle the paperwork created by demobilization.

Meanwhile, the towns and villages, which had been home for many months to the men and women of the RAF, clamoured to throw dances and dinners to celebrate the friendships made as well as the contribution the RAF had made to their communities. In return, the RAF invited these same people to farewell dinners and dances at their respective camps.

On 4 December, the officers of Camp Mohawk hosted a large dance in the assembly hall, attended primarily by guests from Deseronto, Napanee, and Belleville. A Toronto orchestra, hired for the occasion, proved a resounding success.[13]

At Borden, a friendship based on competition and comradeship had developed between those RAF officers who excelled at golf and the scratch golfers at the Borden Golf and Country Club. Other friendships arose from contacts at social events such as camp dances. At the Collier Street Methodist Church concerts had been held in which singers and musicians from the camp performed. Sergeant-Major Pritchard organized the RAF's participation in these concerts, which included solo singers, violin and mandolin solos, duets, trios, and concert numbers.[14]

By the end of November, the cadets at Borden had been demobilized and a few transferred to Deseronto but the mechanics and officers, many of whom had been at Borden since it opened, remained. In appreciation of the generosity shown by Barrie's citizenry, the officers arranged a farewell dance at the camp, which *The Northern Advance* of 19 December described as a huge success. The paper went on to note that, "The breakup of Camp Borden is viewed with much regret in Barrie where the RAF has made themselves very popular."[15]

Hoare, in appreciation for the use of several university buildings, donated a number of airplanes to the University of Toronto, along with a large number of component parts and servicing equipment. This was done to assist the university in setting up an aeronautical engineering department. The university president announced that such a course would be on the curriculum in the coming year. A spokesman for the force made the interesting observation that:

> The mathematical teaching staff of the universities will probably teach most of the courses. It is very unlikely any officers will take on this work because RAF officers who are sufficiently educated in the sciences to teach it in a university course would expect a better position than that of a professor.... Aviation will be one of the heaviest courses in any university because the theory of aviation depends entirely on the working out of mathematical problems, which are very difficult.[16]

Shortly afterwards, Hoare made a similar gift to Queen's University in Kingston. It consisted of two airplanes, four engines, a number of spare parts and the necessary servicing equipment. The engineering department at Queen's did not create a course in aeronautical engineering until 1925, when a course on aeronautics was added to the last year of the mechanical engineering program; an additional course was added the following year.[17]

On 8 December, the RAF announced, "It is expected that by the end of January the RAF will, for all practical purposes, have ceased to exist. So far none of the barracks occupied by the RAF have been closed."[18]

The majority of British officers were anxious to return to England to protect their acting and temporary ranks. A few officers did not return to England. Lieutenant-Colonel Malcom Methven from Lancaster, who commanded the stores depot, married Marion Watson of Toronto in December and opted to stay in Canada.[19]

Tylee was scheduled to take charge of the fledgling Canadian Air Force. With no real challenges left, Hoare was anxious to return to England, not to protect his rank but to avoid the Canadian winter. In January of 1919, Hoare turned his command over to the most competent Canadian available, Captain Murton Seymour.

Seymour continued the winding-down process ably assisted by Major F.W. Hawksford, a British officer who had been in charge of the recruits depot where much of the demobilization had taken place.

The RAF lingered in Canada largely because of airmen injured in training. Longwood House, the convalescent hospital donated by Mrs.

Charles Beattie, was situated eight kilometres north of Toronto. It was furnished for the airmen by the Canadian Aviation Club, been founded by Colonel Hamilton Merritt. It continued to serve as a convalescent hospital for more than a year after the war.

Consequently, winding down the RAF took a good deal longer than anyone had anticipated. By mid-June 1919, total strength stood at 506 men of whom 200 were in the process of demobilization. Another 117 were in use for demobilization purposes, 37 were in the paymaster's office, while 70 were still in hospital. The remainder consisted of 2 medical officers, 67 in Records, and 14 on duty in the States.[20]

In April of 1919, Captain Seymour was called to the bar in British Columbia but remained technically on strength. In the meantime, he turned his administrative duties over to Major Hawksford, who carried them out efficiently. In October, Seymour was called to the bar in Ontario; he then demobilized himself. As all but a few administrative details had been cleared up, he turned these over to Hawksford, who remained in Canada for another few months. By the end of December 1919, the RAF had ceased to exist in Canada.[21] Nevertheless, its impact on the Dominion was both lasting and transformative.

# Chapter Twenty-Four
## The Legacy of the RAF in Canada

It is hardly too much to say that RFC/RAF Canada
was the single most powerful influence in bringing
the air age to Canada. Without it, both the RCAF
and the civil air industry would have been much
less solidly based and inevitably Canadian aviation
would have been dependent upon American flyers
and technicians, and upon American innovations.
As it was, RFC/RAF Canada, and through it a number
of Canadians, had made an impact upon the early
history of United States aviation.

>    — *S.F. Wise, in* Canadian Airmen and the First
>    World War: The Official History of the Royal
>    Canadian Air Force[1]

The demobilization of RAF (Canada) left the IMB lumbered with a large
number of obsolete aircraft. With few civilian or military buyers, the IMB
was forced to unload over 700 JN-4 (Canucks) along with thousands of
parts, engines, and tools. In late January 1919, F.G. Ericson, former chief
engineer at Canadian Aeroplanes, and Roy Conger, a New York City
entrepreneur, purchased all but fifty of these planes. The fifty went to
the Canadian government for use as training aircraft in the CAF. A press
release explained why the IMB believed it necessary to sell these planes,
parts, and related equipment at fire-sale prices:

> All the aeroplanes, engines, and equipment in Canada
> belonging to the Imperial Munitions Board have been
> sold for an unstated figure to a syndicate of American

and Canadian businessmen ... the equipment taken over cost about $9,000,000. But the purchase price is not anything like that figure. "Now that the war is over these machines are of no use to the government," stated the official in Ottawa ... and the Imperial Munitions Board thought this was a good opportunity to get rid of the enormous equipment ... The Government could not hold them indefinitely [stored at Camp Borden] because delicate machinery like aeroplane engines require constant care and might go to waste in a few months if left to rust ... "The syndicate which has taken over is already in the aeroplane business in the States and it is understood that they will inaugurate a service between important centres in Canada."[2]

The Toronto Star interviewed Ericson at the IMB office, asking a number of pertinent questions. Ericson replied:

The operation will be located at Leaside. All the equipment is being centralized there. Toronto should be glad that the company made its headquarters in this city. When will they take possession — formal possession? We took over everything on January 23 when the deal was closed in this office. What was the purchase price? It is not for publication. But the sum was a modest one.[3]

A dispatch from New York City revealed that the British government had stipulated in the agreement that the price not be revealed. In addition to selling the equipment and airplanes at a rock-bottom price, the Canadian government was also persuaded to grant Ericson and Conger the use of the Leaside aerodrome for six months rent-free.

This sweetheart deal enabled Conger and Ericson to sell hundreds of JN-4s at low prices, putting the JN-4 within easy reach of large numbers of aspiring aviators. They also became a cheap source of supply for dozens of entrepreneurs anxious to go into the flying business. Almost overnight, barnstormers made the airplane a common sight at country fairs and city exhibitions across the Dominion. Most of these operations did not survive, but a few went on to form successful commercial enterprises, carrying prospectors into the north, hauling freight where speed was essential, and supplying valuable services to remote corners of the Dominion. For example, JN-4s were used to deliver mail on a regular basis between Ottawa and Toronto, and between Rouyn, Quebec, and Haileybury, Ontario; this service also carried passengers [4] The Jenny was specially modified for this purpose.

By the end of the 1920s, the JN-4 had become obsolete even for civilian use and gradually disappeared. However, a few notable achievements took place in Jennies during this decade. The first two women parachute jumpers carried out their separate feats in the versatile aircraft while the first woman to become a licensed pilot, Miss Eileen Vollick of Hamilton passed her test in a JN-4. She also completed several parachute jumps from these airplanes.[5]

As a consequence of so many affordable airplanes being made available by the wind-down of the RAF, the airplane became part of Canadian commerce with consequences throughout society but with their greatest impact on Canada's north.

Many of the early companies serviced remote northern mining and resource communities such as Fort Norman in the Northwest Territories, Angliers and Rouyn in Quebec, Haileybury and Red Lake in Northern Ontario, as well as Churchill, Manitoba, on Hudson Bay.[6] In addition to supplying a mail service, these pioneer airlines also carried freight and passengers, while several became involved in aerial mapping and prospecting. In these and other ways, the airplane, its colourful and courageous bush pilots, intrepid prospectors, and hardy entrepreneurs began the process of opening up and developing the riches of the vast Canadian North.

Aviation can be credited with introducing the mining industry with its resultant benefits and problems to the sub-arctic. An early example was Gilbert Labine of the Eldorado Gold Mines. While Labine was flying out of Great Bear Lake in the fall of 1929, he spotted a cobalt bloom on the east side of the lake. He returned the next spring and staked a number of sites. In spite of the economic depression, reports of fabulous mineral finds sparked a staking and exploration boom. In the end, only Labine's company actually built an operating mine, but it resulted in the founding of the sub-arctic town of Port Radium. The mine was so important to the Allied war effort in the Second World War that the Canadian government nationalized both the mine and the facility at Port Hope, which processed the ore into radium. It was this mine that supplied the uranium used to create the atomic bombs dropped on Japan, thus ending the war in the Pacific.

The coming of the airplane lessened the settlers' dependence on seasonal ships for the annual delivery of goods and passengers and brought them into more regular contact with the outside world. Medical emergencies were no longer as dire because air travel allowed patients, doctors, and medicine to be airlifted in or out as the situation required. Combined with the radio, the airplane eased the loneliness of the settlers and raised their morale. As one resident of Fort Resolution reported in 1929, "The North has been brought to civilization through the aid of airmail, and the depressing isolation of our winter is soon to be forgotten."[7]

Finding and developing the great riches of the Canadian North is still underway; the diamond mines at Ekati and Diavik developed in the 1990s are two recent examples of the vast riches still being developed in Canada's vast northern frontier. The airplane is crucial to locating, staking, and removing this fabulous wealth. The mines at both Ekati and Diavik were staked by prospectors utilizing helicopters. It is no exaggeration to state that without these aircraft the cost of prospecting the barren lands of the Northwest Territories and Nunavut would be prohibitive. As a consequence, the airplane has been crucial to the discovery and extraction of billions of dollars' worth of mineral wealth. Moreover, its impact on northern communities has been incalculable, ending their isolation and literally airlifting them into the twentieth and twenty-first centuries.

The gift of JN-4s to various universities also had long-term consequences for aviation, leading to the creation of aviation engineering courses at Canadian universities. The universities provided trained aeronautical engineers who were recruited by such companies as Boeing Aircraft of Canada. They located a manufacturing facility in

Toronto shortly after the war and, by the end of the 1920s, had built another plant in Vancouver.[8]

The gift of aeronautical equipment from the IRAF to the University of Toronto, which led to the instigation of a course in aeronautical engineering, impacted the women's movement. In the spring of 1928, University of Toronto's School of Military Aeronautics graduated Elsie Gregory MacGill, the first woman to graduate with a degree in electrical and aeronautical engineering. She went on to earn a master's degree from the University of Michigan and later designed fighter aircraft for the Second World War.

During the period when the RFC/RAF training plan operated in Canada, the British government spent $39,990,000 — a vast amount of money for the time. Put in a comparative context, the total expenditures of the province of Ontario for the years 1917 and 1918 were a little over $30 million, roughly one third less than what the RFC/RAF spent in Canada during the same period.

Not all of the RAF's budget was spent in Ontario. Some money went to the United States to purchase the OX-5 engines, some went to Quebec to purchase linen for the airplanes' coverings, and a great deal was spent in British Columbia for the wooden components. Overall, the RAF's expenditures gave an enormous boost to Canada's economy.

The training plan was crucial to the outcome of the air war. In less than two years, the RFC/RAF plan graduated 3,135 pilots and 137 observers.[*] In addition, the plan trained 456 pilots for the United States. As of 11 November 1918, RAF (Canada) had 240 pilots and 52 observers ready for overseas postings.[9] These were impressive numbers and helped speed the Allied victory and end the war.

In addition, another 7,453 men were trained as ground crew. Although not officially on strength as mechanics with RAF (Canada), several hundred women were also trained in various aspects of airplane servicing and repair. Equally important to Canada's postwar economy were the hundreds of men and women trained in the various skills

---

* Numbers vary depending upon the source. Sir Arthur Kemp, minister of militia and defence, in a speech in London, England, stated that 4,280 pilots and observers had been trained in Canada.[10]

of airplane manufacture at the IMB plant on Dufferin Street. At peak production, approximately 2,000 workers were employed at the plant. These skilled and semi-skilled workers laid the basis for a post-war airplane industry. They further contributed to the public's increased awareness of airplanes and their growing importance to Canada's post-war society.

The importance of the training plan to the Canadian war effort is demonstrated by the statistics; of the more than 22,000 Canadians who served as members of the RNAS, RFC, or RAF during the war, more than two thirds were graduates of the RFC/RAF Canadian operation.

While in Texas the IRFC trained 408 American forces pilots, comprised of 23 U.S naval officers and 385 pilots for the air branch of the U.S. Army Signal Corps. Another 6 had completed all tests except for aerial gunnery while the training of 42 cadets was well advanced. If these cadets are factored in, the IRFC trained a total of 456 pilots for the American forces as well as an additional 1,600 ground trades.[11]

Equally significant was the impetus given to the United States in organizing its aeronautical schools and developing an efficient training plan. After their visit to Toronto in the spring of 1917, American academics and staff officers returned to Washington where they quickly adopted IRFC methods and manuals. As a result, the Americans were able to get an air force trained and fighting in Europe by the spring of 1918.

The influence of the RFC/RAF's air training plan was not limited to its impact on winning the First World War, it also influenced the training plans of the Second World War. The British experience in training pilots in Canada during 1917–1918 was, to a large degree, the template for the British Commonwealth Air Training Plan of the Second World War, but with one significant difference; the BCATP would be totally under the control of the Canadian government.

After the Munich Agreement of 1938, Allen, then employed in commercial aviation, was approached informally by Sir William Mitchell of the Air Ministry who told him that, in the event of war, the ministry was seriously considering an Empire air-training scheme. He also told Allen that the ministry had the experience of the RFC/RAF training plan in mind, but on a much larger scale. Allen stressed, "Any training organization in a Dominion should be under the control of the Dominion authority."[12]

When the British approached Canada's prime minister, William Lyon Mackenzie King, he made it abundantly clear that no training scheme would take place in Canada that was not *completely* under the control of the Dominion government. In his diaries, King commented on his negotiations with the British:

> What was really in the minds of the British Air Force is to keep command in their own hands, though they have been obliged to admit, on many occasions, that Canadian pilots have more skill and judgement than their own.[13]

The British delegation, led by Lord Riverdale, was concerned that British ground crew would be under the command of Canadian airmen. But King held firm to his condition that the RCAF would administer the Air Training Plan and that Canadian airmen would remain under the control of the RCAF even after they had been posted overseas. After some difficult negotiations, the British delegation acquiesced. The agreement arguably created the most successful air-training schemes in the history of modern warfare. It was signed on 17 December 1939.

The RFC/RAF training plan kickstarted Canada into the aeronautical age. Canada was one of the first nations in the world to formally regulate aviation, licensing pilots and certifying aircraft. In the decades between the two world wars, Canada was a leading country in utilizing and developing the potential of the airplane.

Peck's initial airmail flight was quickly replicated in various cities by a number of RAF (Canada) pilots. The result of all this activity led, in the fall of 1920, to the first international mail service between Victoria, British Columbia, and Seattle, Washington. In an age of aerial experimentation, the service survived rather a long time, finally concluding in the summer of 1937. In the autumn of 1928, Canadian Airways increased its thrice-weekly airmail service between Toronto, Montreal, and Quebec City, to a daily mail service; the first of its kind in Canada.[14]

At the level of the individual, a strong bond was forged between the people of Texas and Canadians, which carried over into the Second World War when over 600 Texans travelled to Canada and enlisted in the RCAF.[15]

The links that were established between the United States and Britain re-emerged two decades later when the Nazi menace threatened civilization. If America was slow to join the conflict, many of its young men were not; at least twelve Americans flew with the RAF during the Battle of Britain. And, by early 1941, the RAF was able to establish three fighter squadrons piloted almost exclusively by Americans. When America finally entered the Second World War, facilities were again made available for the training of Canadian and British airmen in Texas and the southern United States.[16]

The shared experience of the First World War, in which the Air Training Plan in Canada played a significant role, fostered a friendship between all three nations and contributed to the United States eventually coming into the Second World War on the British and Allied side not only against its Japanese attackers but against Nazi Germany as well.

The alliances that followed the Second World War were essential to maintaining the peace during the Cold War. These alliances had their beginnings in that first meeting between Hoare and those in Washington. The Texas-Canada training agreement was the forerunner to later shared and more formal defence agreements such as the Permanent Joint Board on Defence, The Canada-U.S. Military Cooperation Committee, CANUSTEP (a memorandum of understanding — Canada-U.S. Test and Evaluation Program, which came into effect in September 2002), NATIBO (North American Technology and Industrial Base Organization, which came into effect in August 1997), Mutual Support and Integrated Lines of Communication Memoranda of Understanding, NATO, and NORAD. In addition, each year the two nations routinely participate in many cooperative land, air, and sea-training exercises.[17]

As recently as the fall of 2005, the Canadian Forces chief of staff, General Rick Hillier, had this to say of the relationship existing between the Canadian and American military:

The U.S. military view the Canadian Forces as a "partner of choice" and on Canada as one of only three or four countries that can actually do a spectrum of operations: humanitarian assistance, rebuilding a country and being tough, "when we need to be tough." He added that U.S. Defence Secretary Donald Rumsfield told him that he had, "Nothing but respect for those Canadians — the only problem is there are too few of you in uniform."[18]

The United States' influence over Canada's economy and political decision-making is regrettable but if you have to live next door to a superpower, the United States is your best choice. Fortunately, while the people of both countries sometimes disagree on issues and values, they share many assumptions and interests and generally have a warm regard for each other.

# CHAPTER TWENTY-FIVE
## THE LOST GENERATION: AN RAF TRAGEDY

> Nothing is here for tears, nothing to wail or knock
> the breast; no weakness, no contempt, dispraise or
> blame; nothing to but well and fair / And what may
> quiet us in [a] death so noble.
> — *John Milton,* Samson Agonistes

No homily spoken at the funeral service of Captain Vernon Castle on that bleak February afternoon could have been more appropriate than this passage by Milton. The manner of the slim dancer's death personified a life of generosity, sacrifice, and nobility of purpose.

The society to which the soldiers returned after the war did not seem worth the cost. Too many profiteers had made fortunes manufacturing shells and weapons while soldiers and nurses fought and laboured for subsistence wages. The war's human and economic waste undermined the old system of beliefs, which were now viewed with cynicism and disillusion.

In Canada, the RAF faced a clamour of protests from former mechanics who claimed their discharge pay was wholly inadequate.[1] The success of the Bolshevik Revolution in Russia unleashed a powerful worker's movement with some labour groups advocating violence and mass strikes. Although illegal in Canada and the United States, the International Workers of the World, a radical organization dedicated to the overthrow of capitalism, was attracting increasing numbers of dedicated disciples. The recession that followed the end of the war unleashed a torrent of unrest amongst the working classes, which peaked in Canada with the Winnipeg General Strike of 1919.

In Paris, a group of writers, sculptors, and poets discarded the traditional constraints of society. They revelled in the sobriquet given them by Hemingway who borrowed the phrase "lost generation" from Gertrude Stein. Dedicated to the café life, they indulged in alcohol, drugs, the arts, and bohemian love, derisively debunking the mores of the previous generation in both their life and their art.

Their story is not typical of RAF officers and flyers, many of whom rose to dizzying heights in the world of commerce, industry, and the professions. But for many young men and women, the high purpose and sacrifice of the war had left them disillusioned; the belief systems of their parents exposed as a sham. Many survivors of the conflict became wastrels and misfits, wandering nihilistically through the postwar years on paths of self-destruction, following *la vie de jouissance*.

The tragic but noble death of Vernon Castle unleashed a torrent of anguish amongst those in the entertainment, social, and aviation worlds who had been touched by his generosity and talent. Nowhere was the anguish felt more deeply than in the small coterie of friends and relatives comprised of Jack Coats, Eardley Wilmot, and his sisters Gwen and Audrey.

When Vernon Castle died, Gwen Wilmot went into mourning and did not emerge from the family home until seven months later when she attended her sister's wedding as maid of honour. With the exception of a French hat of taupe, Gwen was dressed entirely in black satin, surely the most unusual colour ever to adorn a bridesmaid. All of Belleville society knew that the tragic death of her lover was the reason for her mourning.[2]

*Gwen Wilmot dressed for her sister's wedding. Courtesy of Carolyn Heatherington.*

The signing of the armistice on 11 November set off a euphoric reaction to the war's ending and to the privations endured by Canada's civilian population. The populace morphed from the previous despair into a joyful celebration of the victory and a belated return to something approaching normalcy; those celebrations were nowhere more in evidence than in the staunch colonial city of Toronto. Almost every evening, elaborate balls, dinners, and entertainments were held in the homes of the city's best families and finest hostelries.[3]

Audrey and Jack Coats rented a home in Toronto's fashionable Rosedale district and immediately became the centre of a lively group of young officers and society daughters. As the heir to the Coats family fortune, and a holder of the Air Force Cross, Captain Coats was a superb host, especially in the wistful view of colonial elites with daughters of marriageable age.

Gwen Wilmot occasionally attended these soirees. Many a hopeful swain squired Gwen around the dance floor or joined her at the bridge table. But none of the young officers interested her and, eventually, Audrey and Jack abandoned their efforts to find a suitable replacement for her mourned lover. Jack and Audrey sailed for England aboard the SS *Olympic* on 25 January 1919; Gwen followed a few months later.[4]

Although their relationship was frequently stormy, both sisters remained close. Audrey welcomed the presence of her savvy sister to assist her in the daunting task of winning acceptance by the British nobs.

In England, the Coatses moved into a twenty-two-room flat, complete with eleven staff, in London's fashionable Mayfair district. The two sisters were not only superb dancers, but also accomplished horsewomen, a talent they had acquired from their father, Charles Wilmot, who had been an owner, breeder, and trainer of pedigreed horses for jumping, hurdles and show.[5] It was not long before the two sisters were hobnobbing with dukes, earls, and even royalty, as they captivated the aristocracy with their feisty beauty, dancing, and riding skills.[6]

Within the year, Audrey gave birth to a son and, a few years later, a daughter. The son was named Vernon in honour of the man who had brought them all together. Gwen, Audrey, and Audrey's husband, Jack, lived a life of luxury and ease, dividing their time between dancing and

*Audrey Wilmot Coates is seated to the left, while Gwen and her husband, D'Arcy Rutherford, are on the right. The trio is dining at the Café de Paris, where the Castles first came to the attention of the entertainment world. Courtesy of Kaelin McCowan.*

cards in England's finest homes, visiting the salons of Europe, or joining the fox hunts in northern Scotland where Jack was master of the hunt.

In 1930, Gwen married Captain D'Arcy Rutherford, a handsome, debonair playboy with even more diverse talents than Gwen; Rutherford was credited with inventing the sport of water-skiing. A year later, Gwen delivered a daughter whom they named Carolyn. Carolyn was raised as an only, but happy, child.

In the meantime, Eardley Wilmot was following a more adventuresome and entrepreneurial path. When the war ended, he received an early release from the RAF. The Handley-Page Company needed an officer with Wilmot's skills as a flyer and salesman to accompany a shipment of aircraft to Argentina where the government was starting an air force. In late 1918 he left for Argentina, helped set up the air force, and stayed on at the government's request to instruct cadets in the mysteries of flying.

*Eardley Wilmot in Argentina, 17 July 1920. The Spanish translates as "The famous Canadian aviator Wilmot, whose notable acrobatic stunts over the capital have been one of the most impressive spectacles of our National Holiday." Courtesy of Kaelin McCowan.*

In early 1921, he suffered severe burns while flying in Argentina and returned to Belleville where he purchased a JN-4, hired Joe Goold as his mechanic, and began barnstorming Ontario and the United States. The enterprise lasted a little over a year; a normal lifespan in that precarious business. During this period, Eardley received an invitation from the both the Argentinian and Brazilian governments to return with the rank of major and take charge of scout instruction. As the only son of a widowed mother, he felt obligated to turn down those offers.[7]

He then used his contacts and a partner's money to start a Ford dealership in Belleville. Entering local politics in 1926, he was elected to council. The following year he was elected mayor. In 1930, he sold his business and moved to Brantford where he had met Isabelle Cockshutt, youngest daughter of multimillionaire Colonel Harry Cockshutt, the former president of Cockshutt Farm Implement and previously lieutenant governor of Ontario.

On 28 June 1930, Eardley and Isabelle were married in Grace Church, at Brantford; the Anglican archbishop of Toronto, Canon Cody, presiding. Jack and Audrey Coats crossed the Atlantic so that Jack could serve as best man. The reception was held at Dufferin House, the majestic home of Isabelle's parents.[8] It was a glorious June day, the radiant sunlight matched by the well-heeled guests and strikingly attractive couple.

Although the Wilmots and Coatses were at the summit of their lives, dark clouds were already gathering. Despite appearances, Audrey had developed into a serious drinker. She remained much admired in British society partially because of her ability as a colourful raconteur and the life of every party.

Major Coats discovered he had married an independent, hot-tempered, and controlling woman. The tempers of the Wilmot sisters were legendary; Gwen and Audrey often got into violent arguments occasionally ending with both women pushing and slapping each other. This helps to explain why Coats developed into a playboy, often losing heavily at the gambling tables of Monte Carlo where he was much admired for the nonchalant indifference with which he lost huge sums of money.[9]

Coats had been a superb flying instructor, widely liked and respected by both his students and fellow officers. His popularity emerges in a book written by Roger Vee (aka Vivian Voss), who wrote about his CO after Vee had smashed up a plane. Vee, who was far from a natural pilot, provides this account of his conversation with Coats after the accident:

> I'm sorry, sir, about your machine. "Damn it Vee, its all in the game — and your neck is of more consequence than the bus!" It was a sporting view to take of the mishap and was characteristic of the popular officer.[10]

On another occasion Vee gave an example of how Coats understood and guided his student-pilots. Vee had managed only two and a half hours of solo flying when he was dismayed to find he had developing a bad case of nerves.

> One afternoon I had climbed into a machine feeling pretty blue. Lt. Coats came up, carrying a little pup in his arms that some mechanic had brought to the aerodrome. "Isn't he a jolly little chap?" he said, pulling his ear.
>
> "Yes sir," I replied. "I wonder, sir, if I could have a bit of leave. I hate asking for it but I think a few days away from the camp might do me a lot of good."
>
> As usual he was at once sympathetic, but said that it was impossible at present as they were anxious that we should finish our five hours' solo flying so that we could go on to Camp Borden. He promised that he would write to the CO there and try to persuade him to give me a few days.
>
> As he was leaving the machine, he told me to go up and do eight landings. So I taxied out, took off, made one circuit, and landed. Then I took off again, made another circuit, and landed ... I did this eight times.
>
> When I came in, I was delighted to find that my nervousness had completely vanished. This one

afternoon's landings had completely restored my confidence. I should like to stress this fact, as it made a vast difference to me. After this, flying became a sheer delight. It is a most glorious feeling to be able to swoop *confidently* like a bird through the air. When I got in I went at once in search of Lt. Coats.

"I don't think it's necessary any more, sir, for you to write that letter."

"Sure Vee? All right," and there was a knowing twinkle in his eye.[11]

After the wedding, Audrey and Jack returned to England where their lives resumed their downward spiral; Audrey drinking more heavily and Jack gambling ever more recklessly. Unknown to Coats, his heavy losses were partially the result of a crooked gambling ring operating at the Monte Carlo casino. On the last day of June, 1932, Jack Coats took out his service revolver and ended a life that had once been full of promise.[12]

A fine officer and a gentleman during the war, when hostilities ended Coats found himself without purpose. Like many veterans, he became part of the lost generation.

Of the three flying instructors who became close friends at Camp Deseronto, only Eardley Wilmot survived. After his marriage to Isabelle,

*Jack Coats on his wedding day. Courtesy of April Wagrel.*

he developed a large commercial turkey farm. Known as "The Grove," it was one of the foremost turkey farms in Canada. By the standards of the 1930s, the operation was highly mechanized, garnering sufficient interest to be featured in a news film released in theatres across the country.[13]

Despite his success as a turkey farmer, Eardley's first love remained flying. He purchased a De Havilland aircraft and from 1934 until 1939 was either president or vice-president of the Brant-Norfolk Aero Club. He also maintained his status as a member of the RCAF Reserve.

A few months after the outbreak of the Second World War, the British Commonwealth Air Training Plan was created. At forty-nine years of age, Wilmot could not expect to be posted overseas, but the BCATP badly needed experienced instructors. Wilmot's experience during the First World War now encouraged him to apply for an instructor's position with the RCAF. In England, he had flown and instructed in the Auro, the Sopwith Pup, the Camel, the DH-4, the S.E. 5, the Martinade Scout, and the Snipe, but he had no experience with the new fighters and bombers and would have to pass exams in these faster, more powerful aircraft.

In the meantime Wilmot's long association with the local Conservative Party resulted in his nomination as the party's candidate in the federal election of 1940. Mackenzie King's Liberals won a substantial majority and Wilmot, despite local popularity, went down to his first defeat.

He did better as a candidate for flying instructor where he was trained on Oxfords, Harvards, and Fairy Battles. His examiners noted that while his ability was average, he was, "very keen, an excellent pilot, conscientious, hard working, possessed above average initiative and mature judgement."[14] In May of 1941, he was recommended for promotion to squadron leader.

Wilmot was a man of character and determination; he had achieved much and, until the Second World War, had been blessed with good fortune. But bad cess dogged all the Wilmots, even Eardley.

Busy airfields are noisy places. Moreover, they are especially dangerous during wartime, when large numbers of inexperienced pilots are landing, taxiing, and taking off in constrained spaces. This is the likely explanation for what happened on the afternoon of 15 October. Squadron Leader Wilmot was walking across the tarmac towards his airplane when he was struck by the propeller of a taxiing aircraft, killing him instantly. Eardley had been the examining officer at Uplands and in two days was to have been transferred to Camp Borden as its chief instructor.[15] He left behind a broken-hearted wife and three small children.

In the late 1930s, Audrey Coats married an American, Don Haldeman. The couple moved to Nassau where booze came to dominate their lives. One member of the family observed that Audrey mixed milk with her gin during the morning, switched to martinis in the afternoon, and ended up in the evening with two or more large glasses of Scotch.[16] In 1957, she died in her Nassau home after falling down a flight of stairs.

Her younger sister, Gwen, divorced D'Arcy Rutherford noting that, "He could do everything except support his family."[17] Gwen remained in Canada after the war, raising her daughter Carolyn by herself. Carolyn recalls that her mother's great love remained Vernon Castle, whose thick bundle of letters she kept in a large envelope sealed with wax. Near the end of her life, she took out the letters and then, after rereading each one, she cast them, one by one, into the fireplace.

Her daughter, Carolyn Heatherington, although a senior citizen, maintains a busy career as a stage actress in Toronto.

# Epilogue

> He explained that the great quality they [fighter pilots] possessed was a "wealth of optimism and a want of fear.... They also shared a sense of humour and an ability to reduce or abolish fear and worry even in times of great stress."[1]
> — *Thomas Hackett, Harvard professor of psychiatry*

Examining the post war careers of the higher-ranking officers of RAF (Canada) leads to some evident conclusions. First, it is clear that most left the service with an abiding interest in aviation and, for many, a passion for flying. With few exceptions, the success these officers obtained in the Air Force continued into their postwar life, often in business but also in the professions. What follows is an account of the postwar careers of the most prominent of the officers in the RFC/RAF in Canada during the First World War.

Quite a few officers remained in the RAF while a much smaller number were absorbed into the newly created Canadian Air Force or transferred into one of the colonial forces.

Lieutenant-Colonel Gurney Hoare followed the latter course. He had quietly and efficiently substituted for his younger brother on two occasions. In the absence of Hoare and Allen, Gurney Hoare had acted as the CO of the contingent in Texas. In June 1918, when General Hoare was recalled to London, Gurney Hoare was appointed acting CO until his brother's return.[2] As well as his duties as chief of ordinance for the RAF in Canada, he served as technical adviser to the IMB. Blessed with a calm disposition and keen intelligence, he ran his department efficiently with just two staff officers. For his achievements in Canada, he was made a Commander of the British Empire or CBE.

As a fully trained chemist, the elder Hoare had options other than the RAF. Nor did he have any desire to return to England. He had served with the British Army in South Africa during the Boer War and believed it was the only country with a decent climate. Gurney Hoare knew Prime Minister Jan Christian Smutts, whose influence may have helped him obtain the position of chief of ordinance in the South African Army.

He and his family remained in South Africa where he rose to the rank of Major-General. During the Second World War, he led the South African contingent to the Far East Armament Conference and was later posted to India for two years during the turbulent postwar years. He and his family never returned to England but remained in South Africa.[3]

Officers of Wing Commander rank tended to continue as career soldiers in the RAF or, in a few cases, with the CAF. Lieutenant-Colonel Fred Wanklyn, an RMC graduate, was born of prosperous parents in Montreal. Early in life, Wanklyn developed a wanderlust, journeying at his own expense to Port Arthur in Manchuria. Upon graduating from RMC in 1909, he joined the British Royal Artillery in England and, three years later, transferred to the RFC where he gained extensive experience flying nine different types of military aircraft. By the outbreak of the war, he had reached the rank of temporary captain. During 1915, he earned a Military Cross and was mentioned in dispatches. Promoted to major, he was posted to Canada to head the new Wing at North Toronto. On 23 September 1918, he transferred to Deseronto as Wing Commander where he remained until January 1919, when he was posted to HQ staff in Toronto. Wanklyn returned to England in March and transferred to the Royal Artillery, serving in that branch for the next four years. He retired from the service in 1928 and moved to Nassau as general manager of Pan American Airways in the Bahamas. He took up permanent residence in Nassau, holding various airline management positions until his retirement.

Major-General Sefton Brancker was the British officer who, in the face of much skepticism, conceived the plan of a training establishment in Canada and appointed Hoare its commanding officer. Shortly after the war ended, the prescient Brancker left the RAF to take up opportunities in the virgin field of commercial aviation.[4]

James Scott was one of the few officers who remained in the Canadian Air Force. Born to wealthy parents in Roberval, Quebec, Scott had seen just four months of air combat when he was severely wounded while strafing a train well behind enemy lines. For this action he received a Military Cross, but was ruled unfit for further combat and was posted to Canada as staff officer in charge of training. During the winter of 1917–1918, Scott commanded the North Toronto Wing where he supervised the experiment in winter flying. For his role in this pioneer endeavour, he was awarded the Air Force Cross. During much of his time in Canada, Scott was in command of the wing at Camp Borden.

A sophisticated if somewhat arbitrary administrator, Scott had a talent for climbing the promotion ladder, holding various posts in Canadian aviation, including controller of civil aviation, CO of the Canadian Air Force, and finally reaching the top rung as director and CO of the newly formed RCAF, a position he held until 1928 when he resigned to enter private business. Like many of his contemporaries, Group Captain Scott returned to service during the Second World War, retiring at the end of that conflict with the rank of air commodore. He and his elegant wife spent their remaining years in Halifax.[5]

The dashing Captain Peck, who made Canada's first successful airmail flight, settled down after the war, marrying and raising a family while achieving success in private business. A graduate of McGill University and son of a prominent manufacturer, Peck rose to the presidency of a Montreal manufacturing concern. Although he did not return to the Air Force during the Second World War, he remained active in recreational flying.[6]

Keeping a hand in flying was a common denominator for the majority of these men. Murton Seymour, the Canadian who succeeded Hoare as commanding officer in 1919, opened a successful law practice in St. Catharines, but continued his interest in aviation. He incorporated the St. Catharines Flying Club in 1928, and was one of the original founders and directors of the Canadian Flying Clubs Association, holding the position of president of that organization in 1939. In recognition of his efforts in negotiating an agreement between the flying clubs of Canada and the Department of National Defence for the training of military pilots during wartime, he was awarded the McKee Trophy and the gold medal of the CFCA. In 1943, he was named an Officer of the British Empire (OBE) for those same services. His law career was equally distinguished, being elected a Life Bencher of the Upper Canada Law Society in 1951. In centennial year, the government of Canada honoured him for his services to the nation. And, finally, in 1973, for his contribution to aviation and the training of pilots during the Second World War, he was named a member of the Canadian Aviation Hall of Fame.[7]

Dermott Allen followed a more traditional path, remaining in the RAF after the war. As a squadron leader, he served in a variety of theatres including Constantinople, Egypt, Palestine, Iraq, and India before returning to the Air Ministry in England where he was promoted to Wing Commander. Retiring from the RAF in 1930, he took up a post in the Department of Civil Aviation where he was responsible for all ground organization at home and abroad.

In 1937, the lifelong career servant moved into commercial aviation, joining British Airways with responsibility to survey and advise on all aspects on the development of an air service to South America. He was still involved in this project when Hitler marched into Czechoslovakia. In 1939 he was recalled to the RAF and was placed in control of several hundred people in a section that developed and oversaw planning, secret intelligence, security, and civil defence. Allen continued with BOAC, the successor to British Airways, for a number of years after the war, finally retiring to his country home and garden. At the time of his last correspondence with Dodds at the Directorate of History in Ottawa, Allen was spending much of his time in his garden, ruminating over those long-ago days in Canada when he and his comrades had been so young.[8]

Only a few of the higher-ranking officers followed careers as pilots in commercial aviation. One of these was Major Jack Leach, MC, AFC, who eventually became CO at the school at Armour Heights. Despite the loss of one leg, Leach was generally considered the best pilot in the RFC/RAF in Canada. Prior to losing his leg, Leach achieved the status of an ace fighter pilot by shooting down seventeen enemy aircraft. After the war, the slim, handsome flyer went into commercial aviation as chief pilot, instructor, and assistant director of the Ontario Provincial Air Services. On 29 June 1930, Leach was performing loops near Port Arthur, Ontario, when his engine stalled; he was killed in the resulting crash.[9]

The man Hoare considered absolutely indispensable to the Canadian operation, Lieutenant Colonel Arthur Tylee, had studied engineering at the Massachusetts Institute of Technology but did not immediately return to that field. He held the position of acting commander of RAF (Canada) for a few weeks in 1919 but left to head up the newly formed Canadian Air Force. He was made an air commodore and, for his services during the war, was awarded an OBE. After eight months, he returned to business where he applied his considerable talents to building a comfortable fortune, retiring at the end of the decade to spend more time with his wife and children. His obituary sums up a man who epitomized the finest qualities of an RCAF officer:

> Arthur Kellum Tylee ... who kept the RCAF flying through World War II died yesterday at Sunnybrook hospital. He was 73.
>
> In May 1940, he came out of retirement as a wealthy ex-engineer and set up the coast-to-coast repair system that serviced all RCAF craft in Canada... He was a

civilian in the department of Munitions and Supply throughout World War II and preferred to be known as Art. He was an executive who was proud of his ability to operate any machine in any plant he walked into. He was a top-notch organizer but refused to have a telephone on his desk.

Air Commodore Tylee was born on a Quebec farm, milked cows, and rode a horse to school until he was 11. The family then moved to Boston where he finished his education at the Massachusetts Institute of Technology, graduating in 1907 in the same class as C.D. Howe. [The most powerful of Prime Minister King's cabinet ministers, Howe was minister of Munitions and Supply during the Second World War.]

He designed and built heavy machinery in the U.S., opened an office for his firm in Montreal in 1913 and enlisted when the war started ...

He returned to engineering [after the war], went back into the RCAF for nine months in 1920 to organize air force servicing and was the RCAF's first air commodore. He went back into engineering again, retired after 10 years and was dividing his time between Florida and his Forest Hill home when Word War II started. Old classmate Howe, then Minister of Munitions and Supply, put him in the servicing job where he stayed until the end of war then retired for the last time.[10]

Of all the talented people who made the RFC/RAF in Canada such an outstanding success, the man who deserved the most credit was Brigadier-General Cuthbert Hoare. The high esteem in which Hoare was held is evident not just from the comments of Allen and other Canadian officers, but also from what high-ranking Americans had to say of him.

The opinion of one more Canadian officer is worth noting. Murton Seymour, while critical of some of his fellow officers in Canada, had nothing but praise for Hoare. In correspondence with R.V. Dodds at the Directorate of History in 1962, he wrote:

> I am particularly pleased that you paid tribute to Brigadier-General Hoare, C.M.G., who certainly deserves what you said of him and a great deal more. I think you should be able to realize the tremendous drive this man had in order to organize the R.F.C. as quickly, as well as the large force, as he did.
>
> It was always a regret to us other officers on the Staff that he was not granted a higher rank. He had a bigger training Branch than any one or probably any two of the four training commands in England and while the O.C. of each of those commands was a Lieutenant-General, certainly General Hoare should have had the rank of at least a Major-General and I think of a Lt.-General.[11]

Hoare did not remain long in the air force, transferring to the Light Indian Horse in 1919. Nor did he not remain there for long. Allen knew his former commander well, suggesting that, "For one who had been his own master at the head of a big organization, peacetime regimental soldiering in the Indian Cavalry palled. It was too confined, too petty."[12]

In Canada, Hoare and Governor General Devonshire had often spent hours discussing crops, animal husbandry, and the growth in scientific expertise necessary to succeed at modern farming. Hoare came from the rural gentry, that class of men and women who loved fox hunting and farm management, and who had the money to afford it. As the Hoare money came mostly from banking, Cuthbert Hoare may have had sufficient resources to live in the fashion he most desired — that of a gentry farmer.

A few years after the war, Hoare resigned his commission and went to work as a farm pupil with a prosperous farmer in North Lincolnshire. Within two years, he had rented a five-hundred-acre farm on the Yarborough Estate. How he fared in this new venture is not known but he re-emerged in the 1960s, living quietly with his sister in Bradenham, from where he carried on a brief correspondence about the Canadian training plan with his former staff officer, Allen.

He died a few years later. As might be expected, his obituary was brief but was as revealing in what it didn't say about this most singular man:

> On January 31st Brigadier General Cuthbert Gurney Hoare C.M.G. C.B.E., late Central India Horse, of White Cottage, Bradenham, aged 86 years. Funeral service West Bradenburg Church Wednesday February 5th at 2:30 pm. Flowers to church please.[13]

In neither of the two newspaper obituaries dealing with Hoare's death is there any mention of his service in Canada. Nor is there any mention of his wartime service in Europe. The explanation may lie in the romantic view of India held by the British or simply by the greater amount of time spent there by Hoare during his youthful, more adventurous years. Or it may lie in Hoare's modesty and unwillingness to boast of his accomplishments. Another explanation lies in the author of his obituary, who may have been the sister. Hoare may have thought his obituary of no consequence and simply not bothered to write one.

One of the purposes of this book has been to honour the accomplishments of Brigadier-General Hoare as well as the officers and civilians who enabled the RFC/RAF Canada to achieve so much in such a short time. Another is to remedy the failure of British and Canadian historians to credit the RFC/RAF training plan with the massive facilitating effect it had on commercial aviation in Canada. Hopefully, these oversights and omissions have now been remedied.

# Appendix A
## Training Fatalities

Legend:
1 = flying accident
2 = ground accident involving aircraft
3 = other accident

| DATE | NAME | BIRTHPLACE | CAMP | CAUSE |
|---|---|---|---|---|
| **1917** | | | | |
| 4 April | 3/AM. J.M. Talbot | Dorchester, ON | Borden | 1 |
| 17 April | Cad. M. Perrault | Montreal | Borden | 2 |
| 24 May | Cad. A. Pritchard | | Borden | 1 |
| 30 May | Cad. A.W. Fraser | Ontario | Deseronto | 1 |
| 11 June | Mechanic A.M. Pepper [19] | Grey County, ON | Long Branch | 2 |
| 27 June | Cad. S. Callaghan | Ireland | Borden | 1 |
| 8 July | 2nd Lt. W. Donville | Hamilton, ON | Mohawk | 1 |
| 9 July | Cad. C.A. Page [24] | Welland, ON | Borden | 1 |
| 12 July | Cad. S. Teasdale | Toronto | Rathburn | 1 |
| 31 July | Cad. H. Pearson | Comber, ON | Borden | 1 |
| 8 Aug | Cad. Lionel S.R. Walker | Vancouver | Borden | 1 |
| 11 Aug | Cad. A. Haylan (the spelling varies, ie. Heyler or Naylan) | Midland, ON | Borden | 1 |
| 11 Aug | Cad. G.A. Morton | Winnipeg | Mohawk | 1 |
| 14 Aug | Mechanic D.E. Crane | England | Borden | 1 |
| 16 Aug | Cad. Wm. Gallie [21] | Winnipeg | Mohawk | 1 |

| DATE | NAME | BIRTHPLACE | CAMP | CAUSE |
|---|---|---|---|---|
| 17 Aug | Cad. Steven Dore | New Jersey | Armour Hgts | 1 |
| 6 Sep | Cad. A.M. Page | | Borden, ON | |
| 12 Sep | Sgt. Drummond | | Rathburn | 1 |
| 13 Sep | Cad. J. de Beaujeau Donville | Montreal | Borden | 1 |
| 13 Sep | Sgt. Instructor H. Doner | Montreal | Rathburn | 1 |
| 14 Sep | Cad. Kramer | Detroit | Mohawk | 1 |
| 14 Sep | Cad. W.G. Wheadrick | Buffalo | Borden | 1 |
| 15 Sep | 2nd Mech. George Stewart | Birkenhead, England | Leaside | 2 |
| 18 Sep | 2nd Lt. A.C. Williams | Toronto | Borden | 1 |
| 18 Sep | Cad. John E. Ludford [19] | Venezuela | Borden | 1 |
| 23 Sep | Cad. E.A. Austin | Vancouver | North Toronto | 1 |
| 6 Oct | Cad. D.A. Swayze [22] | Dunnville & Lindsay, ON | Borden | 1 |
| 21 Oct | Cad. L.J. Roebuck | Chicago | Mohawk | 1 |
| 26 Oct | Cad. Tom Murphy [23] | England | Leaside | 1 |
| 10 Nov | Cad. Walter A. Jones | | Texas | 1 |
| 11 Nov | Cad. David Edmond | Vital, MB | North Toronto | 1 |
| 12 Nov | 2nd Lt. R.L. Johnson | Canada | Texas | 3 |
| 15 Nov | Cad. James Powers | Chicago | Des. to Texas | 1 |
| 24 Nov | Cad. W.E. Alcock | England | Texas | 1 |
| 24 Nov | Cad. Biddle | England | Texas | 1 |
| 4 Dec | Cpl. Frank E. Mercer [24] | Ontario | Armour Hgts | 3 |
| 4 Dec | 2/AM Harold D. McFaul [24] | Kincardine, ON | Armour Hgts | 3 |
| 7 Dec | Sgt. Fred G. Hill | Blenheim, ON | Texas | 1 |

| DATE | NAME | BIRTHPLACE | CAMP | CAUSE |
|------|------|-----------|------|-------|
| 21 Dec | Cad. A. Eden Webster [19] | Kingston, NY | Texas | 1 |
| 21 Dec | Cad. Cyril A. Baker [20] | Moose Jaw, SK | Texas | 1 |
| 21 Dec | 2nd Lt. J.T. Russell Jenner [19] | Kingsville, ON | Texas | 1 |
| 23 Dec | Cad. A.R Harrison | | Texas | 1 |
| 24 Dec | Cad. E.D. Manson | Northgate, England | Texas | 1 |
| 24 Dec | 2nd Lt. Lawrence Rainboth | Aylmer or Ottawa | Texas | 1 |
| 24 Dec | Mechanic G. Syrad | Philadelphia | Texas | 2 |
| 27 Dec | Cad. D.G. Mott | Campbellton, NB | Texas | 1 |
| 28 Dec | Lt. S.R. Cuthbert | Ithaca, NY | Texas | 1 |
| | | | | |
| **1918** | | | | |
| 7 Jan | Cad. D.H. Rogers | | Texas | 1 |
| 17 Jan | Cad. Vernon Stoddard | Glasco, NS | Mohawk | 3 |
| 21 Jan | Cad. D.E. McMillan | Durham Centre, NB | Armour Hgts | 1 |
| 21 Jan | Cad. M.N. Milne | Malden, MA | Armour Hgts | 1 |
| 21 Jan | Cad. Alex George Bendix | Coppenhagen, Denmark | Leaside | 1 |
| 28 Jan | Cad. W.J. King | | Texas | 1 |
| 28 Jan | 2nd Lt. W.S. MacDonald | Hamilton, ON | Texas | 1 |
| 31 Jan | Cad. R.G. Rundle | St. Marys, ON | Texas | 1 |
| 2 Feb | Cad. P.W. Taylor | | Texas | 1 |
| 1 Feb | Cad. J.D. Brosman | New Brunswick | Texas | 1 |
| 10 Feb | Cad. Frank Fisher [25] | Petrolia, ON | Armour Hgts | 1 |
| 13 Feb | Cad. R. Porter [23] | Long Island, NY | Texas | 1 |
| 14 Feb | Cad. Clifford C. Murray | Wiltshire, UK | Texas | 1 |

| DATE | NAME | BIRTHPLACE | CAMP | CAUSE |
|------|------|-----------|------|-------|
| 15 Feb | Capt. Vernon Castle | England | Texas | 1 |
| 16 Feb | Cad. Fred N. Moore | Quebec | North Toronto | 1 |
| 21 Feb | Cad. J.C. Ringland | Vancouver, BC | Texas | 1 |
| 23 Feb | Cad. F. Fairchild | United States | Texas | 1 |
| 1 March | Cad. L.H. Carter | Boston | Leaside | 1 |
| 3 March | Fitter S. Hays | Seaford, ON | Texas | 1 |
| 7 March | Cad. B.E. Hurlbert | Ottawa, ON | Texas | 1 |
| 18 March | Pvt. Ellis B. Watts | United States | Texas | 1 |
| 19 March | 2nd Lt. R.J. Burley | London, UK | Texas | 1 |
| 20 March | Cad. Armheim (name is spelled various ways) | | Texas | 1 |
| 26 March | Fitter G.V. Webster | Ingersoll, ON | Leaside | 1 |
| 27 March | Cad. Howard Hooten | Montreal | Texas | 1 |
| 29 March | Cad. F.J. Dwyer | Montreal | Texas | 1 |
| 29 March | Cad. J.S. Rowan | | Texas | 1 |
| 8 April | Cad. Milo W. Kirwan | Wallace, NS | Texas | 1 |
| 20 April | Cad. A.H. Webber | | Texas | 1 |
| 17 April | Lt. E.B. Markham | Turin, NY | Texas | 1 |
| 18 April | 2nd Lt. G.L. Grant | New Jersey, U.S. | Beamsville | 1 |
| 17 April | Cad. Edward B. Donynge | New Jersey, U.S. | Beamsville | 1 |
| 25 April | Cad. V.R. Williams | Bayfield, ON | Mohawk | 2 |
| 25 April | Cad. John T. Duval | New Jersey, U.S. | Borden | 1 |
| 2 May | Cad. James Ulson | Orkneys, Scotland | Beamsville | 1 |
| 2 May | Cad. Wm. R. Litchfield (22) | Victoria, BC | Beamsville | 1 |
| 3 May | Lt. W.P. Annis | Toronto [at U of T] | Borden 44 Wing | 1 |

| DATE | NAME | BIRTHPLACE | CAMP | CAUSE |
|---|---|---|---|---|
| 6 May | 2nd Lt. G.A. Ruffridge | Mont Clair, NJ | Borden | 1 |
| 6 May | Cad. H.B. O'Leary | Toronto | Borden | 1 |
| 6 May | Cad. Herbert Paul | Springhill, NS | Mohawk | 1 |
| 11 May | Cad. N.J. Johnston | St. Marys, ON | Borden | 1 |
| 15 May | 2nd Lt. V.L. Murray | | Mohawk | 1 |
| 17 May | 2nd Lt. W. Ewart Clemens | Kitchener, ON | Beamsville | 1 |
| 17 May | 2nd Lt. Gordon F. Birchard | Woodstock, ON | Borden | 1 |
| 18 May | Cad. T.V. Patrick | Souris, MB | Rathburn | 1 |
| 22 May | Cad. Charles A. Mcillagey | New Jersey | Borden | 1 |
| 22 May | Cad. A.D. Hewson [19] | Windsor, ON | Mohawk | 1 |
| 29 May | Cad. Wilf Henry Wimmet | Los Angeles, CA | Borden | 1 |
| 29 May | 2nd Lt. T.H. Heintzman | Toronto, ON | Rathburn | 1 |
| 29 May | Cad. S. Rosenthal | New York, U.S. | Mohawk | 1 |
| 2 June | Cad. Hector S. Miller | Winnipeg | Leaside | 1 |
| 3 June | Cad. R.C. Hamer | Hillcrest, NY | Beamsville | 1 |
| 10 June | Cad. Carl Bender | Winnipeg | Rathburn | |
| 25 June | Cad. A. Burns Laird [21] | Trail, BC | Borden | 1 |
| 27 June | Capt. Dan Callaghan | Ireland | Borden | 1 |
| 2 July | Cad. C.J. Cozier | Mono Mills, ON | Borden | 1 |
| 3 July | Cad. John Robson | Scotland | Borden | 1 |
| 8 July | Lt. William K. Domville [20] | Hamilton, ON | Mohawk | 1 |
| 13 July | 2nd Lt. A.W. Whill | Snetisham, UK | Armour Hgts | 1 |
| 15 July | Cad. J.F. Buchanan | Loreburn, SK | Deseronto | 1 |
| 15 July | Cad. J.C. White | Delhi, ON | Deseronto | 1 |
| 15 July | 2nd Lt. A.W. Hill | Malden, MA | Armour Hgts | 1 |
| 16 July | Lt. C.J. Humphreys | Victoria, BC | Mohawk | 1 |

| DATE | NAME | BIRTHPLACE | CAMP | CAUSE |
|---|---|---|---|---|
| 16 July | Lt. Burton Tait | Toronto | Leaside | 1 |
| 16 July | 2nd Mechanic Belford | Moosejaw, SK | Leaside | 1 |
| 17 July | Lt. Stanley H. Glendinning | Sutherland, ON | Beamsville | 1 |
| 23 July | 2nd Lt. Colin G. Coleridge | Norfolk, UK | Deseronto | 1 |
| 27 July | Cad. Talbot C. Dunbar | Haileybury, ON | Beamsville | 1 |
| 27 July | 2nd Lt. E. L. Morley | London, ON | Rathburn | 1 |
| 8 Aug | Cad. F.R. Cook | Elan, MB | Mohawk | 1 |
| 23 Aug | Cad. Norman Frizell [18-19] | Toronto | Beamsville | 1 |
| 26 Aug | Lt. John M. Cram (or Crem) | Ottawa | Armour Hgts | 1 |
| 6 Sept | Cad. W.D. "Bim" Philip [26] | Kitchener, ON | Leaside | 2 |
| 11 Sept | 2nd Lt. Robert L. Jacks | Los Angeles | Beamsville/ Leaside | 1 |
| 11 Sept | Cad. H.W. Bousfield [22] | MacGregor, MB | Beamsville | 1 |
| 17 Sept | Cad. E. Warden | Calville, WA | Rathburn | 1 |
| 18 Sept | Cad. Harry Saunders [28] | Erin, ON | Leaside | 1 |
| 23 Sept | Cad. A.M. Fromm | Regina, SK | Beamsville | 1 |
| 24 Sept | Cad. Sylvester J. Nightingale | Toronto | Beamsville | 1 |
| 26 Sept | Lt. C.W. Buchan | Moretown, ON | Rathburn | 1 |
| 1 Oct | Cad. Art Richardson | Ireland | Mohawk | 3 |
| 9 Oct | Cad. A.L. Dick | Welland, ON | Borden | 1 |
| 22 Oct | Lt. J.B. Stephens | Toronto | Rathburn | 1 |
| 24 Oct | Cad. J.R. Speer | Moretown, ON | Mohawk | 1 |
| 21 Nov | Lt. E.S. Sexton | Strathroy, ON | Borden | 1 |

| DATE | NAME | BIRTHPLACE | CAMP | CAUSE |
|---|---|---|---|---|
| 22 Nov | Lt. Thomas E. Logan | New Glasgow, NS | Beamsville | 1 |

There were 137 fatal training or training-related fatalities.[1] In addition, during the training operation in Texas, thirty-nine American cadets and officers and one civilian instructor died in training accidents.

# APPENDIX B
## MEALS AND PAY IN THE RAF (CANADA)

### Menu of an RAF Cadet — April 1, 1918[1]

Cadets eat with the enlisted men and are paid the same scale as a third-class mechanic, the lowest rank in the force. The menu includes meat in at least two of the day's three meals. What follows is a sample meal for a typical day:

> BREAKFAST: rolled oats, boiled bacon, baked beans, bread, butter, coffee.
> DINNER: roast beef, baked potatoes, turnips, bread, butter, rice and raisin pudding, tea.
> SUPPER: cold meat, pickles, bread, butter, applesauce, coffee.

### Annual Pay Scales of RAF Officers — April 1, 1918[2]

| Rank | Pay |
| --- | --- |
| General | 2500 |
| Lieutenant-General | 2000 |
| Major-General | 1500 |
| Brigadier-General | 1000 |
| Colonel | 900 |
| Lieutenant-Colonel | 750 |
| Major | 550 |
| Captain | 400, 500 |
| Lieutenant | 350, 300, 250 |

# NOTES

## Chapter One: Canada's First Air Force

1. John English, *Borden, His Life and World* (Toronto: McGraw-Hill Ryerson Limited, 1977), 93.
2. Hugh A. Halliday, "A High Flier, Indeed," *Legion Magazine* (July/August, 2004): 29.

## Chapter Two: The Novelty of Flight

1. *Atlantic Monthly* (October 1918): 435.
2. *Orillia Times,* 24 May 1917, p.1.
3 H.A. Jones, *The War in the Air, Vol. 5* (Oxford: Oxford University Press, 1935), 470.
4. R.V. Dodds, *The Brave Young Wings* (Stittsville, ON: Canada's Wings Inc., 1980), 17.
5. Directorate of History, Allen to Dodds, 1962, p. 12.
6. Ken Molson, "Cartierville: Canada's Oldest Airport," *CAHS Journal* (Winter 1990): 124–126.
7. *Daily Intelligencer*, 17 September 1917, p. 1; *Evening Telegram*, 13 August 1917, p. 7.
8. Directorate of History, Logan to Dodds, 17 March 1962.
9. Directorate of History, A.W. Carter, biographical file, "Difficulties of Enlisting to Serve in Air Services in the Beginnings of Air War in the First World War, 1914–1918," pp. 1, 2.
10. *Ibid.*, p. 2.
11. R.V. Dodds, "When the Canadians Took Over the U.S. Flying Schools," *FLIGHT*, L1X (February 1969): 28–32.

## Chapter Three: Commander Above the Law

1. S.F. Wise, *Canadian Airmen in the First World War: The Official History of the Royal Canadian Air Force, Vol. 1* (Toronto: University of Toronto Press, 1980), 118.

2. Directorate of History, Hoare to Allen, 2 November 1962, p. 4.

3. *Ibid.*

4. *Ibid.*, p. 7.

5. Directorate of History, Allen to Dodds, 22 July 1962.

6. Allen to Directorate of History, 20 September 1962, Appendix B, pp. 1, 3, 4.

7. *The Daily Intelligencer*, 10 June 1918, p. 6. The paper was quoting Hamilton Fyle's article in an English newspaper.

8. Directorate of History, Hoare to Allen, 27 November 1962, p. 4.

9. NA, Air 1/721/48/5, Hoare to Director of Air Organization, London, 28 January 1917.

10. *Ibid.*

## Chapter Four: Keeping Flyers in the Air

1. NA, AIR 1/721/48/5, Hoare to Director Air, 28 January 1917.

2. Alan Sullivan, *Aviation in Canada, 1917–1918* (Toronto: RAF Canada, 1919), 141; NA, AIR 1/721/48/4, Recruitment of Mechanics for RFC in Canada, p. 1.

3. *Mail and Empire*, 15 February 1917, p. 4.

4. NA, RG24, Vol. 2041, HQ 6978-2-131, Vol. 3., Hoare to Air Board, 14 November 1917.

5. *Daily Intelligencer*, 13 September, p. 5; R.V. Dodds, "Canada's First Air Training Plan," *The Roundel* Vol. 14, No. 9 (November 1962): 13.

6. *The Evening Telegram*, 15 February, p. 14.

7. *The Toronto Daily Star*, 14 February, p. 3.

8. *The Mail and Empire*, op. cit., 17 February 1917, p. 7.

9. NA, Air 1/721/48/5, Hoare to Charlton, 12 March 1917, p. 2.

10. NA, AIR 1/721/48/4, Recruiting of Mechanics for RFC in Canada, Final Report for 1917, p. 2.

11. Historical Division, Allen to RCAF, 22 July 1962, p. 3.

12. Bill Twatio, "Lester B. Meets the RFC," *Airforce* (Spring 1997): 55.

13. Joe Goold papers, "Heart-Throbs of Yesterday or Why You Are Here: 1917, the Royal Flying Corps," pp. 1, 2.

14. NA, AIR 1/721/48/5, Hoare to Charlton, 12 March 1917, p. 2, and 11 May 1917, p. 2; Allen to Charlton, 13 April 1917, p. 2; AIR, 1/721/48/4 Recruitment of Mechanics for RFC in Canada, p. 1.

15. National Archives and Library Canada, AIR 1/721/48/48; Hoare to Charlton, 11 May 1917, p. 2.

16. Allen to RCAF Historical Division, 22 July 1962.

17. Smith Collection, Jukes to Smith, 11 January 1983, p. 1.

18. Smith Collection, McWilliams to Smith, 12 March 1973.

19. Sullivan, *Aviation in Canada*, 144.

20. *Ibid.*, p. 145
21. *The Globe*, 17 August 1917, p. 6.
22. NA, Air/1/721/48/5 p. 3 of 3.
23. Directorate of History, Allen to Dodds, 5 December 1962, p. 7.
24. *Toronto Star*, 16 June 1918, p. 2.
25. Directorate of History, Allen to Dodds, 5 December 1962, p. 7.
26. Sullivan, *Aviation in Canada*, 144–145.

**Chapter Five: Training Pilots Dangerously**

1. Editorial, *The Evening Telegram*, St. John's, Newfoundland, 26 January 1918, p. 9.
2. NA, Air 1/721/48/1/4 Hoare's end of 1917 report to the Air Ministry, p. 2.
3. Sullivan, *Aviation in Canada*, 155–156.
4. N.A.C, Air, 1/721/48/5 Hoare to Charlton, 25 April 1917, pp. 1–2.
5. Don Clark, *Wild Blue Yonder: An Air Epic* (Seattle: Superior Publishing Company, 1972), 62.
6. NA, file, 17-1-42-A, Vol. 3, Major Thomas to Lieut. E.E. Scott, 30 August 1917, Department of Militia and Defence, Military District No. 5, Quebec City, PQ, pp. 1, 2.
7. Directorate of History, Diary of C.H. Andrews, pp. 1, 2, 4.
8. Directorate of History, Allen to Directorate, 20 September 1962, p. 4.
9. Smith papers, A.S. Bouttell to Alan Smith 22 January 1974, p. 1.
10. NA, Air 1/721/48/5, Hoare to Charlton, 12 March 1917, p. 5.
11. Smith papers. Letter dated 25 November 1973 from Captain RAF (ret.) J.W. Askham to Captain (ret.) RCAF Allan Smith, including a report written by Askham dated 30 November 1918. Askham was then living at R.R. 1, Cobble, B.C.
12. *Toronto Star*, 17 November 1917, p. 4.
13. Sullivan, *Aviation in Canada*, 155, 156, 159, and 166.
14. Directorate of History, Gibbard to Directorate, 3 August 1962.
15. War Museum of Canada, letters of Alan McLeod, 19 June 1917.
16. *Ibid.*, 7 July 1917.
17. Joe Goold papers, "Heart-throbs of Yesterday," pp. 1, 2.
18. *Daily Intelligencer*, 9 April 1917, p. 1; *Northern Advance*, 12 April 1917, p. 1; Base Borden Military Museum pamphlet, "A Noble Young Life," 2002.
19. Directorate of History, Diary of C.H. Andrews, pp. 15 and 20.
20. *Ibid.*, p. 6.

**Chapter Six: Canada's First Airplane Factory**

1. NA, Hoare to Dermott Allen, undated but received on 27 November 1962, p. 3.
2. *Toronto Daily Star*, 3 January 1921, p. 4; *Who's Who in Canada, 1917*, Toronto,

Ottawa, Montreal, p. 1410; Interview with Aubrey Baillie, grandson of Frank Baillie, 14 June 1999.

3. Sullivan, *Aviation in Canada*, 44, 47; Molson, K.M. "The Canadian JN-4," *Canadian Aeronautics and Space Journal*, Vol. 10, No. 3 (March 1964): 58 and 59.

4. Sullivan, *Aviation in Canada*, 44, 47.

5. K.M. Molson, "The JN-4 (Can)," *AAHS Journal* (Summer 1973): 86–87; Interview, Bob Fredericks, 5 May 2004. An engineer with Stephens-Adamson, Fredericks was told by Ed Butcher, assistant plant superintendent at Stewart-Warner Alemite, in the 1960s that the plant still had hundreds of these instruments in stock. They were later sold for scrap metal.

6. Molson, "The JN-4 (Can)," 86.

7. *Ibid.*

8. NA, Air 1/721/48/5, Hoare to Charlton, Directorate of Air Organization, 30 June 1917.

9. NA, Air, Memorandum On Development Of the School Of the Royal Flying Corps In Canada. 1/721/48/4, p. 1.

10. NA, Air, 1/721/48/5, telegram dated 13 April 1917, pp. 1 and 2.

11. NA, Air 1/721/48/5, Allen to Charlton, 13 April 1917, p. 2.

12. William E. Chajkowski, *Royal Flying Corps: Borden to Texas to Beamsville* (Erin, ON: Boston Mills Press, 1979), 39.

13. NA, Air, 1/721/48/4: RFC Final Report for 1917, p. 9; Hoare to Charlton 15 June 1917, p. 3; NA, Air 1/721/48/4, Hoare Memorandum on Development Of the Royal Flying Corps In Canada, December 1917, p. 9; NA, Air 1/721/48/5, Hoare to Charlton, 15 June 1917, p. 2; Sullivan, *Aviation in Canada*, 251.

14. NA, Air 1/721/48/5, 11 May 1917, p. 2, 3; *Ibid.*, Hoare to Charlton, 12 July 1917, p. 5.

15. *Toronto Star*, 6 May 1918, p. 1; *Northern Advance*, 9 May 1918, p. 1; *Daily Intelligencer*, 22 May 1918, p. 1.

16. NA, Air 1/721/48/5, Hoare to Director of Air Organization, London, 6 June 1917, pp. 3, 4.

17. NA, Air 1/721/48/5, Hoare to Charlton, 17 July 1917, pp. 4, 5.

18 Sullivan, *Aviation in Canada*, p. 50; R.V. Dodds, "Canada's First Air Training Plan," part 4, *The Roundel* (March 1963): 22, 23.

19. *The Intelligencer*, 6 June 1918, p. 5.

## Chapter Seven: Finding Flyers

1. NA, Air 1/721/48/4, Hoare's Final Report for 1917, Recruiting, p. 2.

2. Sullivan, *Aviation in Canada*, 160. At the end of the war only 9,200 cadets had

been accepted, out of some 35,000 applications processed; NA, Air 1/721/48/5, 1 of 3, Hoare to Director of Air Organization, 26 January 1917, p. 4.

3. Directorate of History, Gibbard to Directorate, 8 March 1962; Wise, *Canadian Airmen in the First World War*, 100.

4. J. Castell Hopkins, *The Canadian Annual Review 1911* (Toronto: The Canadian Annual Review Publishing Company Limited), 395; Wise, *Canadian Airmen in the First World War*, 641, table 7.

5. Robert Laird Borden, *Robert Laird Borden, His Memoirs, Vol. 2* (New York: The MacMillan Co.), 601–602.

6. NA, Air 1/721/48/5 Hoare to Charlton, pp. 1, 4.

7. Directorate of History, 75/394, Hoare to Sir Robert Falconer, 24 April 1917.

8. Directorate of History, op. cit., Major Allen to Sir Robert Falconer, 16 May 1917.

9. Sullivan, *Aviation in Canada*, 147.

10 NA, MG 40, D-1, Vol. 15, Air 1/721/48/5, Hoare to Charlton, 12 March 1917, *Globe and Mail*, 8 August 1917, pp. 7, 8.

11. *Daily Intelligencer*, 13 September 1917, p. 5.

12. Sullivan, *Aviation in Canada*, 147–148, 312.

13. *Toronto Daily Star*, 16 August 1917, p. 5; *Daily Intelligencer*, 5 January 1918, p. 1.

14. NA, HQ 6978-2-131, Vol. 3. Hoare to Gwatkin, 23 October 1917; Captain Daag to Hoare, 26 October 1917; NA, HQ 6978-2-131, Vol. 3, Hoare to Major Gore, 15 November 1917.

15. Wise, *Canadian Airmen in the First World War*, 113 and 114.

16. NA, Air 1/721/48/5, Hoare to Charlton, 11 May 1917, p. 1.

17. NA, Air 1/721/48/5, Hoare to Charlton, 20 April 1917, p. 1.

18. NA, op. cit. Hoare to Charlton, 30 June 1917; p. 3; Sullivan, *Aviation in Canada*, 142.

19. *Toronto Daily Star*, 16 August 1917, p. 15.

20. NA, Air 1/721/48/5, Hoare to Charlton, 12 September 1917, p. 1.

21. NA, Air 1/721/48/5, Hoare to Charlton 28 September 1917, pp. 1–2.

22. NA, G22, vol. 9 (2), Governor General Devonshire to Colonel Long, 29 July 1918.

23. NA, Air 1/721/48/5, Hoare to Hearson, 15 October 1918; *Daily Intelligencer*, 22 August 1918, p. 5.

## Chapter Eight: The Making of a Fighter Pilot

1. *Vancouver Sun*, Editorial, 19 September 1917, p. 4.

2. Lieutenant Pat O'Brien, *Outwitting the Hun: My Escape from a German Prison Camp*, (New York: Harper & Brothers Publishers, 1918), 9.

3. Bill Lambert, DFC, *Combat Report* (London: Corgi, 1975), 25.

4. Vivian Voss, *Flying Minnows: Memoirs of a World War 1 Fighter Pilot* (London:

John Hamilton, 1935 [pseudonym Roger Vee]. Amended reprint, London: Arms and Armour Press, 1977), 20.

5. NA, AIR 1/721/48/5, Hoare to Charlton, 15 June 1918, p. 2.

6. Canadian War Museum, letters of Alan Arnett McLeod, VC, to his parents.

7. J. Stirling Halstead, *A Mission to the Royal Flying Corps* (Ottawa: Directorate of History), 9–11.

8. Voss, *Flying Minnows*, 21.

9. Canadian War Museum, letters of Alan Arnett McLeod, VC. His record with the RFC Higher Training Squadron shows McLeod with five hours of dual instruction and forty hours of solo flying.

10. Directorate of History, Allen to Directorate, May 1962, pp. 13, 14; *Ibid.*, p. 8.

11. Canadian War Museum, McLeod letters, training documents and certificates of McLeod.

12. Op. cit., McLeod to his father, 10 or 11 July 1917, p. 1.

13. NA, Air 1/721/48/4, Photography Report of Lt. E.F. Hall, December 1917.

14. Canadian War Museum, McLeod papers, letter of 11 July 1917.

15. *Ibid.*, letters dated 24 and 28 July and 1 and 4 August 1917.

16. Honours and Awards web site created by Hugh Halliday, pp. 128–129.

17. Wise, *Canadian Airmen in the First World War*, 65.

## Chapter Nine: Social Life in Belle Époque Canada

1. Elizabeth O'Kiely, *Gentleman Air Ace: The Duncan Bell-Irving Story* (Madeira Park, BC: Harbour Publishing, 1992), 25.

2. Directorate of History, Allen to Directorate, 1962, 76/199.

3. NA, MG 40, D AM, Vol. 1, Air 1/10/15/1/37; *Toronto Daily Star* 25 May 1918; *Daily Intelligencer*, 20 August 1918.

4. J. Stirling Halstead, *A Mission to the Royal Flying Corps*, 42.

5. Cadet Wing Review, September 1918, p. 16–17.

6. Directorate of History, Diary of C.H. Andrews, 21 October 1917, p. 15.

7. Op. cit., pp. 10, 11.

8. Directorate of History, Diary of C.H. Andrews, 21 October 1917, p. 15.

9. Unpublished memoirs of Joe Goold.

10. *Ibid.*, Goold letter to Al Smith, 27 March 1973.

11. Don Clark, *Wild Blue Yonder*, 26.

12. Smith collection, Alex Hunter to Al Smith, 21 December 1973.

13. Op. cit., undated letter to Al Smith from Maude Tullock.

14. *The Globe*, 8 August 1917, p. 7.

15. *Daily Intelligencer*, 3 May 1918, p. 7.

16. Don Clark, *Wild Blue Yonder*, p. 51.

17. Smith collection, Webster to Smith, 5 November 1973, pp. 1, 2.

18. *Ibid.*, pp. 2, 3.

19. *Ibid.*, p. 5.

20. *Daily Intelligencer*, 14 February 1918, p. 2.

21. *Cadet Wing Review*, September 1918, p. 1.

22. NA, Air 1/721/48/4, Report of Major B. O'Reilly MD, dated 4 December 1914 at Fort Worth Texas.

23. *Toronto Star,* 3 June 1918, p. 5.

24. House of Commons Debates, Vol. 2, 1918, p. 1365 and p. 1617.

25. *The Toronto Star*, 3 June 1918, p. 5.

### Chapter Ten: The Sine Qua Non of Athletics

1. "Sports De-Luxe," *Cadet Wing Review*, Special Issue, 20 July 1918. The quotes of Hoare and the editor are both taken from this source.

2. *Northern Advance*, 12 September 1918, p. 1.

3. The following sources were incorporated into the text: *Toronto Daily Star*, 4 June 1917, 13 and 19 February 1917, 1, 3, 4, 6 June 1917, 20 August 1917, 17 September 1917, 29, 30 October 1917; 28 November 1917; 13, 19 February 1918, 3, 4, 6, 9 June 1918, 19 August 1918, 9, 17, September 1918, 11, 16, 18 December 1918; *Globe and Mail*, 30 July 1917, 17 September 1917; *Northern Advance*, 1 August, 12 September 1917; *Daily Intelligencer*, 8 August 1918; Chajkowski, *Royal Flying Corps*, 107; *Cadet Wing Review*, 20 July, 3 August, 9, 19 September 1918; letters of Alan A. McLeod, 3, 25 May 1917; Dodds, "Canada's First Air Training Plan," part 4: 21.

### Chapter Eleven: Hijinks on the Ground and in the Air

1. Thornton Wilder, *Theophilius North* (New York: Harper & Row, 1973).

2. Directorate of History, Diary of C.H. Andrews, pp. 14, 15.

3. Smith papers; information from Lloyd Carbert, son of Charles S. Carbert, a mechanic at Mohawk when Castle instructed there.

4. Frank H. Ellis, *Canada's Flying Heritage* (Toronto: University of Toronto Press, 1954,) 127.

5. *Toronto Star*, 23 April 1918, p. 11.

6. Ellis, *Canada's Flying Heritage*, 127–128.

7. *Evening Telegram*, 14 August 1917, p. 5; *Daily Intelligencer*, 15 August 1917, p. 1.

8. *Kingston Whig Standard* and *Daily Intelligencer*, 11 September 1917. Both papers assert it was the first time airplanes had been used to hunt for criminals.

9. Information on Monette and the IRFC hunt obtained from *The Daily Intelligencer*, 11 September, p. 1; 12 September, p. 1; 19 September, pp. 6, 8; 21 September 1917, p. 1.

10. *Toronto Star,* 10 January, p. 5.

## Chapter Twelve: The Dancers — Vernon and Irene Castle

1. Irene Castle, *My Husband* (London: Charles Scribners, 1919), 86 and 87.
2. *Ibid.*, 34.
3. *Ibid.*, 58.
4. *Toronto Daily Star*, 16 February 1918, p. 6. Castle's friend Captain W.II. Wilde, in an interview with *The Star*, said, "He had a contract for about a hundred thousand a year which he got the holder to tear up so that he could join."
5. *Napanee Express*, 1 June 1917, p. 1; Kenneth W. Spafford, "As I Remember," *Picton Gazette*, 18 January 1978.
6. Interview with April Wagrel, daughter of John Coats, 7 November 1998; interview with Carolyn Hetherington, daughter of Audrey Wilmot, 31 October 1998.
7. Smith papers, letter of Joe Goold, 5 August 1974, p. 2.
8. *The Daily Intelligencer*, 31 October 1918, p. 5; Allen to RCAF Historical Section, May 1962. Allen describes an incident at an American hospital where he conned a Texas administrator with Lord Wellesley, who demonstrated a quick wit in assisting. Allen had a high opinion of Wellesley.; Smith papers, in a recorded interview with Cadet Carbert, who served at Camp Mohawk in 1917. Carbert describes Wellesley's car stalled on the train tracks and Carbert's successful attempts to move it. Wellesley was extremely grateful and gracious. Carbert thought highly of both Wellesley and his wife, Lady Louise Pamela, and believed the townspeople shared his sentiments.
9. PAC Air 1/10/15/1/37, Casualty Return 87/9926; Irene Castle, *My Husband*, 170–171.
10. *Daily Intelligencer*, 25 September 1918, p. 5.
11. Interviews on 31 October 1998 with Carolyn Hetherington, daughter of Gwen Wilmot, and Edith Gould, nanny and servant to Audrey and Gwen Wilmot for over three decades. Both women confirmed the existence of a voluminous sheaf of letters written by Castle to Gwen and the large engagement ring he gave her; interview with Ed Day (b. 1908), who heard from his parents and their contemporaries that Castle was a frequent visitor at the Wilmot home. Smith collection, letter to Al Smith from Sheila (Burrows) Chapline, 16 April 1983, wherein she states that Gwen fell in love with Vernon Castle. Sheila grew up in the Glanmore Mansion. Her mother witnessed the romance and told her the story of Coats landing in their backyard, which ran south for about a kilometre. Letter of Sheila B. Chapline to Smith, 16 April 1983, Smith Collection.
12. Interview with Jim Graham, grandson of George Graham, 19 January and 4 February 1999.

## Chapter Thirteen: How to Succeed by Breaking the Rules

1. Directorate of History, Hoare to Allen, 27 November 1962, p. 2.
2. G.A. Fuller, J.A. Griffin, K.M. Molson, *125 Years of Canadian Aeronautics* (Willowdale, ON: Canadian Aviation Society, 1983), 25.
3. NA, Air 1/721/48/5, Hoare to Charlton, 1 June 1917, p. 1.
4. Wise, *Canadian Airmen in the First World War*, 635. Professor Wise's chart shows the rate of enlistment per thousand population for B.C. at 2.08 percent; Ontario is second highest at a rate of 1.38 percent; Manitoba and Alberta have only slightly lower percentages.
5. Hiram Bingham, *An Explorer in the Air Service* (New Haven, CT: Yale University Press, 1920), xiii.
6. Directorate of History, Allen to Department of History, undated report titled "Royal Flying Corps, Canada," p. 6.
7. *Toronto Star*, 20 August 1917, p. 13.
8. Hiram Bingham, *An Explorer in the Air Service*, xiii.
9. Sullivan, *Aviation in Canada*, 67; Jones, *The War in the Air*, 467. At the conclusion of the war, Sullivan calculated the cost of training in Canada at $9,835, which he reduced to $9,660 after the disposal of assets. Jones states that the cost in England was £1,030, or C$4,944. (The exchange rate at that time was C$4.80 per £1.) These calculations are distorted by the inclusion of capital costs, all of which are divided by the number of pilots trained. As the Canadian plan ran for less than two years, its output of pilots was far less than the plan in England, which ran the entire four years of the war. Had the Canadian plan ran the same length of time, costs per pilot would have been far less as capital costs (including HQ buildings, hangars, sewer and water lines, water treatment plants, and large equipment purchases) are one time only. All these assets were sold at the war's end at fire-sale prices.
10. Directorate of History, Allen to Department of History, op. cit., p. 7.
11. *Ibid.*, p. 8.
12. NA, Air 1/721/48/5, Hoare to B.C.H. Drew, 26 December 1918, p. 4.
13. NA, Air 1/721/48/5, Charlton to Hoare, 12 April 1917, p. 2.
14. NA, Air 1/721/48/5 Vol. 15, 3 of 3, Charlton to Hoare, 9 August 1917, p. 3.
15. NA, Air 1/721/48/5 Vol 15, 3 of 3, Benous to Hoare, 31 August 1917, pp. 1, 3.
16. NA, Air 1/721/48/5, Hoare to Charlton, 22 October 1917, p. 2.

## Chapter Fourteen: Forging an Historic Alliance

1 Directorate of History Allen to Directorate, undated, pp. 9–10.
2. L.L. Smart, "Training in Canada, 1917," *CAHS Journal* (Winter 1972): 121.
3. *Ibid.*
4. Don Clark, *Wild Blue Yonder*, 22.

5. Smart, "Training in Canada, 1917," 121.

6. Don Clark, *Wild Blue Yonder*, 31.

7. *Daily Intelligencer*, 8 August, 1917, p. 1.

8. Directorate of History, Allen to Dodds, 7 November 1962.

9. Halstead file, "Mission To The RFC," Historical Section, p. 46.

10. Directorate of History, Allen to Directorate, 20 September 1962, pp. 6, 10. NA, AIR 1/721/48/5, Hoare to Charlton, 9 October 1917, p. 1.

11. NA, Air 1/721/48/5, Hoare to Charlton, 9 October 1917, p 1

12. *The Toronto Evening Telegram*, 16 November, p. 22; *Daily Intelligencer*, 17 November 1917, p. 1. The body of the airman was found on the train tracks the day after the train left Deseronto. Power may have intended to go AWOL, as his wife lived nearby. The IRFC would not have attempted to force him to return, as it might have endangered Hoare's recruiting program in the United States.

13. R.V. Dodds, "Canada's First Air Training Plan," part 3, *The Roundel*, (January–February 1963): 21.

14. NA, Air 2/166/RO 4869, D.L. Roscoe, Commanding Officer Taliaferro Fields, to Chief Signal Officer of the Army, Washington, D.C., 6 May 1918, p. 7.

15. Diary of C.H. Andrews, Historical Section, p. 23.

16. Don Clark, *Wild Blue Yonder*, 90.

17. *Ibid.*, 87.

18. *Ibid.*, 87. Letter from Joe Goold to Captain Al Smith, 3 June 1975.

19. Texas researcher Glen Martin, letter of 5 December 1997. Mrs. McCluer was the last surviving member of the World War One Flyers' Club in Fort Worth. Her late husband, Charles, had been a Lieutenant in the U.S. Army Signal Corps and an instructor at Hicks Field in the First World War. Martin obtained the details of the McCluer interview from articles in the November and December 1992 issues of *Aeroplane Monthly Magazine* titled, "Royal Flying Corps in Texas."

20. Don Clark, *Wild Blue Yonder*, p. 71. Ironically, Cadet Tolchan of New Mexico, a source for this story, was one of the cadets who received a cold reception from the ladies.

21. *The Toronto Star*, 29 December 1917, p. 9.

22. *The Toronto Star*, 9 February 1918, p. 21.

23. Glen Martin, op. cit. This information was provided by the oldest man in Benbrook, Hershal Montgomery, who told Martin he heard this from Florence Carter, daughter of Mrs. Lee Rodgers, who owned the house rented by Castle.

24. Glen Martin, op. cit., letter of 5 April 1998. Martin has a photograph of the postcard.

25. Irene Castle, *My Husband*, 172–173; Don Clark, *Wild Blue Yonder*, 67.

## Chapter Fifteen: Friction Between the Allies

1. Allen to Dodds, Directorate of History, 20 September 1962, pp. 16–17.
2. *Ibid.*, p. 8.
3. *Ibid.*, p. 18.
4. NA, 1/721/48/5, Hoare to Charlton, 22 October 1917, p. 2.
5. NA, AIR/2/166/RO4869, Report of General Roscoe, Commanding Officer, Taliafero Fields to The Chief Signals Officer of the Army, through Chief Air Division, Washington, D.C., 6 May 1918, pp. 5, 6.
6. Sullivan, *Aviation in Canada*, 243; R.V. Dodds, op. cit., p.19.
7. NA, AIR/2/166/RO4869, op. cit., p.8.
8. Hoare to Allen, Directorate of History, 27 November 1962, p. 3.
9. Op. cit., Allen to Dodds, 22 July 1962, p. 3.
10. AIR 1/721/48/5, Hoare to Lieutenant Colonel Drew, Military Aeronautics Directorate, Air Board Office, London, 26 December 1917, p. 3.
11. J. Stirling Halstead, "A Mission to the Royal Flying Corps," Directorate of History, from the original manuscript as filed at the U.S. Naval Base at Pensacola, Florida, p. 44.
12. Allen to Directorate of History, "Canada in Retrospect," undated, p. 33.
13. Allen to Directorate, op. cit., 22 July 1962, p. 3.
14. Dodds, "Canada's First Air Training Plan," part 3: 19.

## Chapter Sixteen: Frostbite Flying — Beating the Canadian Winter

1. F.G. Ericson, "Aviation in Canada, 1919," *CAHS Journal* (Summer 1969): 37.
2. NA, Air 1/721/48/5, 1 of 3, Hoare to Charlton, 28 February 1917, pp. 2, 3.
3. Ellis, *Canada's Flying Heritage*, 126.
4. *The Daily Mail and Empire*, 13 February 1918, p. 4: "the weather was the coldest in the past five years"; *The Toronto Star,* 8 August 1918: "[January was] one of the coldest in the history of the Meteorological Station"; Sullivan, *Aviation in Canada*, 122.
5. Directorate of History, 76/199, Allen to Directorate, 5 December 1962.
6. *Toronto Daily Star,* 12 to 18 January 1918.
7. Sullivan, *Aviation in Canada*, 125, 126, 130.
8. Canadian War Museum, excerpt from a text written for the museum based on a copy of a logbook held at the Directorate of History.
9. NA, Air 1/721/48/5 Allen to Lt.-Colonel Drew, Military Aeronautics Directorate, 2 February 1918, pp. 1, 2.
10. Approximate Thresholds, Wind Chill Graph, Wind Chill Program, Meteorological Service of Canada, p.1. See www.msc.ec.gc.ca/education/windchill/history_e.cfm
11. Directorate of History, Allen to Directorate, RCAF, Historical Section,

undated, p. 18. For every 1,000 feet above sea level, the air temperature drops an average of 3°F. A pilot at 8,000 feet flying at 100 kilometres per hour when the sea level temperature stands at -23°C is therefore experiencing a temperature of -36°C. The wind chill factor lowers this to -64°C.

12. Sullivan, *Aviation in Canada*, 126; Dodds, "Canada's First Air Training Program," part 3: 20, 21.

13. *The Daily Intelligencer*, 11 February 1918, p. 2. Lieutenant Edwards was the son of Doctor J W Edwards, M.P. for Frontenac.

14. NA, Air 1/721/48/5, Allen to Lieut-Colonel Drew, op. cit., p. 2.

15. Sullivan, *Aviation in Canada*, 131; *The Toronto Daily Star*, 8 August 1918, p. 2.

16. Sullivan, *Aviation in Canada*, 131.

## Chapter Seventeen: Surviving Training

1. *The Daily Intelligencer*, 21 February 1918, p. 4.

2. J. Stirling Halstead, *A Mission to the Royal Flying Corp* (Directorate of History, 1964), 26.

3. Voss, *Flying Minnows*, 33–34.

4. War Museum of Canada, letter of Alan Arnett McLeod to father, 12 June 1917.

5. Halstead, *A Mission to the Royal Flying Corps*, 36.

6. NA, Air 1/721/48/ 5, Hoare to Charlton, 22 October 1917, pp. 1, 2. Sullivan, *Aviation in Canada*, 24, 25. Flavelle and Morrow were directors of the IMB in 1919. Sir Joseph Flavelle was chairman and G.A. Morrow was director of aviation. Brand is not listed by Sullivan but was almost certainly a director at the time of their meeting with Hoare.

7. RG 24, Vol. 2043, Hoare to Chief of Staff, Department of Militia and Defence, 8 November 1918, "Accommodations in Buildings Created for RAF Canada." This document provides the square footage of the Westinghouse factory. *Toronto Star*, 3 June 1918, p. 14.

8. Sullivan, *Aviation in Canada*, 145. Sullivan lists number of women in various Wings and Sections. The number of male officers and staff was determined from the photograph on page 171.

9. NA, Air 1/721/48/5, Hoare to Air Ministry, 18 June 1918, p. 2.

10. *Toronto Star*, 27 August 1918, p. 2.

11. Chajkowski, *Royal Flying Corps*, 34. Chajkowski notes that, during the autumn, accommodation for 2,500 officers and cadets plus a new hospital was completed. *Cadet Wing Review*, 9 September, 1918, p. 1; *Daily Intelligencer*, 8 August 1918, p. 7; the newspaper notes that a new hospital would open on 12 August at Camp Rathbun to serve both camps.

12. *The Daily Intelligencer*, 17 June 1918, p. 2.

13. *Ibid.*, 18 August 1917, p. 12.

14. H.A. Jones, *The War in the Air, Vol. V.* (Oxford: Oxford University Press, 1935), 431.

15. Log book and training records of M.P. MacLeod from private collection of B. Campbell; Shores, Franks, & Guest, *Above the Trenches: A Complete Record of the Fighter Aces and Units of the British Empire Air Forces 1915–1920* (Stoney Creek, ON: Fortress Publications, 1990), 251; Hugh Halliday, Honours and Awards, p. 129.

16. NA, MG 40, Air 1/721/48/5 (3 of 3), Hoare to Secretary of the Air Ministry, 28 May 1918. Decline in percentage of fatalities of cadets under training. Directorate of History, Allen to Dodds, op. cit., p. 18.

17. *The Vancouver Daily Sun,* 21 September 1918, p.3. *Northern Advance,* [Barrie newspaper] 3 October 1918, p.1.

18. Sullivan, *Aviation in Canada,* 230–231.

## Chapter Eighteen: Pummelled by Typewriters

1. NA, HQ 6978-2-131 Vol. 4, Chambers to Allen, 4 March 1918.

2. Smith papers, U. M. Wilson to Barnsdale, 1 May 1918, p. 1.

3. Edwin G. Guillet, *The Story of Canadian Roads* (Toronto: University of Toronto Press, 1967), 148.

4. Op. cit., Barnsdale to Wilson, 15 May 1918.

5. Op. cit., Alkenbrack to Smith, 31 October, year not given.

6. *Daily Intelligencer,* 17 January 1918, p. 1.

7. NA, HQ 6978-2-131 Vol. 4., Chambers to Colonel Allen, 28 February 1918, p. 2.

8. *The Toronto Daily Star,* 18 February 1918, p. 3.

9. NA, HQ 6978-2-131 Vol. 4., op. cit., p.1.

10. MG 40, D-1, Vol. 35, Air 2/13/058/4066, Report by Lieutenant Colonel, C.J. Burke, on Personnel, 20 January 1916, p. 1.

11. Op. cit., Chambers to Colonel Allen, 28 February 1918, p. 1.

12. *The Toronto Star,* 3 June 1918, p.11.

13. Op. cit., Chambers to Gwatkin, 1 March 1918.

14. Op. cit., Chambers to Gwatkin, 28 February 1918, p. 2.

15. *The Toronto Star,* 6 June 1918, p. 21.

16. *The Toronto Star,* 20 April 1918, p. 8.

17. *Daily Intelligencer,* 25 May 1918, p. 1.

18. D.B. Rhodes, "The Star and The New Radicalism, 1917–1926" (master's thesis, Queen's University, 1955), p. 11.

19. *The Globe,* 21 May 1918, p. 4.; *The Windsor Record,* 23 May 1918; *Daily Intelligencer,* 23 May 1918, p.1.

20. *The Star,* 3 June 1918, p. 10.

21. *The Star*, editorial, 19 June 1918, p. 16.

22. *The Orillia Packet*, 13 June 1918, p. 7.

## Chapter Nineteen: Towards a Canadian Air Force

1. NA, RG 9 III, Vol. 80, Borden to Perley, 22 May 1917, os 10-9-27, Vol. 1.

2. *The Toronto Star*, 10 June 1918, p. 10.

3. NA, Air 1/721/48/5 Air Board to Hoare, 27 September 1918, p. 2.

4. *Ibid.*

5 *The Daily Intelligencer*, 23 September 1918, p. 1.

6. *Ibid.*

7. *The Daily Intelligencer*, 15 August 1918, p. 6.

8 Allen to Directorate of History, 22 July 1962, p. 4; *Toronto Daily Star*, Report of Captain Seymour, 6 June 1918, p. 14.

## Chapter Twenty: Perfecting the Training Program

1. *The Morning Bulletin*, Edmonton, 30 January 1918, p. 7. Similar ads appeared around the same time in many major (and a few small-town) newspapers across the Dominion, including *The Toronto Star*, *Northern Advance*, and *Montreal Gazette*.

2. Sullivan, *Aviation in Canada*, 166, 169; Dodds, "Canada's First Air Training Plan," part 4: 20–21; *The Daily Intelligencer*, 17 June 1918, p. 2.

3. NA, Air 1/721/48/6 Hoare to Secretary, Air Ministry, 28 May 1918, p. 2; Sullivan, *Aviation in Canada*, 75.

4. *Daily Intelligencer*, 8 August 1918, p. 7; Smith collection, report on Wing Headquarters, pp. 5, 10.

5. Sullivan, *Aviation in Canada*, 145, 275, and 276.

6. *Ibid.*, 162, 166.

7. *The St. Catharines Standard*, 11 April 1918, p. 3.

8. Numbers obtained by combining information from the following: Hugh Halliday, "Beamsville Story," *CAHS Journal* (Fall 1969): 75–76; Sullivan, *Aviation in Canada*, 75.

9. NA, AIR 1/721/48/5, Hoare to Secretary, Air Ministry, 28 May 1918, p.1, in reply to their cable of 22 May 1928.

10. *The Intelligencer*, 6 June 1918, p. 5. The men at Rathbun photographed the new trainer.

## Chapter Twenty-One: A Pandemic Engulfs Canada

1. *The Daily Intelligencer*, 18 October 1918, pp. 1, 6. Doctor Ackrill's credibility was weakened by his prominence as a local bootlegger. On the day his letter appeared, a newspaper article noted a suggestion had been made to the

federal government to temporarily remove Prohibition. The article argued that as whisky was used extensively in the treatment of pneumonia, with which many influenza cases become complicated, it should be made more readily available to those suffering from the Spanish flu. Despite these arguments, no changes were made to Prohibition.

2. *Toronto Daily Star,* 21 October 1918, p. 1. Toronto undertakers reported that in 600 deaths in the previous three weeks, 65 percent were of people between the ages of twenty and thirty.

3. Arthur Bishop, *Our Bravest and Our Best: The Stories of Canada's Victoria Cross Winners* (Toronto: McGraw-Hill Ryerson Limited, 1995), 93–94; Carl A. Christie, "Alan Arnett McLeod, VC: Canada's Schoolboy Hero," *CAHS Journal,* Vol. 34 (June 1998): 21.

4. *The Toronto Star,* 25 September 1918, p. 7.

5. *The Daily Intelligencer,* 4 October 1918, p. 1.

6. *The Toronto Star,* 28 October 1918, p. 3.

7. Eileen Pettigrew, *The Silent Enemy: Canada and the Deadly Flu of 1918* (Saskatoon: Western Producer Prairie Books, 1983), IX and X.

8. Population statistics released by Toronto's chief of the assessment department, *The Toronto Star,* 7 September 1918; 23 October 1918, p. 13. This information was released to the press by Major O'Reilly, Chief of the RAF Medical Staff.

9. *Daily Intelligencer,* 31 October 1918, p. 7

10. *The Toronto Star,* 30 November 1918, p. 10.

11. *Northern Advance,* 12 December 1918, p. 6.

12. Sullivan, *Aviation in Canada,* 75 (chart).

13. Directorate of History, Allen to Dodds, 5 December 1962.

14. *Daily Intelligencer,* 25 October 1918, p. 4.

### Chapter Twenty-Two: Canada's First Airmail

1. *Daily Intelligencer,* 6 July 1917, p. 1.

2. *The News Record,* 17 September 1917, p.1.

3. *Intelligencer,* 5 June 1918, p. 7.

4. *Ibid.,* 15 August 1918, p. 6.

5. R.K. Malott, "Fifty Years Ago," *CAHS Journal* (June 1968): 15.

6. Material for the first postal flight was obtained from the following sources: James Hornick, "They Carried Old Mull and Air Mail to Toronto," *The Globe Magazine* (28 June 1958): 25; R.K. Malott, "Fifty Years Ago": 13–17.

### Chapter Twenty-Three: Winding Up the RAF in Canada

1. *Daily Intelligencer,* 14, 18, 21 November 1918.

2. *Ibid.,* 22 November 1918, p. 7.

3. *The Montreal Gazette*, 21 November 1918.

4. NA, RG 24, Air 1/721/48/5, Hoare to Brancker, 28 July 1918, p. 1.

5. *The Toronto Globe*, 26 November 1918, p. 8.

6. *The Toronto Star*, 4 December 1918.

7. *The Toronto Star*, 3, 4 December 1918.

8. *The Toronto Star*, 28 February 1919.

9. Chajkowski, *Royal Flying Corps*, 9, 116.

10. *Daily Intelligencer*, 29 December 1921; Research paper prepared by Ryan Barberstock, Deseronto Archives, 10 May 1967, p. 28.

11. Ryan Barberstock, op. cit., p. 29.

12. *Toronto Star*, 30 November 1918, p. 7.

13. *Ibid.*

14. *Daily Intelligencer*, 5 December 1918, p. 7.

15. *The Northern Advance*, 9 and 16 May 1918, p. 8.

16. *The Northern Advance*, 19 December 1918, p. 8.

17. *Toronto Daily Star*, 9 December 1918, p. 11.

18. *The Intelligencer*, 13 December, p. 5; Queen's University Archives, Minutes of Faculty of Science, 12 May 1925, pp. 20, 32–33.

19. *The Toronto Globe*, 9 December 1918, p. 8; *Daily Intelligencer*, 9 December 1918, p. 1.

20. *The Toronto Star*, 11 December 1918, p. 8.

21. NA, RDS/1/AC/87/96a, Hawksford to Chief of the General Staff, Dept. of Militia and Defence, Ottawa, 10 June 1919, p. 1.

22. Directorate of History, Murton Seymour, OBE, QC, to Dodds, 28 May 1962, p. 1.

## Chapter Twenty-Four: The Legacy of the RAF in Canada

1. Wise, *Canadian Airmen in the First World War*, 120.

2. *Toronto Star*, 30 January 1919, pp. 1, 2.

3. *Ibid.*, p. 2.

4. Fuller, Griffin, Molson, *125 Years of Canadian Aeronautics*, 117–121; *Intelligencer*, 8 August 1918, p. 2.

5. Fuller, Griffin, Molson, *125 Years of Canadian Aeronautics*, 139.

6. *Ibid.*, 119, 123, 127.

7. Morris Zaslow, *The Northward Expansion of Canada, 1914–1967* (Toronto: McClelland and Stewart, 1988), 180.

8. Fuller, *125 Years of Canadian Aeronautics*, 151.

9. Sullivan, *Aviation in Canada*, 57, 75; Dodds, "Canada's First Air Training Plan," part 4: 24.

10. *The Toronto Star*, 3 March 1919, p. 8.

11. NA, AIR 2/166/RO-4869, Colonel Roscoe, Commanding Officer Taliaferro Fields, Texas to the Chief Signal Officer of the Army, Washington, D.C. 6 May 1918, pp. 3 and 4.

12. Directorate of History, Allen to Directorate, May 1962, p. 12.

13. J.W. Pickersgill, *The Mackenzie King Record, Vol.1, 1939–1944* (Toronto: University of Toronto Press, 1960), 52.

14. Fuller, *125 Years of Canadian Aeronautics*, 147.

15. Directorate of History, Allen to Directorate, 5 December 1962, p. 9, re. page 249.

16. Sebastian Cox, "Aspects of Anglo-US Co-operation in the Air in the First World War," *Air & Space Power Journal* (Winter 2004).

17. Website maintained by the Deputy Minister (Public Affairs)/DAM(PA), last modified 28 July 2006.

18. Christopher Gully, "Tough Talk from Canada," *Forever Young* (November 2005): 4.

## Chapter Twenty-Five: The Lost Generation

1. Complaints of mechanics and cadets found in the following: *Toronto Daily Star*, 5 September 1918, p. 10; 2 December 1918, p. 7; 20 December 1918, p. 5; 24 December 1918, pp. 2, 4; 30 December 1918, p. 18; 10 January 1919, p. 9; 18 January 1919, p. 7. The strike threatened by police unions first surfaced in February 1919 when *The Star* reported the threat in an article on 21 February (p. 12). *The News Record* in Kitchener reported an attempt by the IWW to infiltrate western farm workers on 6 September 1917 (p. 1). On 18 September 1918, *The Toronto Daily Star* reported the trial of Constantine Goshuik, who was charged with starting a Bolshevik Society in Toronto the previous June.

2. *Daily Intelligencer*, 25 September 1918, p. 5.

3. Accounts of the various balls, entertainments, luncheons, dances, and dinners were described in *The Toronto Star*: 2 December 1918, p. 12; 3 December 1918, p. 8, 17; 4 December 1918, p.16; 5 December 1918, p.21; 7 December 1918, p. 24; 12 December 1918, p. 23; 15 December 1918, p. 25; 16 December 1918, p. 9; 20 December 1918, p. 25; as well as in *The Hamilton Spectator*, 13 December 1918, p. 19.

4. *Toronto Star*, 20 December 1918, p. 25; 18 and 23 January 1919.

5. *Daily Intelligencer*, obituary of Charles Wilmot, 19 March 1941, p. 1.

6. Interview with Edith Goold, 31 October 1998. Miss Goold was the personal attendant to Audrey and Gwen for eighteen years. She was hired by Audrey in 1932 and came to Canada with Gwen Wilmot during the Second World War. Interview with Carolyn Heatherington, 28 February 1998. Carolyn is

the only child of Gwen Wilmot and D'Arcy Rutherford. She has enjoyed a long career in the theatre as a professional actress. In 2007, she was still active on the Toronto theatre scene.

7. NA, Personnel Records, box 92-W-102, letter of W.E. Tummon of 18 November, 1929 to Deputy Minister of National Defence; Various letters in the Goold papers; *The Intelligencer*, 12 December, 1993, Remember When section, p. 4.

8. *Brantford Expositor*, 30 June 1930, p. 8.

9. Interviews Carolyn Heatherington, 28 February, 1 March 1998; *The Daily Mail*, [London, England], 16 March 1934; Interviews with Edith Goold, 13 March, and 31 October 1998. Interview with Anna Johnson, former dancer with the Winnipeg Ballet, daughter of Eardley Wilmot, 22 February 1998;

10. Voss, *Flying Minnnows*, 35.

11. *Ibid.*, 39–44.

12. *London Times*, 1 July, 1932; Interviews with Carolyn Heatherington, 28 February and 1 March 1998; Interview with Edith Goold, 31 October 1998; Interview with April Wagrel of London, England, daughter of Jack Coats, 11 March 1998.

13. *Daily Intelligencer*, 17 December 1936, p. 2.

14. NA, Personnel Records, DND, file 415-W-26, PR3-7-6-41.

15. *Ibid.*, 16 October 1941, p. 1. NA, Personnel Records, DND, file 415-W-26.

16. Interview with Carolyn Heatherington, 28 February 1998.

17. *Ibid.*; Interview with Edith Goold, 31 October 1998.

## Epilogue

1. *The Intelligencer*, 31 January 2002, p. 10.

2. *The Toronto Star*, 4 June 1918, p. 14.

3. Directorate of History, Hoare to Allen, undated letter titled "Notes by Brigadier-General C.G. Hoare, concerning Major General F.R.G. Hoare, C.B., C.B.E."

4. Directorate of History, file of F.A. Wanklyn; *The Toronto Star*, 28 November 1918, p. 23; 5 December 1918, p. 21; 7 December 1918, p. 24; Allen to Directorate of History, 1963, p. 27.

5. *Toronto Star*, 21 January 1919, p. 8.

6. Directorate of History, file of J.H. Scott, Box 8725-30; Honours and Awards website created by Hugh Halliday, pp. 154, 155.

7. Directorate of History, file of Captain Brian Peck, Box 7693-6; *The Globe Magazine*, 28 June 1958, p. 25; R.K. Malott, "Fifty Years Ago": 14–17.

8. Directorate of History, file of M.A. Seymour, Box 339.

9. Op. cit., Allen to Directorate, Appendix B, September 1962, p. 4.

10. Directorate of History, J.A. Leach file, Box 5482-3; Honours and Awards, op.

cit. pp. 104–105; *Toronto Star*, 3 June 1918, p. 12.

11. Op. cit. S. Murton file, Box 338, Murton to Dodds, 1 May 1963, p. 1.

12. Directorate of History, A.K. Tylee file; NA, Air 1/721/48/5, Hoare to Brancker, 28 July 1918, p. 1.

13. Directorate of History, Allen file, Allen to Directorate, September 1962, p. 38.

14. *Eastern Daily Press,* 4 and 8 February 1969.

## Appendix B: Meals and Pay in the RAF

1. *Toronto Daily Star*, 11 June 1918, p. 16.

2. NA, MG 40, D AM, Vol. 1, Air 1/10/15/1/37.

## Books

Borden, Robert Laird. *Robert Laird Borden: His Memoirs, Vol. 2*. New York: Macmillan, 1938.

Chajkowsky, William E. *Royal Flying Corps: Borden to Texas to Beamsville*. Erin, ON: Boston Mills Press, 1979.

Clark, Don. *Wild Blue Yonder: An Air Epic*. Seattle: Superior Publishing Company, 1972.

Ellis, Frank H. *Canada's Flying Heritage*. Toronto: University of Toronto Press, 1954.

English, John. *Borden: His Life and World*. Toronto: McGraw-Hill Ryerson Limited, 1977.

Jones, H.A. *The War in the Air, Vol. V.* Oxford: Oxford University Press, 1935.

O'Kiely, Elizabeth. *Gentleman Air Ace: The Duncan Bell-Irving Story*. Madeira Park, BC: Harbour Publishing, 1992.

Parkin, J.H. *Bell and Baldwin: Their Development of Aerodromes and Hydrodromes at Baddeck Nova Scotia*. Toronto: University of Toronto Press, 1964.

Pettigrew, Eileen. *The Silent Enemy: Canada and the Deadly Flu of 1918*. Saskatoon: Western Producer Prairie Books, 1983.

Pickersgill, J.W. *The Mackenzie King Record, Vol. 1, 1939–1944*. Toronto:

University of Toronto Press, 1960.

Sullivan, Alan. *Aviation in Canada 1917–1918*. Toronto: Rous & Mann Limited, 1919.

Voss, Vivian. *Flying Minnows: Memoirs of a World War 1 Fighter Pilot*. London: John Hamilton, 1935 (under pseudonym Roger Vee). Reprint (amended), London: Arms and Armour Press, 1977.

Wise, S.F. *Canadian Airmen and the First World War: The Official History of the Royal Canadian Air Force, Vol. 1*. Toronto: University of Toronto Press, 1980.

Zaslow, Morris. *The Northward Expansion of Canada, 1914–1967*. The Canadian Centenary Series. Toronto: McClelland & Stewart, 1988.

## Other Published Sources

*House of Commons Debates*, 1917 and 1918. Edited by Colonel Ernest John Chambers, Gentleman of the Black Rod, Senate of Canada, Ottawa.

*Parliamentary Guide*. Edited by Colonel Ernest John Chambers, Gentleman of the Black Rod, Senate of Canada.

## Private Collections

Campbell, Beth. She loaned the complete records, including training and pilot's log books, of her cousin, Lieutenant Malcom Plaw MacLeod, DFC and Belgian Croix de Guerre. Plaw scored seven kills in the last few weeks of the war. He also served in the RCAF during the Second World War.

Smith, Alan, Captain (Ret) RCAF. Smith spent twenty years accumulating papers, photos, and correspondence. He interviewed several people who had served or worked at the Deseronto Camps. A bomb aimer during the Second World War, he was shot down over France, captured, and survived for eighteen months in various prisoner of war camps.

**Magazines and Periodicals**

Anonymous. "They Wanted Wings." *Sentinel* (May 1967): 24–29.

Cox, Sebastian. "Aspects of Anglo-US Co-Operation in the Air in the First World War." *Air & Space Power Journal* (Winter 2004): 27–33.

Dodds, R.V. "Canada's First Air Training Plan." *The Roundel*. (Part 1, Nov. 1962; Part 2, Dec. 1962; Part 3, Jan.–Feb. 1963; Part 4, March 1963.)

Halliday, Hugh A. "High Flyer Indeed." *Legion Magazine* (July/August 2004).

Halliday, Hugh A. "Beamsville Story." *CAHS Journal* (Fall 1969).

Molson, K.M. "The JN-4A (Can)." *CAHS Journal*. (Summer 1973).

Russell, Colonel Ronald D. (Ret). "Canada's Airmen and Airwomen in the First World War." *Airforce Magazine* (Spring 2004 and Summer 2004).

Shannon, Norman. "Sam's Air Force." *Airforce Magazine*, 15 (Oct–Dec. 1991).

Stewart. Robert. "The Obsessions of Sam Hughes." *The Beaver* (October/November, 2003).

**Unpublished Thesis**

Rhodes, D. Berkley. "The Star & The New Radicalism, 1917–1926." Master's thesis, Queen's University, 1955.

**Newspapers**

Newspapers were consulted from the following communities: Barrie, ON; Belleville, ON; Calgary, AB; Deseronto, ON; Edmonton, AB; Fort Worth, TX; Fredericton, NB; Halifax, NS; Hamilton, ON; Kingston, ON; Kitchener, ON; Montreal, QC; Napanee, ON; Orillia, ON; Ottawa, ON; Picton, ON; St. Catharines, ON; Saint John, NB; St. John's NF; Sydney, NS; Vancouver, BC; and Windsor, ON.

**Photo Collections & Sources**
Camp Borden Museum, Deseronto Archives.
Charles Snell Carbert Collection, Hastings County Archives.
Robert Crossman Collection, National Defence Collection.
Sullivan, Alan. *Aviation in Canada, 1917–1918.*

**Appendix A**
NA, AIR 2/166/RV 4869, Report of Col. Roscoe, Commanding Officer, Taliaferro Fields, to the Chief Signal Officer of the U.S. Army, 6 May 1918, p. 5. He lists the number of men in the Air Division killed in training with the RFC in Texas.

NA Casualty Returns (Statistical) April 1917 to May 1918 inclusive. The reports are not complete; those after 30 May 1918 are missing. Our researchers also found fatalities in newspapers which were not listed in the period covered by the Official Reports.

Directorate of History, The Commonwealth War Graves Commission, file 73/1376.

Halliday, Hugh, "Beamsville Story," *CAHS Journal* (Fall 1969): 75–77.

Various Canadian and U.S. newspapers, particularly *The Toronto Star, Globe and Mail, St. Catharines Standard, Northern Advance,* and *The Intelligencer.* A few fatalities listed in the Official Reports as accidents later became fatalities; they were reported in newspapers but not in the Reports, which were prepared at the time of the accident and filed at the end of the month.

# List of Abbreviations

| | |
|---|---|
| AEA | Aerial Experimental Association |
| AFC | Air Force Cross |
| BCATP | British Commonwealth Air Training Plan |
| BOAC | British Overseas Airways Corporation |
| CAC | Canadian Aviation Corps |
| CAF | Canadian Air Force |
| CANUSTEP | Canada-United States Test and Evaluation Program |
| CBE | Commander of the British Empire |
| CEF | Canadian Expeditionary Force |
| CFCA | Canadian Flying Clubs Association |
| CO | Commanding Officer |
| CPR | Canadian Pacific Railway |
| CTS | Canadian Training Squadron |
| DFC | Distinguished Flying Cross |
| DH-4 | Curtiss airplane, training aircraft |
| FAI | Fédération Aéronautique Internationale |
| GTR | Grand Trunk Railway |
| GNR | Great Northern Railway |
| IMB | Imperial Munitions Board |
| IRFC | Imperial Royal Flying Corps |
| JN-3, JN-4 | Curtiss airplanes |
| MC | Military Cross |
| NATIBO | North American Techology and Industrial Base Organization |
| NATO | North Atlantic Treaty Organization |
| NORAD | North American Aerospace Defense Command |
| NCO | Non-Commissioned Officer |
| O/C | Officer Commanding |
| OBE | Order of the British Empire |
| OX-5 | Curtiss engine for JH-4 Canuck |
| RAF | Royal Air Force |
| RCAF | Royal Canadian Air Force |
| RCNAS | Royal Canadian Naval Air Service |

| | |
|---|---|
| RFC | Royal Flying Corps (British) |
| RFC Canada | Royal Flying Corps Canada |
| RFC/RAF | British Air Training Plan (1 April 1918) |
| RNAS | Royal Naval Air Service |
| VC | Victoria Cross |
| YMCA | Young Men's Christian Association |
| YWCA | Young Women's Christian Association |

# Index

# About the Author

C.W. Hunt is a former history teacher, business executive, and entrepreneur. He retired from business in 1996 in order to devote more of his time and energy to writing. Hunt has written six books on the history of Canada, including *Booze, Boats and Billions* and *Gentleman Charlie and the Lady Rum Runner*. He lives in Belleville, Ontario.

# Other Books by C.W. Hunt

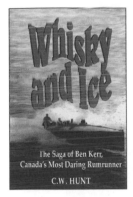

## Whisky and Ice
978-155002-249-0
$16.99

Travel back to the Prohibition era, when Canada and the United States were obsessed with "demon liquor," and Ben Kerr was known as the "King of the Rumrunners," landing him at the top of the U.S. Coast Guard's most-wanted list.

# Of Related Interest

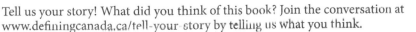

### Day of the Flying Fox
*The True Story of World War II Pilot Charley Fox*
by Steve Pitt
978-155002-808-9
$19.99

### The Sky's the Limit
*Canadian Women Bush Pilots*
by Joyce Spring
978-189704-516-9
$24.95

### Generally Speaking
*The Memoirs of Major-General Richard Rohmer*
by Richard Rohmer
978-155002-518-7
$45.00

In July 1944, in France, Canadian Second World War pilot Charley Fox attacked the car that contained the famed German general Erwin Rommel, and succeeded in wounding him. Author Steve Pitt focuses on this seminal event, but also provides fascinating aspects of the wartime period.

Exciting and daring stories of early Canadian women bush pilots from the late 1940s onwards. From aerial surveys, water bombing of fires, to the operation of a float-plane flying school, these women have left little undone.

The engaging memoirs of Major-General Richard Rohmer. Arguably Canada's most decorated citizen, Rohmer is a commander of the Order of Military Merit, an Officer of the Order of Canada, and received the Distinguished Flying Cross for his service during the Second World War.

🏛 **DUNDURN PRESS**
www.dundurn.com

Available at your favourite bookseller

Tell us your story! What did you think of this book? Join the conversation at www.definingcanada.ca/tell-your-story by telling us what you think.